T0356312

TORONTO BLUE JAYS

A Curated History of the Jays

KEEGAN MATHESON

TRIUMPH
BOOKS

THE FRANCHISE

Library of Congress Cataloging-in-Publication Data available upon request.

This book is available in quantity at special discounts for your group or organization. For further information, contact:
    Triumph Books LLC
    814 North Franklin Street
    Chicago, Illinois 60610
    (312) 337-0747
    www.triumphbooks.com

Printed in U.S.A.
ISBN: 978-1-63727-792-8
Page production by Nord Compo
Design by Preston Pisellini

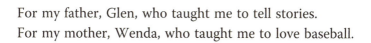

For my father, Glen, who taught me to tell stories.
For my mother, Wenda, who taught me to love baseball.

Part 1 Origin Stories

Part 2 Only in Toronto

Part 3 Faces of the Blue Jays

CONTENTS

Part 4 Stories of the Seasons

Part 5 The Glory Years

Part 6 The Storytellers

Foreword

I OWE MY WHOLE BASEBALL CAREER TO THE TORONTO BLUE Jays.

I got drafted by the Mets in the first round back in 1980 and sure, I got a brief little stint up there, but my playing career never really materialized. I started my coaching career over there, too, and that wasn't really going anywhere either...until I got an opportunity to go to Toronto. Looking back, it's everybody's goal to be in the big leagues, whether you're a player or a coach. That's where I served all my time, in Toronto.

My mind goes back to when I first got to Toronto. This happened in my first go-round as manager, then again when I came back, it happened again. We'd always hear from people around the city that it had been forever since those '92 and '93 seasons, but just wait...if you guys are relevant at the end of the year, just watch what happens. Well, we finally found out.

There was something different about that group in 2015 and '16, wasn't there? I got a couple months in with the '86 Mets. It was the same type of thing. The personalities on the team were what made it all so unique. Both teams had a ton of talent, but there was just something unique about it. Being the manager wasn't easy, no question, because you had some big personalities and some volatile guys, but that's what made them so damn good. On any given day, they might tell me to beat it. There was always something going on. I don't care how good things were going, there was usually something about to crop up, but that was the beauty of it.

I think this is the important part. You've got to let them be who they are. We had a bunch of guys who were late bloomers. Josh Donaldson didn't get his career going until later, then there was José Bautista and Edwin Encarnación. It wasn't like these guys were the golden boys from day one. They'd grinded, they'd had their ups and downs and their disappointments. Some of those things that happened along the way probably had something to do with their personalities, too. I just let them be themselves and got out of the way. It's about them. That's all. It's the guys. It's the individuals. It's the personalities.

Those teams were easy to love, too. They weren't boring. They felt a lot like those '86 Mets I was talking about…. Well, maybe not that extreme, but people could latch onto those guys. People weren't just saying, "OK, we'll go out and watch a boring game, have a beer, and they'll win 2–1." There was some personality to it. There was some fight. People fell in love with those guys. Even if we hadn't had as much success in those two years as we did, I think people still would have loved those teams.

I'll never forget those years. Toronto is so special to me, not just because of the people I met and how that whole country took care of me. It's just such a special place. I remember some players, before they went up to Toronto, they'd worry about it. It's a different country, blah blah blah, you name it. All of that stupid stuff. I have never come across a player that I managed or talked to who, when their time in Toronto was over, they didn't just absolutely love it. That said a lot about Canada. There are a lot of people who are apprehensive before they ever get there, but then they end up falling in love with it and a lot of them never want to leave.

If it wasn't for the Blue Jays, the lone team out there—not even in the United States—that gave me a shot, I wouldn't have had a major league career. I really don't think I would have. The Blue Jays made me who I am in baseball.

You never really appreciate anything until you're not there anymore, you know? Not until you look back. That's what's happened when I think about Toronto, when I think about Canada. I look back and I smile at all the good times. And I'll tell you what, we sure had some good times.

—John Gibbons
July 2024

Introduction

I grew up asking to watch the Blue Jays bat one more time before bed.

Those 7:30 PM starts of the '90s landed at 8:30 in Nova Scotia, and for years, Carlos Delgado was my ticket to seeing the second inning. Delgado was the Blue Jays' cleanup hitter in those days, so if the Blue Jays went down in order in the bottom of the first, I'd begin to plead my case. *At least let me watch Delgado hit,* I'd say, *and then I'll go to bed.*

This is how baseball began to grow in my mind. Another year would pass and I'd learn that the Blue Jays were more than just Shannon Stewart, Shawn Green, and Delgado batting in the top half of the lineup. At the time, I didn't exactly understand pitching as an art form, only a 10-minute nuisance that got in the way of me watching the Blue Jays bat again. Soon, I saw how foolish I'd been and learned that, every fifth day, I should probably pay attention to this Roy Halladay guy.

Baseball grabbed me and it hasn't let go since, even though my relationship with it has changed. As a kid, we made more trips to Fenway Park than SkyDome. The east coast of Canada is still full of Red Sox fans. There are too many old photos of me wearing a Blue Jays hat with a Red Sox shirt, the name of Mo Vaughn, my favourite player, across the back. I regret that no one stepped in to correct this fashion faux pas.

As the old story goes in my family, I threw a tantrum at my first Blue Jays game because they fell behind 1–0 in the first inning. The day was soon saved, along with my parents' sanity, when the Blue Jays hit a grand slam. It's comforting to know that my mood swings in that stadium are nothing new.

The story also goes on to tell that I lost a tooth in a SkyDome cheeseburger one game and another tooth in a SkyDome ice cream cone the next. I must have been terrified walking through those gates for Game 3.

I've since drifted away from baseball and back to it. My work covering the Blue Jays for MLB.com takes me on the road for 125-plus nights a year, and while each season eventually wears me thin, it will forever beat working a real job. So much of my life has come to orbit around Blue Jays baseball. I struggle to remember birthdays and important dates, but the fried wiring in my brain will always remember which hotel rooms, airports, or dive bars I was sitting in when the news of a trade or a free-agent signing broke.

Covering the Blue Jays as a beat writer, which I've done since 2017, has changed my relationship with the game. I struggled in the early days, more with life in "the big city" than the job itself, and too quickly became jaded, a mistake I've worked to shake with the years. This game has already given me so much, and while I'm no longer a fan of a team, a writer should still never fall out of love with the game. Nothing lights my heart on fire like a good story. Rarely do I feel more alive than the moment I sit down to write with some good quotes in front of me.

This job has also shown me the different realities we all grew up in with the Blue Jays. As this organization creeps up on its 50th year, you can so clearly see the eras, the generations of fans. When I sat down to write this book, for the first time and for the hundreds of times that followed, I wrestled with how to capture the Toronto Blue Jays in their entirety. What I soon realized is that can't be done. If it could, you'd be holding a volume of encyclopedias right now, not this one book.

My hope is that these stories add to your experience as a Blue Jays fan, whether they are new to you, add to the memories you already have, or bring back some you've forgotten. These pages do not hold the story of every major moment or every star, but I hope they do hold something that is meaningful to you.

This book, like the work I do each season on the Blue Jays beat, does not exist without the fans of the Toronto Blue Jays and the passion they have for their team. It's important for me to always remember that.

This book is for you. I hope you enjoy it.

PART 1

ORIGIN STORIES

1
Opening Day, 1977

IT SNOWED. OF COURSE IT SNOWED.

On the day Major League Baseball tilted its head north to watch Canada's newest team, the Toronto Blue Jays, play their inaugural game, the baseball world saw a Zamboni of sorts, slowly circling the snow-covered infield at Exhibition Stadium.

It was an absolute mess and the perfect moment for the Blue Jays to be born into. That April 7, 1977, it all began.

Exhibition Stadium was a wretched place, a football stadium with the furniture rearranged to wedge Major League Baseball onto the shore of Lake Ontario, like playing baseball in the untamed wild. Those who had the blessing and misfortune to call Exhibition Stadium home look back on it through the same romantic lens, like how you would talk about an old college apartment. Sure, it was a run-down shack with mice in the walls and water dripping down through the ceiling when it rained, *but it was our first place.*

"It was an abomination," Paul Beeston said, "but it was our abomination."

Exhibition Stadium wasn't just baseball's worst venue, though. It went further.

"It was not the worst stadium in baseball, it was the worst stadium in sports!"

For many of the Blue Jays' players and so many of the staff who'd built this organization, it was enough just to be invited to the party. Toronto was in the big leagues; it didn't matter if the Blue Jays didn't exactly play at the Ritz yet. Around baseball, though, Exhibition Stadium had its own folklore, the snowy northern outpost that players from other organizations whispered and warned one another about.

In the days surrounding Opening Day, local news coverage spoke of Exhibition Stadium as if Torontonians were preparing for their first mission to a new planet. Tickets, which ranged from $2.00 for general admission to $6.50 for a field-level chair, were snapped up quickly as fans flooded in from across southern Ontario, bundled in coats and scarves and blankets to watch baseball. On the day of the first game, the *Toronto Star* ran a fashion story on how people dressed at the stadium, from the trenchcoat and warm tweed suit worn by the police chief to the slacks, sweater, and red jacket lined with white fur worn by Anne Murray, who performed the first national anthems.

In 1977, Buck Martinez was playing with the Royals, who came to Toronto at the end of April for the first time. It wasn't hovering near freezing, as it had been on Opening Day, but it was still brutally cold as the winds whipped in off the lake. Coming to Toronto was still such an adventure for some players in those years and Toronto itself was growing...but the stadium simply hadn't caught up.

"The thing that we really enjoyed was the exchange rate. At that time, the dollar was really good. We stayed at the Royal York, and I can still remember we saw Barbara Eden in a concert," Martinez remembers, smiling at the memory. "She was one of my favorites, from *I Dream of Jeannie*. We saw that, then we sat in our room one of those first nights after we'd been rained out and we looked up at the CN Tower. Lightning was hitting the CN Tower and causing sparks to come off of it. It was just awesome."

"The stadium? Oh, when we came from the Royals' stadium to Exhibition Stadium, it was like, 'What the hell is this?' I had been on an expansion team in 1969, so I kind of related to a lot of those guys. It was fun. There were some cold, cold days. I probably had more cups of chicken noodle soup in that place than anything else. I'd sit down in that bullpen, and you'd be freezing cold."

Even working at the stadium was a challenge in April. When Jerry Howarth arrived in 1982 to join Tom Cheek in the Blue Jays' radio booth, he'd never called baseball games in April and May, especially not on the shores of a Canadian lake.

"Oh, it was freezing at the ballpark," Howarth remembers. "For a month, when Tom and I were calling the games at Exhibition Stadium, there was a window in front of us. Tom would always close the window, so he would broadcast behind that window in a warmer booth. When it was my turn to do the third, fourth, seventh, and eighth innings, I would open it. He'd ask me why and I said to Tom, it's not for the weather, I need to have the crowd noise come in. I need to have a feel for the game. I'll just dress warmer. A lot of times, when I would do my innings, he'd get up and leave because he was freezing."

This wasn't supposed to be a ballpark. Exhibition Stadium had long been the site of a racetrack, which brought the long bleachers that stretched past the outfield, and was home to the Toronto Argonauts. The Blue Jays even shared the facility with a soccer team, the Toronto Blizzard, who played their home games there in the NSL from 1979 to '83.

Like SkyDome in its early years, Exhibition Stadium was home to anything and everything. Michael Jackson, Bruce Springsteen, The Who, The Police, U2, and every other headliner you can name played there. In 1986, it played host to The Big Event, a WWF production that headlined that year's Canadian National Exhibition. The main event was between WWF World Heavyweight Champion Hulk Hogan and "Mr. Wonderful" Paul Orndorff.

"When I walk in Exhibition Stadium and thousands upon thousands of Hulkamaniacs are going crazy, my blood turns to ice-cold water running up through my veins and I can't help but say you turn me on, Toronto. I can't wait," Hogan shouted, flexing and shining and staring into the camera.

The Ex had seen some things over the years.

When a stadium is built to host everything, it's ideal for nothing, but that didn't matter. It was all the Blue Jays had, and even as the years stretched on, there was this strange sense of pride that grew around the misfit stadium.

"I still remember walking back from Ontario Place one day after lunch and it said, 'Yankees vs. Blue Jays,'" Beeston said so proudly. "You knew you'd made it. It wasn't like the Mariners or someone. It said, 'Yankees vs. Blue Jays' on the marquee over the stadium."

The Blue Jays had arrived. It didn't matter if they were late to the party and underdressed.

* * *

When it came to the games themselves, playing at Exhibition Stadium was unlike any experience in baseball, even before the first pitch was thrown.

"We had to use the water-removing Zamboni quite a bit," remembers Gord Ash. "Unfortunately, the suction was so significant that it used to lift the turf right off the ground. That created some issues."

Over the years, the Blue Jays tried to frame all of this as a home-field advantage. It was like playing golf at your home course. You know all the breaks, all the bounces, how to hit the blind shots over the hill.

"There's no question it was...different," said Ernie Whitt, who debuted with the Blue Jays in May of 1977.

"As a catcher, I'd look out to our centre fielder and I could only see him from the waist up. I couldn't see the legs of the centre fielder."

What?

"The field was a football field, and it was crowned so that the water would run off the football field," Buck Martinez said. "If I looked out to centre field, I couldn't see the centre fielder. All I could see was his thighs and up. He was downhill. That's why balls would go over the crest and into the alley in left-centre. They'd just roll all the way to the fence. Ground balls would speed up."

The wind was just as much a factor. In those early days at Exhibition Stadium, members of the Blue Jays' front office and coaching staff would gather on the field at different times of day to launch balls into the air, trying to track the chaotic wind patterns. Perhaps it could be another advantage if they could figure it out, but more often than not, it was a guessing game, the gales turning without warning.

"We had the pigeons, we had the wind, we had the rain," Beeston said. "Jim Clancy got blown off the damn mound and Clancy was a big guy! It was windy enough one night we ended up having to cancel the game. Not for rain, not for lightning, not for anything else. Clancy got blown off the mound."

He's right. In May 1984, just five pitches into his start, Clancy was knocked off balance by the raging winds at Exhibition Stadium and the game was called. The home-plate umpire, Don Denkinger, said in the *Toronto Star* that "it was like getting sandblasted."

The year prior, Exhibition Stadium was the scene of the famous seagull incident involving Dave Winfield, then a 31-year-old outfielder for the Yankees. Winfield was throwing a warmup ball that struck and killed a seagull, and when the game finished, he was taken into police custody in Toronto and charged with cruelty to an animal. He was held on a $500 bond, which the Blue Jays paid, and the matter was soon dropped, but it lives on in the lore of Exhibition Stadium, the only place in baseball where so many of these stories could have ever happened.

As the Blue Jays lurched out of their early growing pains and began to blossom in the mid-'80s, fans continued to fill Exhibition Stadium.

"When they talk about us doing four million people here at SkyDome, the real amazing thing was how did we put 2.8 million people into Exhibition Stadium?" Beeston said "It's unbelievable! It's an unbelievable story. People were coming."

There was just this one thing...they wanted beer.

"We want beer! We want beer! We want beer!" Beeston can still hear the chants.

A Major League Baseball team, owned by a group that included Labatt, couldn't sell beer. It's like if Rogers Centre didn't get cell phone service. This was a provincial government issue, banning the sale of alcohol at professional sporting events, and the province was slow to relent. This was still a more conservative version of Toronto. On Opening Day in 1977, Ontario Attorney General Roy McMurtry took a carton of milk with him to the game. How refreshing.

"Before that, the biggest thing you had to do was clean up all the mickey bottles. Everyone brought it in," Beeston said. "We didn't really check for it. We were supposed to, but we didn't. They'd bring in their flasks, so you had all these bottles sitting there at the end."

If the Exhibition Stadium era had lasted any longer, there would be no "but" when players and executives look back on their time there. The Blue Jays got out just in time, after they'd tasted the success of the mid-80s and just before they went on their World Series runs of 1992 and '93. They moved out of that old college apartment that made them appreciate just how nice their new home was.

There's still this odd sense of appreciation for The Ex, though, even these 35 years later.

Executives remember the small, square office, where people like Pat Gillick, Paul Beeston, or Howard Starkman would have their offices around the edges with desks in the middle. No one was stuck in a silo. Everyone was involved, frantic, right in the middle of it all, a beehive building something from scratch.

"It was the perfect incubator for Blue Jays fans," Buck Martinez said. "It was Canadian. It was outdoors. It was on the water. It was hard to sit on those aluminum benches. I thought it was a wonderful place."

By the late 1980s, though, the Blue Jays needed a serious stadium. They weren't just about to move to a nicer part of town; they were moving into a mansion.

2

Springtime in Dunedin

THE BLUE JAYS NEEDED A SPRING HOME, BUT 1976 IS CENTURIES ago in baseball.

This was not the time of sprawling player development complexes, complete with computer labs, analytics departments, and cameras capturing every breath, every movement. There were no player parking lots lined with BMWs, Lamborghinis, and Range Rovers. The Blue Jays just needed some land, a place to play games, and a few shacks to put their stuff in.

"I can tell you how it all worked," said Paul Beeston, because of course he can. "I started back in 1976 with the team."

"When we first started out, we were Metro Baseball. We didn't even have a name. That was May of 1976. Each one of the owners had what you'd want to call a representative on the board."

So the faceless, nameless, not-quite-yet Blue Jays hit the road. Gerry Snyder represented Montreal businessman R. Howard Webster, who owned a share of the team alongside Labatt, and Snyder set out for Florida. Snyder was a big name in Montreal who had helped bring the Expos and 1976 Olympics to the city—Mayor Jean Drapeau's "right-hand man," as Beeston puts it. It was time for the first scouting trip in Blue Jays history.

The first mention of Dunedin appeared in the *Toronto Star* on April 29, 1976. There were six Florida locations offering to work with Toronto's new MLB club on their new spring training home, according to Dave Cashen, the Ontario sales manager for Labatt: Dunedin, Clearwater, Sarasota, Jacksonville, Venus, and West Palm Beach.

"Snyder was charged with finding a place to go. He obviously looked all over Florida, but mainly looked at the area around the Tampa Airport," Beeston explains. "Gerry came back, after [going] through the three or four different places he really looked at, said the best place he looked was Dunedin. Dunedin had been the home of the Tigers and it had a small ballpark. It was close to the Tampa Airport."

If this same scene played out today, there would be hundreds of millions of dollars of future revenue on the line, a golden ticket of tourism that different cities and towns would be fighting over. Looking back, that was still at stake in 1976, but no one knew it yet. Spring training is a big business, especially when a small corner of Florida like Dunedin can tap into the entire market of Canada for one month a year.

There was a ticking clock behind all of this, though. Snyder and reps from Toronto's new team weren't traveling the globe or carrying out profound economic studies. They just needed a place to warm up for the season, and if it was convenient for their players and staff, that was a bonus.

"It was easy to get to from Toronto and who knows what, exactly, Gerry promised them. But he came back and he and Cecil Englebert bonded very, very tightly."

Englebert, Dunedin's mayor at the time, is a key character in all of this. He wasn't just open to the Canadian club coming down to crash on Dunedin's couch, he wanted them there.

"They would always have their issues with us because they thought of us as being owned by a bank, a rich industrialist out of Montreal and Labatt Brewery, so we could pay for everything that we wanted and we were really bringing nothing to the party, they were bringing it to us," Beeston said. "Cecil Englebert and that group, they saw us as being a magnet for bringing tourists down there, which in fact has happened. A lot of people who are down there originally came down to see the Blue Jays, bought a condo, and they're still there."

In August 1976, the Blue Jays finally signed their deal with Dunedin, a city of just 29,000 at the time.

"I want to find a place where we can establish an identity with Toronto," then GM Peter Bavasi told the *Toronto Star* in 1976, "so that next year, the year after and five or 10 years from now, people from Toronto will know where our team will be training when they are planning their winter vacations."

Dunedin was so different then, still tucked away in its own quiet corner before the recent boom of tourism in the surrounding areas—particularly Clearwater Beach, which has become overbuilt with hotels and overrun by college kids on spring break. It still works for all the same reasons, though, a short and simple drive from the Tampa Airport. To this day, there's something special about the moment you drive across those long causeways, stretching toward Clearwater until you reach Gulf to Bay Boulevard. A new year starts the moment your tires hit those causeways, palm trees lining the pavement, water stretching out as far as you can see from either side.

Back in 1976, there was almost nothing built along Highway 19, fields sitting empty for miles. There was Innisbrook to the north, which offered a place to golf and some accommodations for the staff, but there wasn't much to see in between. The Blue Jays set up their first headquarters at a Ramada Inn, and much like the life they'd soon know at Exhibition Stadium, found some charm in how rugged and rudimentary it all was.

Their first home was Grant Field, which had been built in 1930 and played the role of spring home to some other clubs over the years, including the International League's Buffalo Bisons, now the Triple A affiliate of the Blue Jays.

"The ballpark wasn't much of a ballpark," Beeston said. "It had some stands behind home plate and some bench seats out in right field, then a little bit of left field. It really didn't have a clubhouse. It didn't really have anything. We didn't have a place for a minor league team, but we didn't have a minor league team at that point. Cecil said, 'OK, we'll take you over to Solon Avenue and we'll build you a field or two there.'"

The player development complex was then born on a few patches of grass, the same land that now houses the Blue Jays' massive facility, which just underwent a $100 million makeover.

"The clubhouse wasn't much bigger than this office, and I don't exaggerate when I say that. We put up trailers for the offices. The visiting clubhouse? They probably dressed at their own stadium or in the hotel."

The Blue Jays' first spring exhibition game was scheduled on March 10, 1977, against the Phillies, but there was a torrential downpour that day, wiping out the game. The next morning, spread across the top of the *Toronto Star's* C1 Sports page, was the image of a big, ugly bullfrog, sitting atop the wet mound at Grant Field, the sparse bleachers soaked behind the frog. It wasn't much to look at.

If a Major League Baseball team from 2025 stumbled across a field like this, they wouldn't get off the bus, but these were different times. Spring training wasn't viewed as much of a money-maker in those days.

"It was more of a fraternity as opposed to a factory," Beeston said. "Quite honestly, back then, baseball was more of a sport than a business."

Imagine, for a moment, if Toronto's search party had eaten a bad meal at a diner in Dunedin or stayed at a hotel with noisy guests in the next room. What if Mayor Englebert, so enamored with the idea of Major League Baseball coming to his precious Dunedin, hadn't lobbied? There are so many years, so many moments, that could have spun off in a different direction entirely.

Perhaps the Blue Jays would be the exact same club they are today—same players, same reputation, same stories—if they'd spent the past 50 years gathering in Venus or West Palm Beach each February. That's hard to imagine, though.

There's something so right about Dunedin and the Blue Jays, Canada's lone team flying south each year to prepare for the season in a city so small. Other organizations who train nearby, like the Phillies in Clearwater or the Yankees in Tampa, have their stadiums and training facilities surrounded by sprawling parking lots, close to the highway for fans to flow in and out. The Blue Jays' stadium, now TD Ballpark, feels like a small-town field that grew up and stayed put.

Driving down Douglas Avenue on a game day in Dunedin, you'll see Dunedin residents on their front lawns with flags, waving Blue Jays fans in to park on their grass. Twenty bucks will get you within a couple of blocks of the stadium; 10 bucks will leave you with a walk.

TD Ballpark shoots up in the middle of it all, but on all sides, it's surrounded by houses, a big-league ballpark in the middle of a quiet neighbourhood. It comes complete with all the classics, too, from Home Plate, the diner across the street, to Bauser's up the road, the beloved local bar where Blue Jays fans gather—and park—before a home game.

Dunedin has grown up alongside the Blue Jays, each side with something to thank the other for. You can see it in Dunedin's downtown, in particular its Main Street and the blocks surrounding it, which are now a dense, wonderful collection of shops, restaurants, and breweries. It's all so underrated, so untouched by the "Florida" of it all, a secret that Blue Jays fans get to keep. Catching a Blue Jays game in the afternoon then wandering up Douglas Avenue to Main Street in Dunedin is one of the best days you can have in baseball.

The Blue Jays wouldn't fit in Tampa, in Jacksonville. From sharing Canada with the Expos to being the country's lone team, geography has always mattered to the Blue Jays. They're the hometown team for a country of nearly 40 million people and Dunedin captures that hometown feeling so wonderfully.

The Dunedin of today, with Clearwater on one side and Clearwater Beach on the other, feels like stepping into a different world each spring. By the middle of February, when the weight of winter has become too heavy, the drive across those causeways comes best with the windows down for the first time in months, warm air whipping through. By the time everyone makes the drive back across those causeways in the other direction at the end of March, the air is heavy and humid with the heat that's crept in over the last six weeks.

The snow has melted, you hope, in Toronto. It's time to begin.

3

SkyDome

THERE'S STILL MAGIC IN THE OLD DOME.

If you stand inside on the right afternoon—when they begin to open the roof before there's any music echoing through the dead air—you can still hear the sound of the stadium moaning and groaning to life. It's the sound of metal on metal, concrete on concrete, the low, grumbling howl that comes from a creature deep in the ocean.

These days, Rogers Centre grabs the heart more than the mind. When it opened in 1989, SkyDome was a marvel of modern engineering, a breathtaking project that announced Toronto to the rest of the baseball world. No longer were the Blue Jays baseball's other team, the Canadian outpost playing their home games in a seaside dump. These were the new Blue Jays, the Blue Jays who won, who spent money, who innovated.

All these years later, this organization has few strengths greater than the plot of land this stadium sits on. Other locations were thrown around, including a development plan for Downsview Park, but in 1985, the Blue Jays landed on this hunk of undeveloped railyard land near the CN Tower and Union Station.

Architects went to work, trying to push the limits of what we understood a stadium to be. After all of those years suffering through the exposure of Exhibition Stadium, the Blue Jays wanted control. A roof when it rained, open air when the sun was shining. They wanted it all.

This stadium also needed to work for everyone, not just the local baseball team. It would need to work for the CFL's Toronto Argonauts, who were drawing far greater crowds in that era, and would eventually play home to the NBA's Toronto Raptors from 1996 to '99. It was the Raps' own version of Exhibition Stadium, a strange, rearranged stadium that couldn't have suited their needs less, but it worked. Then came the concerts, beginning with Rod Stewart just a few days after the first Blue Jays game in June 1989 and the countless stadium shows that have followed. The monster truck rallies came, along with soccer matches, WWF events, and track meets, including the famous 150-metre race between Canadian Donovan Bailey and American Michael Johnson to crown the "World's Fastest Man." Bailey won the race, along with the $1 million prize, and famously said that his rival didn't pull up injured...he was just a chicken.

Few major league stadiums can boast a resume like Rogers Centre's. It's seen so much, changed so much, and aged so much. We look at the concrete behemoth so differently now.

As architects began to work on their designs, trying to score the unlikely contract, the challenges were obvious. This stadium needed to lean into technology, lean into grandeur, lean into newness. In the years that followed SkyDome's opening in 1989, baseball saw the birth of retro classics like Camden Yards in

Baltimore and Jacobs Field in Cleveland. If the idea and money for SkyDome had come along a few days later, perhaps we'd live in a much different baseball reality in Toronto, but this stadium was one of its time.

How, then, would the retractable roof work? Would it slide on and off the stadium, covering some of the land outside? Would sections of the roof tilt up and out? Would this be one big, sliding chunk of roof or dozens or sections, pulling apart like pieces of an orange from the centre?

Architects Rod Robbie and Michael Allen, who won the contract, found inspiration where you would least expect it.

"The inspiration was the idea of crustacea, all of these shells moving on a lobster or a sea animal of that kind," Rod Robbie said in an old History Channel documentary, *The Demand for a Dome.*

Think of a lobster. The long abdomen stretching down from the body is typically called a "lobster tail" if you're ordering at a restaurant. The lobster's tail curls and straightens, curls and straightens as it moves itself backward, the strong exoskeleton protecting the soft organs underneath. When you hold a live lobster out of the water, this tail will curl quickly and powerfully, whipping back and forth to free itself. As that happens, you can see the sections of the lobster's back sliding along the edges of one another, fitting perfectly into an armor that moves with the lobster's body instead of limiting it.

There it was, on the back of a lobster, the answer to it all.

Robbie called SkyDome a "secular cathedral," wanting the building's movements to hold elegance, not just process and purpose. There was some romance to this project from the very beginning.

Construction crews from EllisDon typically numbered between 600 and 700 people on-site at a time, 24 hours a day, six days a week. In the final push to complete the project, there could be up to 2,000 workers at SkyDome at any given time. The winters became particularly difficult, especially with the amount of steel and concrete work needed for the build. The initial roof construction itself required a quarter-million bolts.

The roof was constructed in a mostly open position, meaning that the first movements of the roof were to close it, not open it.

This was not just another stadium. We've become so comfortable with it now, the old dome that's always been there, but it's so important to hold onto the time when SkyDome was something beautiful and new. There are stories of the workers, standing down at what we'd now call field level, looking up at the roof moving above them for the first time with tears in their eyes.

In that first test, the panels of the roof slipped out from their stack on the north side of the stadium, sections of the lobster's shell moving together along the same body, and moved to the south. "As if it was born from the rest of the structure," Robbie said in the documentary.

SkyDome, in all its wonder, was born.

Now, it was time for the Toronto we know today to grow up around it.

* * *

Find an aerial view of Toronto from the late 1980s, when SkyDome construction was underway.

To the northeast side of the stadium, Yonge and Bay Street were lined with buildings, but that area stands above the rest. It's jarring, quite frankly, to see how much of Toronto has appeared in just the past 35 years.

The areas directly north of SkyDome and west, from King St. West down through Fort York, were not littered with condo buildings and the insufferable construction projects that continue to pull those towers from the earth. Much of it was completely bare.

"This area had nothing. Nothing!" Paul Beeston said, pointing out the window of the office he still keeps at Rogers Centre. "It ended at Reese Street. You didn't go down Bremner to York, it ended right here. All of these places were parking lots. That was a bus parking lot, then across the street there was nothing there at Navy Wharf and Bremner. There was nothing. This was the start of the development of this whole area. When the Leafs moved down here, you started to have restaurants. Toronto already had the entertainment district. Ed Mirvish had built Princess of Whales and already had Mirvish. We're not as lucky as the Leafs. When you get off the subway or the GO Train you're right there, but we're not that far away. It works."

Toronto was already well on its way, but the birth of SkyDome kicked things into overdrive. There was still so much space downtown to build up at that time, but the presence of this stadium blew the opportunities wide open. If 50,000 people would be spilling out of SkyDome on any given night, all of those people needed to park. Some of those people needed to have dinner before the game. Some of them needed a beer or six after the game. The area around SkyDome began to grow with it.

What a gift it is now, to have this stadium in the heart of downtown. It doesn't work for everyone—no stadium can—but the number of people who can easily access the stadium each night by walking, cycling, or public transit is rare. In so many other cities, stadiums are placed on the outskirts of a city or outside of it entirely, surrounded by parking lots for thousands of cars to come in and out. SkyDome was built in the middle of it all. If you live in Toronto today, chances are you know at least one person with a view of the dome from the balcony of the 300-square-foot condo they rent for $3,100 a month.

This part could have gone all wrong, though.

"We got lucky because there were some of us, of which I was one.... We could have moved out to the Woodbine Racetrack," Beeston said. "That was an option, but Trevor Eyton said no, we're staying here. Trevor was with Labatt at the time, and the bottom line was we were staying here, it didn't matter what we said. Our thought was that we could build a baseball-only stadium and we could have all of the parking and everything else. It would have been a mistake. It would have been a huge mistake. This is what's worked for the city."

"I'm for downtown. It's great for the city and it's great for the team. Right here is particularly good because you have one end anchored by Rogers Centre, you have the other end anchored by Scotiabank Arena. In between, you've got the Metro Toronto Convention Centre, Ripley's Aquarium, and the CN Tower. You have the open area where the train museum is, too. I wouldn't be changing this location for anything."

They won't need to, either.

Recent renovations, pushing $400 million, have completely overhauled the interior of Rogers Centre, setting it up to survive the years ahead. The bones and organs of the stadium have aged well, that magnificent roof included. These decisions are often less about the aesthetic features we can see and more about the foundational elements of a building, like the plumbing and electrical components, the steel and concrete. It's all rock solid, like an old Honda that hasn't missed an oil change.

Why go anywhere else? Besides, the land the stadium sits on is zoned for stadium use only until the year 2088.

"It's special. It's got a 100-year lease," Beeston said. "What are we in here, our 35th year from 1989? There's another 65 fucking years left, right here! I don't see them changing that. It's great for everybody."

We don't marvel at SkyDome today like we once did. That relationship has changed. She's old faithful now, the stadium that may not belong on a postcard, but which still holds so many memories, all of them etched into the infinite weight of concrete. That said, you will never appreciate Rogers Centre more than the moment you attend a game at another MLB stadium and it begins to rain.

What's next, though?

It feels too abrupt to even ask now, so soon after the Blue Jays poured $400 million into renovations over the course of two winters. It's like asking your friend what's next for them, professionally, a month after they've landed their dream job.

It was once Toronto's job to catch up to SkyDome. Now, it's Rogers Centre's job to catch up to Toronto.

* * *

Rogers Centre needed some life. The stadium itself had lost its swagger.

Sentimentality aside, Rogers Centre can be a brilliant venue on the right day and dreadful on the wrong one. Catch the Blue Jays down 7–0 with the roof closed and a light crowd? The grey, grey, and grey of it all really become noticeable as sounds echo and clang around the empty airplane hangar. All stadiums are built to be full...but especially this one.

The bones were good, though. The Blue Jays and Rogers ownership needed to find the right way to do this—and the right amount to do—but they explored some other options first.

First on Mark Shapiro's plate were the renovations to the Blue Jays' player development complex and TD Ballpark in Dunedin. The Blue Jays did well with both, upgrading their complex from one of the worst in baseball to one of the best, while TD Ballpark remains a gem of the Grapefruit League circuit and will for years to come.

Rogers Centre was more complicated and, naturally, more expensive. Everything in Toronto is.

As the deal and planning stages of the Dunedin renovations wrapped, the Blue Jays turned an eye to the stadium project and worked with a consultant. The group came up with a plan that had three options, giving them some flexibility to move up or down the list based on the initial reaction from Rogers ownership. That was pitched to Joe Natale soon after he was named CEO of Rogers Communications, but with other high-cost priorities already in play for Rogers, ownership couldn't allocate the capital at that time. It was kicked a little further down the line.

Then, for a moment, the attention shifted elsewhere.

"We diverted focus toward a different concept of tearing this place down," club president and CEO Mark Shapiro said. "It was something that was kind of a pie-in-the-sky idea. Really interesting, but pie in the sky. That was about a two-year diversion."

Talking with people throughout the organization, that pie was truly up in the sky—we're talking way up there. These are the conversations that organizations need to have, though. If you're renovating your house to add a third bathroom or fourth bedroom—and if you're smart—you'll look at a few different options, maybe chart out a few different cost levels. Expand that budget to a half-billion dollars and you'd probably toss around a few more options, even if they're a little dreamy.

It's nearly impossible to beat Toronto's current stadium location, but to create the space surrounding the stadium for a more expansive project would require either some serious imagination, some serious cash, or a full move. Many modern stadium developments, particularly in the NFL, are turning into small villages of their own, complete with shops, restaurants, and hotels, each one an opportunity for the organization to pull in more revenue.

This "pie in the sky" idea would have seen the stadium rebuilt "closer to the Gardiner," Shapiro said, but recognizing the long-shot odds of the idea, Shapiro soon distanced himself from that, deciding it was no longer the best use of his time. Besides, if the Blue Jays tore down and rebuilt—or did anything significant involving the land around their current building—they would likely need to play elsewhere for a season during construction. No thank you.

"Once that started to die, we resuscitated the lowest version of the original plan," Shapiro continues. This was when the momentum began to build.

"Let's think about the highest areas of need from a fan experience perspective and the highest areas of need from a revenue generation perspective. The bones of this building are still in pretty good shape. We need to really think about our competitive disadvantages in this marketplace for sports and entertainment dollars, which was a lack of fan experience other than just the team, and that made it 100 percent dependent on winning. We didn't have any premium, even when we were filling the stadium, which really muted our revenue."

Premium seating and premium experiences are where pro sports teams make money; it doesn't matter which sport we're talking about. Fans paying $30 or $70 or $107 for a ticket are crucial to sustaining a club's dollars and cents, but if a pro sports team wants to really *make* money, it needs to corner the premium market, people with money who aren't afraid to spend it at the ballpark.

The Blue Jays wanted to add club lounges. They wanted to add bars and entertainment options within the stadium. If you're a hardcore baseball fan who wants to sit in one seat and watch the game for all nine innings, fantastic. It's the more casual fans—often younger fans who wanted to experience a baseball game as more of a social event and less of a sporting event—who they were targeting. Besides, they're all Blue Jays fans just the same and they're all willing to pay.

From that point, the Blue Jays began to focus on what Marnie Starkman calls "medium term impact." The club's executive vice president of business operations was heavily involved in each stage of this process along with Anuk Karunaratne, who left the organization to join the St. Louis Cardinals in January of 2024.

"We were able to convince ownership that this was needed regardless, even if you are going to knock this place down 20 years from now," Starkman said.

It was set. In the 2022–23 offseason, the Blue Jays handled the 500 Level and much of the outfield, now labeled as the Outfield District, full of new destinations to grab a cocktail and maybe take a glance at the game between sips. The next offseason, from 2023–24, was for the lower bowl and completion of the player facilities, clubhouses, and more. It was a massive undertaking, but even the plan the Blue Jays eventually ran with began with a different shape.

"The reality is that the real renovation was only supposed to be the second phase," Starkman explains. "When we started to see the potential of the outfield, Mark did a great job of saying, 'Hey, we'd be silly not to do these together.' We actually reversed the order and did the outfield first, which we needed to do to explain what it means to renovate Rogers Centre. Then, in the second phase, we did the infield."

An advantage in all of this, Starkman said, was private funding.

This was about speed. When a stadium project goes through a provincial or state government, things can slow down. There are more voices involved, more interests to shape the project around. By the time the funding is secured and you're ready to knock down the first wall, the designs could be a bit dated. Using private funding for this project, the Blue Jays were able to design and build immediately with the full focus of 225 business operations employees on the renovations.

In this case, speed really mattered.

There was no "goal" date here. There was a hard date, with the Blue Jays coming home in April of each season for their home opener. If there were delays, the Blue Jays and the endless stream of construction crews going through those doors needed to adjust on the fly, making up hours and days.

Down in Dunedin at the Blue Jays' facilities, they had live feeds of the progress at Rogers Centre so that executives, like Shapiro, could keep an eye on things from afar. There were a couple of what Starkman calls "hold-your-breath" moments along the way, one of which came in January during one of the offseasons of work. Starkman was on-site with Karunaratne when her phone rang. It was Shapiro.

"I remember him calling and saying, 'Marnie, there's nothing.' Anuk and I were standing down there thinking, 'We're playing baseball in 15 weeks. What are we doing?'"

They pulled it off, even if some of the paint was still drying the night before the 2023 and 2024 home openers. Even though some other larger, loftier ideas were batted around before they landed on this, the Blue Jays kept their greatest strength.

"You can't beat our location," Starkman said. "Any team you talk to, sure, it's great to have millions of dollars of revenue from parking that some of these teams have, but the idea that we're at the core of the city, the idea that you can stumble in or stumble out on the subway, that was one of the biggest focuses of the outfield. It was a mind shift for the staff. It's OK that someone comes here for four innings to have a drink. It's OK that you're in the Corona Rooftop Bar, it's a tie game with Jordan Romano pitching and there are 50 people up there who don't care. They're just there to have fun. That's a mind shift, right? That's how our game has to be consumed to get a younger, new fan."

So, what's next?

Rogers Centre is already the seventh-oldest stadium in Major League Baseball, which doesn't feel quite right. Only the Red Sox, Cubs, Dodgers, Angels, Athletics, and Royals played in older stadiums in 2024.

These renovations should set up Rogers Centre for another 15 to 20 years, though, and who knows what the hell the baseball landscape will look like by then? Twenty years ago, the Blue Jays were wearing black jerseys. Twenty years ago, we hadn't heard of Instagram or Twitter yet. Attention spans were different. Interests were different. Fans were different.

The stadium itself will need to continue to change and adapt to the city around it. When SkyDome first opened, its Jumbotron, standing 33 feet high and measuring 110 feet across, was considered a marvel. Today, we all carry around a screen in our pocket that would blow that one out of the water. Plasma TVs were cool once, but time moves on.

That time will come again. Time will move again. It already is.

"We need to answer the question: What, of the major potential alternatives, do we want to go down and why?" Mark Shapiro asks.

"Do we want to build a stadium somewhere entirely different downtown or not downtown? That's unlikely, but I'm just giving you everything because we can't move forward without it. Do we want to keep renovating this place but in an extreme way? I'm talking about tearing down a wall and putting glass in. I'm talking about tearing up the roof and putting in a sliding roof, but keeping the same location. Or do we want to go back and do a more realistic version of that two-year wild goose chase to look at acquiring other land in this area?"

It's all possible. It all has to be possible. SkyDome's build, like the recent renovations to Rogers Centre, was just one idea of many.

The day will come again, years down the line, when the Blue Jays will need to decide what the future of baseball looks like in a bigger, bolder way. The day will come again when someone looks at the back of a lobster as it moves and dreams of something new.

PART 2

ONLY IN TORONTO

4

The Canada Problem

THE TORONTO BLUE JAYS HAVE ALWAYS BEEN MAJOR LEAGUE Baseball's other team.

They had a cousin in the Expos until 2004, but for this organization's entire existence, the Blue Jays have lived on the other side of a border that is six inches high to some and six miles high to others.

The truth and the narrative of this have always existed in a strange dance with one another, but there have been two things—and two things only—that have eliminated the "Canada problem" for the Blue Jays: money and winning.

"I've watched this and I believe it. Until I'm convinced otherwise, I'll believe it," said Paul Beeston. "You can get any player you want as long as you have a chance to win and if you're prepared to pay. That's the key. You can always get the B player. Getting the A player? Getting that superstar…. Robbie Alomar could have left here, but Robbie stayed. Jack Morris loved it here. Dave Winfield wanted to sign on. Everyone had some type of connection here."

Winning is undefeated. If you build a ball club capable of winning the World Series and are willing to pay a player five bucks more than the next team is, it doesn't matter if you play your home games on Jupiter.

"I'll be quite frank with you. We never really had a problem getting players here or getting them to stay here…once we started to be good," Beeston said. "The money was good, and the team had a chance to win. By the time that happened, and we signed those guys at the end of the 1980s and early '90s, we were playing indoors here under the only roof that could open and close."

That's why so many executives have experienced different realities over the years in Toronto. Getting players to come to Canada hasn't always been easy. At times, it's been a big, ugly hurdle, particularly when the Blue Jays have tried to compete as a low-budget team, which a team in a city like Toronto never should be.

In recent years, Rogers ownership has shoveled money into this organization, both at the infrastructure level and in terms of player payroll. The renovations to the player development complex and TD Ballpark in Dunedin blew past $100 million. The renovations to Rogers Centre eventually landed in the neighbourhood of $400 million. The club's payroll has steadily climbed alongside all of this, setting a new high-water mark in 2023 and again in 2024. Money isn't a problem anymore, but it has been over the years.

The city has changed, too. Look at downtown Toronto now, where anyone from a young, single 22-year-old to a married 36-year-old free agent can find their slice of life within blocks of Rogers Centre. It's a city with its problems, like anywhere else, but ball players don't have to do much driving of their own, which already eliminates one of Toronto's biggest pains. They can experience every bit of the vibrant, diverse, modern downtown. If you can't find something you'd like to do in Toronto on any given night of the week, your eyes are closed.

Think back to 1979, though, or 1983. The Blue Jays were playing at Exhibition Stadium. Toronto was still a big city, but it hadn't quite grown into its oversized suit yet. More importantly, the Blue Jays weren't seen as threats yet. They were still that other team up north, the ball club that had to play through the snow every once in a while.

"Clearly, in that first decade or so, it made a difference," said Gord Ash. "Players didn't want to come to some place where they didn't have a chance to win. In the mid-80s and late '80s, that started to turn, and once we got the stadium built, it became a more permanent factor. The other thing we did—and the Cardinals always did this very well, I thought—was to trade for a player, and once he gets there, he'll stay. We had more luck paying players like that than we did attracting them. They then had a comfort level. That was part of our strategy. Get players into the system, get them acclimated and then when the opportunity came to re-sign them, it was much better."

These days, the Blue Jays don't have to do gymnastics to get a player to come to Canada.

Sure, they might need to lean in another inch to break the odd tiebreaker. Think of Hyun Jin Ryu's four-year, $80 million contract or George Springer's six-year, $150 million deal. Whether it's a little extra cash or going one year further than most others are comfortable with, this can still be a challenge for the Blue Jays, but they sit at the adults' table. They don't need to convince anyone of much at this point.

The on-field results haven't been there under the front office led by Mark Shapiro and Ross Atkins, but it's hard to argue with how this club has spent money.

On top of Ryu and George Springer, this organization signed Kevin Gausman to a five-year, $110 million deal and extended José Berríos with a seven-year, $131 million deal soon after acquiring him from the Twins. Chris Bassitt came to Toronto on a three-year, $63 million deal.

"Nine years ago, I was told free agents wouldn't sign here," Mark Shapiro said in early 2024, soon after the club's near-miss on courting Shohei Ohtani. "You had to pay a premium. That's clearly not the case right now. I'm sure there are still some, but for me, that was definitely not the case. We were having a conversation with the most preeminent free agent in the history of modern baseball. We were among the few teams he was considering."

Now, the Blue Jays need to stay here. They need to live in the top 10 payrolls in baseball, maybe even flirt with the top five.

When this club isn't spending big—and isn't winning—Canada starts to feel awfully far away.

* * *

These days, the Blue Jays want to demystify Canada to their young players.

We focus so much on the big-money free agents like Springer or Gausman choosing to come to Canada, but what about the 16-year-old kids signing contracts out of the Dominican Republic or Venezuela?

Players coming up through the system today have the Vancouver Canadians, the Blue Jays' High A affiliate. The Canadians are a fantastic organization, drawing great crowds for years by minor league standards. It's been a good first step for many NCAA draft picks joining the organization, or those young Latin prospects who have finally earned a promotion from Single A Dunedin and have finally gotten their ticket out of Florida, where some of these young players can spend the first four or five years of their professional careers.

Vancouver was affiliated with the Oakland A's organization before aligning with the Blue Jays, which began in the 2011 season and has continued since. When Minor League Baseball was realigned, the Blue Jays made it a priority to keep their foot in Canada. It's worked wonderfully.

Back in the day, the Blue Jays had the Medicine Hat Blue Jays, their affiliate from 1978 to 2002. From 1986 to 1999, they also had an affiliate in St. Catharine's, Ontario. Between the two Canadian clubs, players like Pat Hentgen, Carlos Delgado, Vernon Wells, Lloyd Moseby, Chris Carpenter, David Wells, and Jimmy Key got a taste of playing baseball in Canada before they ran out of the Blue Jays' dugout for the first time.

"The good ones got their exposure in Medicine Hat," Paul Beeston said. "You ask people in downtown Toronto where Medicine Hat is? They don't know! So how are these guys from the Dominican or from Tennessee going to know?"

"One of the things about going to Vancouver, and it's the reason Medicine Hat was also good—and we had some very good players go through Medicine Hat—they found out that our money was different, but it still spent. They found out that the country was not a third-world country. They found out that the people are nice, and quite frankly, that there was a high level of knowledge about the game of baseball. We're always talked down to about our game of baseball, but the reality of the situation is that there's a high level of it. We didn't have to sell the game of baseball here. Everyone was already a Yankees fan, Cleveland fan, or Detroit fan. Everyone was a two-hour-drive fan. They knew the World Series, they knew the system, they knew the playoffs. They knew Willie Mays and Hank Aaron and Ted Williams. They knew all of that and Toronto had good minor league baseball, too, when they had the Maple Leafs. You had everything there to sell."

This was all part of building the foundation. Even Canadian affiliates for other MLB organizations helped indirectly.

It's taken a while for Toronto to get its swagger back, though. Once you lose it, it takes years and years.

When the Blue Jays won the World Series in 1992 and '93, those moments were built atop those incredible teams of the mid and late '80s. Those teams, led by Dave Stieb, George Bell, Tony Fernández, Jimmy Key, Tom Henke, Devon White, Fred McGriff, Lloyd Moseby, and so many more, were undeniable. Who gives a damn if they had to go through customs on their way in and out of the country? Those are names you couldn't look away from in that era of Major League Baseball. By the time those World Series runs rolled around, as the Blue Jays built up for '92 and retooled significantly for '93, getting stars to come to Canada wasn't as challenging as it had been, at the very least.

Then came the drought.

The Blue Jays didn't reach the postseason again until 2015.

Over those 22 long years, Canada drifted further and further from the United States, further and further from being an option for the types of players the Blue Jays so desperately needed. Sure, they were able to develop superstars like Roy Halladay and Carlos Delgado, but they struggled to surround them with enough talent.

The Blue Jays became caught in the middle. Of the full-length seasons over those 22 years, they dipped below 73 wins just once (2004) and topped 87 wins just once (2008). For the most part, they hovered around .500, not quite falling off the map, but not doing enough to change the narrative. Without any recent banners to wave around and without much cash to spend at times, they had little luck luring players north.

The Canada problem was a problem again.

"Oh, 100 percent," said JP Ricciardi, GM of the Blue Jays from 2001 to 2009. "Whether people in Toronto want to believe it or not, when players have options, Toronto isn't the first option. That's what I found, so this is just me. Toronto wasn't their first choice. It was the first choice when the Jays were rocking and rolling, because they were paying guys and they were a high, big-payroll club. They were packing the stadium. Everybody wanted to come to Toronto, but the No. 1 thing was that they were paying people back then. All I can tell you is that, in my situation, we didn't have the resources.

"On certain occasions we did, and when we did, we tried to strike, but even when we had it—whether it was BJ Ryan or Frank Thomas or Scott Rolen or Troy Glaus or AJ Burnett or Rod Barajas or Ted Lilly—it wasn't their first choice. A lot of it comes back to the families who don't want to be hassled going through customs. Most players are either Latin American or American. The Canadian player would love to play in Canada and that's great, which we were able to do with Matt Stairs, but most of the players aren't from Canada. Canada, for their families, is a totally different perspective. A lot of players, once they get to Toronto, I think they realize what a great city it is and realize what a great place it is to play, but it's about getting them and their wives over that initial, 'Oh, I have to go through customs every time? I've got to have a letter?'

"When people are free agents, they have choices. The path of least resistance is a lot of people's choice when it comes to their family. It wasn't the easiest place to bring people. I had to work really hard to get people to drop their no-trades. Troy Glaus didn't want to give up his no-trade. Scott Rolen didn't want to give up his no-trade. We had to convince them that we were doing something big and important and that they were going to be a part of it."

Ricciardi uses BJ Ryan as one example of when the Blue Jays had to stretch further than the rest of the pack to land a top-end player. When the Blue Jays signed the lefty closer to a five-year, $47 million contract in late 2005, it was the largest contract ever given to a reliever, topping even Mariano Rivera's deal with the Yankees.

Ricciardi is quick to riff back through the payroll details of those eight years he spent in Toronto. When he arrived from Oakland, ownership had asked him to reduce payroll... and quick.

His front office shaved, shaved, shaved away, trying to get the club's payroll down in the range of $50 million, which made it so difficult to build a lineup around Carlos Delgado. Midway through Ricciardi's tenure, Rogers ownership told him that payroll could increase gradually over the next three seasons to $70 million, $80 million, and $90 million, but he got this news in January, which limited his ability to jump the market in the first year.

This was a different version of Rogers ownership than we see today. The scope of how we see the Toronto Blue Jays was so different, particularly from a business and revenue-generating standpoint.

If you win, people buy tickets, beer, and jerseys. If you don't, they don't. It's that simple.

"I don't think Rogers really understood what they owned," Ricciardi said, thinking back to those years. "I think they were nice people—great people—and I think it was nice that they bought the team. I just think that if they had better communication about what the team could do for them and what the team meant to the country, I think Rogers would have had a different approach than the approach they had when I was there. Even when I was there, if you go back and look, three of those years in today's game, we would have made the playoffs with the way the playoffs are set up now. We had competitive teams; we just didn't have the resources. We were told we couldn't go over-slot or overpay in the draft. There were a lot of mandates given to us which we had to follow. I don't make the rules, I follow them. I just wish from my end that I could have had better communication with Rogers. I had to go through the team president at the time, who was Paul Godfrey. I just wish I could have been the one talking to Rogers, and I think we would have been able to convince them a little bit more of what they had.

"They did a great thing in buying the team and they did a great thing in keeping the team. I just wish they would have had someone who was a little bit more aware of what baseball actually was. I think they lacked that, and I think because they lacked that, they didn't invest money in the team. We tried to do the best we could, but you're in a division with the Yankees and the Red Sox."

That relationship has changed—slowly—to allow for the spending we see today.

That began through the Alex Anthopoulos years, looked upon so romantically by Blue Jays fans for reigniting baseball in Canada. With Anthopoulos at the helm and Paul Beeston back in the big chair, the connection between the baseball people and the business people improved.

By the time Ross Atkins and Mark Shapiro arrived in late 2015, the hard work had been done. Toronto had its swagger back. The Blue Jays were baseball's beloved bad boys, fresh off an electrifying trip to the ALCS and about to make another run. José Bautista had just flipped his bat. The city was alive, vibrating.

The two ingredients were there again: money and winning.

Again, like it had in the late '80s, Canada started to drift back toward the United States, no longer another planet.

Shapiro, in his time with the Blue Jays, has never viewed this as a challenge.

"I don't understand why that is," Shapiro said. "When it comes to the unknown, it's frightening. Different currency, the border, this is a different country. What does that mean? A little bit of this is about the lack of clarity. One part of our effort was just education. The border is easy to manage. Get Nexus and it's largely no different than traveling domestically. We can help with these things. For the currency, you can still use your credit card. It's manageable, right?"

One of Shapiro's strengths, from a business standpoint, is a stern, direct approach to problems.

The field has ugly dirt cutouts around the bases instead of a full dirt infield? Great. Fix it. The turf sucks? Great. Fix it.

Rogers Centre has its many constraints between the tons of concrete and the challenges of maintaining natural grass, but the Blue Jays have tried to chip away at these small problems over the years. Then, with their recent $400 million renovations spread across two frantic offseasons, they took some of the big bites they'd been waiting for.

"They're little things. They're all little, but if you take all of those little things, players start saying that it's not just OK to play here, it's a really good place to play."

The Blue Jays need to staff themselves differently, too. They can't just rely on teammates and coaches to help players figure out how to get across the border and set up their lives in Canada. It's always the little things that will snag in a player's mind. Ricky Romero tells a story about landing in Canada for the first time after being drafted by the Blue Jays in the first round of the 2005 draft to find that his cell phone didn't work here. He later learned that only Sprint had a Canadian plan at the time, but he was on AT&T, so he had to live with two cell phones for a while.

It's those small things. How does banking work? How will my cell phone work here? How do my taxes work? Should I buy a car here or take my own? Should I rent an apartment or buy one? Should I just stay in a hotel? What if I rent an apartment and get optioned to Triple A? What's the "normal" grocery store here? Does my family need paperwork to come through the border?

The Blue Jays have had to build this support into their organization. It's something other clubs don't need to worry about as much, but it's helped close off so many of those small reasons for players to hesitate.

"I think the segment of the population that's still hesitant to play here, that's more about it being urban," Shapiro said. "There will always be guys who want to be in a rural setting, who want to be in a suburb and drive into the stadium. We're not the right team for that. Is it possible? Robbie Ray did it, but that was during COVID. The best alternative to that is players who live in Lawrence Park and have a yard, but it's still pretty urban. If you're averse to being in a big city, this is probably not for you. It has nothing to do with Toronto and nothing to do with Canada. We're a city. We're a big city, a really big city. We sell that as a point of pride."

Over and over again, Shapiro comes back to the same idea. Toronto is different. That's not a problem, it's a selling point.

This organization hasn't won a postseason game since those incredible runs of 2015 and '16, but it's stayed close enough to call itself "competitive" until 2024's letdown. Pair that with a payroll that just keeps growing, and it's been enough.

Ask the players who have signed these massive contracts lately and their decision to come to Canada doesn't sound all that difficult. That's just how the Blue Jays want it.

* * *

In late November 2021, Kevin Gausman and his wife, Taylor, were on vacation.

There was just one problem. Gausman wouldn't get off his phone.

Gausman felt the MLB lockout looming in December, so he was up against the deadline of that as much as anything, choosing between the Toronto Blue Jays and New York Mets. The clock was ticking, so Gausman didn't have the time for the traditional free-agent tour of Toronto, relying instead on his many trips over the years with the Orioles.

He sat on Zoom calls with Ross Atkins, Pete Walker, and Shannon Curley, then the Blue Jays' senior manager of player relations and community marketing, a title that rolled 10 jobs into one as she worked with players and their families.

"Well, it was funny. We went to...it was called a wellness resort," Gausman said. "You're not supposed to have your phone on you. We got there and we were there for four days. My wife was like, 'Kevin, you're attached to your phone.' So I was like, 'Well, I have to be. It's kind of a big deal.'"

Gausman is as open-minded as anyone you'll find in the Blue Jays' clubhouse, beloved by players of all backgrounds and temperaments for good reason. He'd been to Toronto plenty of times, but that didn't shake the reality he'd come up with in the league.

"The consensus over the majority of my career has been that, if guys had to pick between a team in the United States or the Blue Jays, they'd probably pick the team in the States."

"The biggest thing for me, which might be different than other free agents, was talking to them about my family. What were they going to do for my family? How were they going to help my family get passports? I think Global Entry was a big thing that was talked about."

Over those days on the wellness retreat, Gausman sneaking looks at his cell phone the entire time, he debated where he would sign. He and Taylor had already looked at houses in both New York and Toronto, picking out which neighbourhoods they'd like to raise a family in. These things don't matter as much to players swinging through town for a year, but if you're signing on for five, you need to set up a life.

By the time Gausman left the resort, he'd made his decision.

He was going to sign with the New York Mets.

The Gausmans had to take two flights to get home. Before boarding the first plane, he called his family and told them the news. He was going to sign a deal with the Mets and pitch in Queens next year.

Then, his plane landed.

"I thought it was a done deal [with the Mets]," Gausman said. "When I got off the first flight, I turned on my phone and I had six missed calls from my agent. I was like...what's going on here? He called again and told me that Toronto was where we wanted them to be. Done deal. He asked me if I wanted to be a Blue Jay and I said, 'Let's do it...and I've got to call my family back.'

"That's how close we were."

On December 1, Gausman's five-year, $110 million deal was made official. A day later, the MLB lockout began, meaning Gausman had no contact with the Blue Jays for the next couple of months, an absolutely bizarre way for one of the biggest free-agent signings in franchise history to begin their tenure.

On the day he signed, Gausman stood alongside Taylor, his hat backward with a blue dress shirt on, and did his press conference over Zoom. It was the only way to thread the needle and pull it all together in time.

Since then, Gausman has come to embrace Toronto along with Taylor and their young daughters, Sutton and Sadie.

"I always knew that Toronto was a very diverse city, but I don't think you realize until you live there how much, day in and day out, you're around so many different ethnicities, cultures, and languages. That's so different from Kansas City or Detroit. It's just different.

"The whole recruiting process of one team for an entire country...I don't think I could really process that until I was actually on the team. You meet people and run into people around the city, and it might sound bad to say, but they'll love you no matter what because you're a Blue Jay, because you represent the one team, because you represent baseball in Canada. That's one thing I didn't understand coming here and it's been really cool to see."

One thing Gausman has preached to teammates, though, is the importance of staying together. This comes easily now, with so many players from the 2023 and '24 teams having young children around the same age. If you play in Chicago or Detroit, Gausman said, you might have a friend nearby, an old college teammate, a buddy from the minor leagues who you can grab dinner with. Playing in Canada, despite the many advantages he lists, still separates you from the baseball culture of the United States. If you don't hang out with your teammates on an off night, you might not have anyone else to hang out with, he said.

It's the same story, over and over again, in this situation. Once a player comes to Toronto, they fall in love, but other people in their life still need to get over that hurdle.

George Springer has run into the same thing, owner of the biggest contract in Blue Jays history at six years, $150 million.

He's a northeastern kid. He grew up in the cold and the snow. This doesn't bother him. Canada felt closer to him as a kid born in Connecticut than it would have to a kid growing up in Florida, Texas, or California. Living in between Boston and New York, he already knew what a snowy, crappy day felt like.

"I could hop in a car and go to Montreal, go to Toronto. My dad actually took me to Ottawa a bunch because he's a big history guy, to do all of that stuff," Springer said. "The country of Canada didn't seem so far away. Other guys think it's on the other side of the world."

Going through the 2020–21 offseason, a year before Gausman signed in Toronto but after the Ryu signing had signaled to the rest of baseball that the Blue Jays were willing to spend, they were circling Springer. He was one of the jewels of the offseason, a supremely talented leadoff hitter who the Blue Jays envisioned alongside Vladimir Guerrero Jr. and Bo

Bichette, taking this organization from a good young team to a great championship-caliber team.

In January, Springer and his wife, Charlise, were having a quiet day on the couch when his agent called to tell him where the Blue Jays were at financially. Six years, a club record $150 million. He hung up, turned, and told his wife.

"We were just sitting there and she goes, 'OK, what's your point?'"

Springer sat silent for a moment, then realized he didn't have a point. There was no "but." His head was already wrapped around the idea of playing baseball in Toronto—in Canada—so Charlise asked her husband what they were going to do.

"We're going to go to Toronto," Springer told her. "We're going to enjoy it. We're going to go represent a country and start a life not that far from home. I think it's a great opportunity for us."

The Springer signing is the type of news that put the Blue Jays on the map again with some permanence. The little team up north wasn't screwing around.

It's one thing to bottom out, like the Blue Jays had done in 2019, and develop a young core for the future. That's the easy part. The hard part comes with the "something else," and that "something else" has been a thorn in Toronto's side too many times over the years. This time, the organization chose to lean in, a decision it had failed to make too often in the past. The Blue Jays did not want Vladdy and Bo to play out their careers like Delgado, an elite player who was never given enough running mates to make a memorable run in Toronto.

Four years into his deal, Springer has done what everyone else does. He's fallen in love with Toronto.

"It's a very good place to live. It's a great place to have a family. I'm a mountain guy. I love being in the mountains and by the lake, the river, the stream. It was built toward what I like to do, which is all stuff you can find in Toronto. You can drive an hour in either direction and find what you're looking for."

"What's cool about our games, then with the Leafs, Raptors, and every team in Toronto, is that it provides something for people to do. They can come out to enjoy themselves and enjoy their lives a little bit. Playing in Toronto on the road, you got that feel. It would be a random Saturday in April and the place would be packed. It's such a great atmosphere to play in. If you go outside the stadium after a day game on a Saturday afternoon, there's three million people hanging out. There's restaurants, bars. Anything you want to do, you can do. That gets back to the common misconception. When you go to Toronto, what are you going to do, sit in the woods? No. If you want to, you can, but you'll have to drive. There's so much more. It's an attractive place to go now because of guys like Gausman, like José, who have made this jump and they love it."

So many of these problems have fallen away naturally with the passing of time.

A cell phone plan isn't a problem now. Players understand now that, if they have a credit card, it works no matter which country you tap it in. Add a Nexus or TSA PreCheck card to the mix and going through the border isn't all that different from taking a flight from New York to Chicago.

These hurdles used to be physical. You could see them, touch them, be terribly annoyed by them in the real world. Now, they're more mental, and the players who have experienced Toronto—fully wrapped their arms around the experience of Canada—will say, to a man, that it's all worth it.

"There's a misconception about how long stuff is, what you have to do every time, the taxes, how you do X, Y, and Z,"

Springer said. "I think the word has gotten out that you just have to take five extra minutes to get through the border. It's really not as bad as you think it is... and Canada is not as far away from home as you've been told it is."

5

Famous in a
Small Town

THE CITY OF TORONTO HAS GROWN UP WITH THE BLUE JAYS,
taking on so many different shapes over the years.

The explosion of this city, both out and up, has been so
recent. You don't need to go all the way back to the Blue Jays'
inaugural season of 1977. Even in 1989, when SkyDome opened,
the city around the stadium looked absolutely nothing like the
mess of towers we see today.

In '89 and through the early '90s, only Yonge St., stretching
up from the northeast of SkyDome, looked like a major city.
To the west of SkyDome and most of the north, there were no
towers, no sprawling buildings, no condo construction projects
torturing traffic. Neighbourhoods like CityPlace and Liberty
Village weren't even ideas yet. Stretching to the west along
Bremner and Fort York was just...nothing.

There's one thing that hasn't changed over the years, though. Toronto is a great place to be young and famous with a few bucks in your pocket, especially when your ball club is the hottest ticket in town.

"Listen, Toronto is a great city. It's diverse. But Toronto also knows how to have fun and a lot of that happens after hours," José Bautista said. "There are definitely a lot of different options in the nightlife around the city. It's good to live in a place where, if you choose to and you want to partake, you have plenty of options. Toronto does know how to have fun and we experienced a little bit of that when we were here."

Bautista walks the line beautifully here, but what he's getting at is this—you can have some fun in Toronto.

This truly started to take off around the building of SkyDome. As businesses and hotels began to pop up around the stadium, which brought in more than just ball games back in those days, more players started living nearby. That location has become one of this organization's greatest strengths, right in the heart of a vibrant city, but you can't exactly hide.

As the Blue Jays turned into a powerhouse through the mid to late '80s and eventually went on their World Series runs, this all jumped to a new level.

"You have to remember that from '91 through '93, we sold out every single game," said Ed Sprague. "It was hard to go out anywhere in the city for dinner without somebody coming up to your table and asking for an autograph, and this was before a few hundred thousand more people moved in downtown and they surrounded SkyDome with high-rises. Life in the city was great. I always loved Toronto. I lived in a number of different parts of the city. It was hard to go out without being interrupted, whether you were Joe Carter or the 25th man on the team. Not to mention they gave us cars with big logos on the side, too. Don't have a bad game then get a flat tire after dinner."

Those players in the early '90s experienced life in the city prior to social media, which had to be a blessing. If they pulled their hat down low enough and grabbed a pair of sunglasses dark enough, they could fit right in, maybe even slip out the side door unnoticed.

Year by year, though—and condo building by condo building—Blue Jays players became more centralized. Unless a player is on a lucrative, long-term deal and buys a home on the outskirts of the city, many players over the past couple of decades have lived within blocks of the stadium. While some players—think Vladimir Guerrero Jr.'s level—leave via the parking garage to keep some level of privacy, many walk out the Gate 13 doors, right onto the sidewalk of Blue Jays Way, where they're met by fans. From there, it's only a few blocks to King St. West and the heart of Toronto's Entertainment District, depending on how you define the word *entertainment*.

In an average year, the stars are popular in Toronto. When this team is competing for a World Series, every single player on the roster turns into a celebrity. The perfect storm rolled back around for those 2015 and '16 clubs, as baseball exploded in popularity. Sure, the Blue Jays were good, but baseball was cool again in Toronto. It wasn't the slow old game your dad watched on TV each night, it was a social destination.

Those players, many of whom lived, worked, and had their fun within a few block radius in downtown Toronto, were suddenly celebrities in the biggest small town in Canada.

"The city was on fire," Josh Donaldson remembers. "It was one of the coolest moments and times of my career. What people told me when I got traded over here was, 'If you win here, people will go crazy.' That's what happened."

These teams weren't boring old ballplayers, either. They had an edge, a personality, an aura that everyone wanted a piece of.

"It was crazy. I can't say that it was the Michael Jackson treatment...but it certainly felt like it to me," Bautista said. "It went way beyond personal success, too. I was in a good groove there for about eight, nine years, and a lot of those were before we started experiencing the playoff success. That just took it to another level."

It wasn't just in their bubble of downtown Toronto, either.

"I used to always joke that there were times you felt like Justin Bieber," Ryan Goins remembers. "I remember doing the Winter Tour. We'd show up at some mall and the mall was absolutely insane, just packed, people everywhere, lining up the whole concourse of the mall. That is something I don't think any other team would have."

Goins and Kevin Pillar are such unique examples of the phenomenon. Blue Jays fans always have—and surely always will—loved the hard-nosed role player. You might not be able to relate to the gifted top prospect or the man making $25 million a year, but the 32nd-round pick who has to climb walls and slam his body into the concrete turf every night? That's a little closer to reality.

Goins remembers that sensation so vividly, and it's not something you see in every market. Hell, there's still a breakfast spot a couple of blocks from the stadium with a smoothie called "Goins, Goins, Gone" in the year 2024. Lower down on the menu? Another smoothie called "The Superman."

Superman was born in 2015, when Pillar went from a fringe outfielder known for his defence to a cult hero in Toronto. He scaled walls twice his height, launched into the air for diving catches, and threw his body in front of a truck every night.

Almost overnight, he became one of the club's most beloved players, even if he wasn't exactly a star.

"Honestly, robbing that home run changed my life," Pillar said. "It definitely changed my popularity in the city, and I think it kind of snowballed after that. I felt like I was going out and making plays nightly, and I pretty much became famous overnight. There was nowhere I could go in that city and not be recognized. During the second half of the year, after that trade deadline…it felt like we never lost a game. I think all of our lives changed. There was nowhere we could go in that city where we weren't recognized, appreciated, encouraged, idolized.

"We went out and enjoyed the nightlife a little bit and we were recognizable if we went to certain places, especially if we went to places with younger crowds or places that would be considered Blue Jays bars. You'd get that face recognition. People would think it was cool you were there, buy you drinks, take pictures."

All of these young men were suddenly in the right place at the right time at the right age. Pillar was 26. Goins was 27. Donaldson was 29. Aaron Sanchez at 22 and Marcus Stroman at 24 were right in the middle of it all.

"It was alive, buzzing," Marcus Stroman remembers. "It was just always good energy, everywhere you went. It was never overwhelming. It was just people coming up to you, telling you to keep it going. It felt like everybody in the city was in tune with what we were doing. It was just a really good time to bring the playoffs back after the drought in this city. We had such an incredible squad. We had such a good balance of veterans and young guys."

Some players were young and single. Others were married with children. Fame meant different things to different players, but whether it came at breakfast or at midnight, they were getting recognized.

They lived in a different era than those World Series teams from the early 1990s, though. They lived in the time of Instagram, Twitter, and Facebook. They weren't just getting recognized; they were being photographed every step of the way. This has changed so much about the dynamics of media, too.

In my earlier years covering the Blue Jays, I was in my late twenties and frequented some of the same areas, too often investigating which spots downtown had the latest last call after covering a game. Older writers tell stories from the '80s and '90s of bumping into players outside of the ballpark, particularly on the road, but that came before social media, when players and media had a much different relationship than they do today.

Some veteran players still took the same approach, though. Several times over the years, I'd unexpectedly catch the eye of a player—or table of players—across the bar at an hour that can only be described as "after the game." Sometimes, there would be only a silent nod exchanged. Other times, a beer would appear in front of me, a quiet understanding that neither of us saw one another. If they went 0-for-4 or I asked a stupid question the next day, it didn't matter and we hadn't seen one another.

The newer generation of players, broadly speaking, is more cautious. As this city has grown, there are more and more places for players to spend their time that you or I don't exactly frequent. Some young stars are more apprehensive now, understanding the power of social media and the importance of not showing up there for the wrong reasons. I've watched a young player dart out of the bar after seeing me, their drink still full, forgetting their cell phone on the bar behind them. Looking back, the baseball writer taking tequila shots on a Monday night with the two bartenders who'd just finished their shift probably had more of an image to worry about than the player eating a chicken sandwich with a vodka soda.

There's a balance. It's impossible to find at first, but players who have been around Toronto long enough to sink into it eventually find it. What stands out from speaking with all these players who have experienced it, though, is their appreciation for the love.

"Trying to get tables and be taken care of has never been a problem in Toronto," Bautista said in the confident tone only he can pull off. "It was even easier at that point, but enjoying the meal without having somebody tap you on the shoulder or wanting a picture or an autograph? That was a different story. But listen, any time as a player, when you get that much love, you've got to embrace it. Roll with the punches. If your meal gets interrupted every now and then, so be it. You want to foster that love and the relationship between the fans and the franchise. We know we are stewards of the team at that point and we tried to do our best at it."

As these players mature, they experience the love in different ways.

Looking back, there's this piece of advice that has been burned into Pillar's mind. He's played in other cities now, bouncing around baseball to carve out a fine career, but nothing has compared to his time in Toronto.

"When I was married and had my first kid, you kind of wanted to get away from it sometimes. You really couldn't escape it," Pillar said. "You're at breakfast with your wife and your kid and you just want to be normal, but the trade-off...I wouldn't trade it for anything. I don't remember if it was Justin Smoak or his wife, Kristin, who told me this, but they told me, 'At some point, no one is going to give a shit who you are.' No one is going to want your autograph someday. Embrace it while it's there. That's been pretty true of my career post Toronto. If you're at the field, you're still idolized. You're still a celebrity and people want to take photos with you, but that's really only at the baseball field. There aren't many places in the other cities I've played where you get recognized. Honestly, I still mostly get recognized by Blue Jays fans."

All the players describe Blue Jays fans the same way, too. They're passionate, even obsessive at times in their fandom, then there comes a loving "but..."

They never go too far. They respect a player's boundaries. There will always be outliers, of course, but they won't take it too far. Players can feel the fans' appreciation and love, but then move on with their lives. If you're on the right team in the right season, it can be a perfect balance.

"Canadians, in general, are pretty respectful," said Russell Martin, who starred in those postseason runs of '15 and '16. "They don't go out of their way. Even if they're fans, they'll notice you, but if I'm walking around with my girl or one of my buddies, they won't let it show that they noticed you. They're always super respectful. If we were out for dinner, people would stop to say, 'Hey, it's good to meet you' and stuff like that, but that's an honour. Especially if the team's playing well."

This particularly comes across in speaking with players who have young families. We're not talking about midnight at the bar, we're talking about 9:00 AM at Eggsmart or some other version of a chain breakfast spot downtown. It's nice to be appreciated, but some days, you just want to live your life, and they're typically given that space.

"That's exactly how it is," George Springer said. "I don't venture out that much and when I do, I'm with my wife and my kids. Every interaction I've ever had has been so positive. It's extremely respectful. They don't want to get in your way, they just want to say hello, thanks for how hard you play, whatever it is. I never feel invaded or like my space is violated."

"I remember me, my wife, and my kid went to that Jurassic World place in Mississauga. It got obvious that I'd been noticed, but I didn't feel like I had to leave. It was so cool. These fans are so proud of their team, and they just support their players."

Blue Jays fans have never limited their love to the stars, though, like Pillar, Goins, and so many others have experienced. Even some coaches and managers over the years have become celebrities in their own right.

In John Gibbons' first stint as manager, he felt the heat. He wasn't yet the beloved "Gibby," and since he was on TV every night, often explaining the night's losses toward the end of his tenure, everyone knew what Gibbons looked like and sounded like. He lived a few blocks from the ballpark like most players do, and most Saturday mornings, he'd walk to a nearby movie theatre, buy a ticket for himself, and "try to hide."

"I remember when I came back the second time, I made a point to get out more, see the city and enjoy it," Gibbons said. "I didn't know how long it was going to last, because even that second go-around didn't start off good. When it finally came together and that team took off, I'd walk around and when people would see me it was the total opposite. They'd come up and want to give me a hug, take a picture, you name it. They went from throwing things at me to hugging me."

This is about baseball and about fandom, but also about the Canadian market. The Blue Jays have always been Major League Baseball's "other" team, and even though narratives of players not wanting to come to Canada have disappeared over the years, as Toronto has grown into one of the largest cities in North America, this dynamic still creates a deep affection between fans and the players who stay here for a few years.

José Bautista wasn't just beloved because he hit 54 home runs that season and flipped his bat, he's beloved in Toronto because he gave Canada something the rest of baseball didn't have. He stayed, embraced the city, and claimed it as his own. Each player who's done that speaks with such love for this fan base.

They've given them so much, but they've gotten so much in return.

6

The COVID Years

It felt a million miles away until it wasn't.

That first month of spring training 2020 rolled by like it always does. The mornings were early, the afternoons were hot, and the days were long.

We were still in the early days of learning about COVID-19, at least in North America. Early cases had been identified in China in late 2019, but it wasn't until one month before players arrived in Dunedin, on January 10, 2020, that the World Health Organization first used the term "novel coronavirus."

On January 20, the first case was confirmed in the United States, in Washington. Three days later, Wuhan, China, with a population of more than 10 million people, was placed into a lockdown. This still felt so far away, though, and by February 13, the day Blue Jays pitchers and catchers reported to camp, there were just 15 confirmed cases in the United States.

That first month of spring training carried on as usual. The spread of COVID-19 appeared more in the news, adding some daily reality to the situation, but most people involved did something we no longer have the luxury of doing: they carried on without a worry. The conversation around COVID-19 and its spread grew within Blue Jays camp, though, from an unexpected source.

The Blue Jays had just signed Hyun Jin Ryu to a four-year, $80 million deal in December. This was a monumental moment for the club, announcing to the rest of baseball—a year earlier than anyone expected, perhaps—that it was willing to spend big to surround its new core of Vladimir Guerrero Jr. and Bo Bichette with MLB talent. Tearing a club down to gather young talent is the easy part, but by landing Ryu, the Blue Jays had taken one giant step in the direction of the hard part.

With Ryu came a crush of media attention. In those early days of camp, more than a dozen Korean reporters followed Ryu's every move. If Ryu threw a 20-pitch bullpen session, Korean media would film every moment of it, then interview pitching coach Pete Walker, Ryu's catcher, even the pitchers who were throwing on the mounds next to Ryu. For a few weeks, Danny Jansen may have been the most televised man in Korea.

The questions came first from those Korean reporters, who at the time were taking the global spread of COVID-19 far more seriously than the general public in Canada or the United States. It felt early when a handful of Korean reporters asked Ross Atkins about the COVID-19 situation, midway through that spring training, but they were right to do so. Atkins answered as he should have at the time, stating that the organization was monitoring the situation and prioritizing player health.

Days later, the world shut down.

History books will show that on March 11, 2020, the World Health Organization officially declared COVID-19 a pandemic. Sports fans will remember it as the day that Rudy Gobert tested positive.

If you could freeze that day in time and unpack it, you'd need years. The NBA was the first major domino in pro sports to fall, all others toppling moments after it.

Just before 8:30 PM ET that night, as the Utah Jazz and Oklahoma City Thunder warmed up for their game, the teams' head coaches met with the referees and learned about Gobert's positive test for COVID-19. The game was immediately canceled, and nearly one hour later, news broke that the NBA was suspending the season, effective immediately. It all happened in what felt like an instant.

The next day, March 12, the Blue Jays had two games. One squad was in Bradenton, playing the Pirates, while another was in Dunedin, playing Canada's Junior National team.

Mark Shapiro was sitting in Charlie Montoyo's office at TD Ballpark in Dunedin, Ross Atkins right next to him, watching the game in Bradenton, trying to get a grasp on what was happening. The phone rang. It was Dan Halem, the deputy commissioner of Major League Baseball.

"We're shutting it down," Shapiro was told. "We'll have a call tomorrow to explain, but you need to get everybody out."

The Blue Jays had to scramble. These days, the "border issue" isn't much of a narrative with the Blue Jays, but it was suddenly serious. The Blue Jays were a Canadian team with Canadian employees. They had to move. Right now.

Shapiro started to make calls.

"I remember Mark calling and he said, 'We need to get everyone home,'" Marnie Starkman said.

A charter plane was arranged for Blue Jays staff as some media members bolted for Tampa International Airport, scrambling to find the first flight out of the country. The fear was that international borders would close, and with everything moving so quickly, it was best to get across before that became possible.

The next morning, March 13, Blue Jays leadership met with players in the staff and media dining room of TD Ballpark, underneath the bleachers that stretch up the right-field line. Some players were more engaged with the news, understanding the gravity of what was happening, but for the most part, these were young men trying to make a baseball team. The scope of a professional athlete's focus often doesn't leave as much room for the real world to get in. Each person in that room stood on new ground and no one had answers.

"I remember there being a lot of questions and uncertainty, some disbelief," Shapiro said. "There was definitely no understanding that we wouldn't be able to use the facilities."

For players on the big-league roster who keep accommodations nearby in Florida, this was simple enough. For young prospects from the Dominican Republic, for example, this was more challenging, working with the organization to arrange flights home while travel advisories changed by the moment. A group of young Venezuelan prospects weren't able to leave Florida at all, instead staying at a hotel in Florida provided by the Blue Jays.

The next day, those facilities sat empty.

They thought, even amid the fear of those days, that they'd be back soon.

* * *

The rest of March, April, and May carried on without baseball. By the end of May, the death toll from COVID-19 in the United States passed 100,000, according to the WHO. Soon after, COVID-19 cases in the United States surpassed 2,000,000.

Nothing was in the distance anymore.

In Major League Baseball's world, this became a labour issue as both the league and Players Association wanted to play...but wanted to do so in a way that followed public health guidelines and kept players safe. Given the air travel involved, particularly as the players came back together from their home states and countries, this was extremely risky.

As June wore on, the two sides worked on what this shortened season would look like. Players reported on July 1 to summer camp, a bizarre version of spring training, with the 60-game regular season scheduled to begin on July 23. Given all the logistics that were involved and the stakes of doing this properly, it was easy enough for 29 teams to pull off.

The Blue Jays, on the other hand, were staring at one of the biggest challenges in the organization's history.

Shapiro and Blue Jays leadership were already well into their discussions with government at the city, provincial, and federal levels, wrangling with what no other club had to. While the NBA eventually set up a bubble to finish its season in Florida, MLB would be traveling between stadiums, leaving the Canada-U.S. border a glaring issue.

The Blue Jays held their summer camp in Toronto in July of 2020, but that came with extreme restrictions. Players had to undergo intake testing before even arriving at Rogers Centre, but once there, they couldn't leave.

The Blue Jays had to create their own bubble. Nothing comes in. Nothing goes out.

"There was so much public pressure on following rules, so part of how we got approval was that the players were going to live in this bubble in the building," Marnie Starkman said. "What our team had to do was create that bubble. It was everything from turning the suites into lounges for the guys, making sure that food was delivered, making sure basketball nets were set up.... Not because we were trying to spoil our players, but because we had to tell them, 'You need to come to Toronto, and by the way, when you get to Rogers Centre, you're staying at the Marriott and you can't leave the building.' We built outdoor patios and we were so worried that the media would see one of the guys out. I remember telling Charlie [Montoyo], 'You can't go running by the water. People are going to see you. You have to run in the building.'"

Players would wake up in the Marriott hotel attached to Rogers Centre; shuffle through their own, controlled corridors; and reach the ball field. Significant measures were put in place to keep players distanced, along with frequent testing.

Attempting to keep the focus on baseball—partly for the players' sanity and partly because an MLB season started in a few weeks—the Blue Jays ran through drills each day and eventually built up to intrasquad games. Media were permitted to attend, undergoing a strict screening process upon entering. Temperatures were taken and questions were asked. I will always remember the fear of failing that first temperature check, red in the face after standing outside the Rogers Centre media gate in June's heat.

Desks were spread across the upper ring of the 100 Level. After the intrasquad games, a player or coach would speak with masked reporters via Zoom from a level below, inside the stadium.

The mental toll is something those involved have only begun to appreciate with time, long after the tension and momentum of it all has faded.

Looking back, John Schneider remembers "21 days of darkness."

"It was weird, crazy, lonely. It was kind of nerve-wracking. We didn't know what this thing was, so we were kind of scared of it, but at the same time, we thought we were tough guys so we were like, 'This can't hurt us.' We would do the same shit every day. We'd go up into the Budweiser lounge and they'd have food and drinks for us. They actually made, outside of Gate 13, a little lounge area where you could be outside, but there would be security guards out there. It was like we were in prison. We could not leave."

Nights were hardest. Once the baseball was over, there were entire evenings to kill. These are professional baseball players, completely unfamiliar with having so much free time in the evening in July.

"We did nothing. You sat in the hotel," Schneider remembers. "You'd go to someone else's room, sit 10 feet apart, talk shop and drink beers. It was all we could do."

This all challenged different players in different ways. Younger players were kept afloat by the newness of the big leagues, and even with the challenges around them, an MLB season was weeks away. Some veterans struggled with this new reality, so far from the life they'd become accustomed to as a big leaguer, often separated from their families for weeks or months at a time.

Charlie Montoyo, the Blue Jays' manager at the time, saw the definition of his job fundamentally change. He was suddenly a manager of people, of families, of emotions. Those people just so happened to be baseball players.

"You're talking about human beings, and we could not get out of that place, but they all followed the rules. Nobody went outside, not even for one minute," Montoyo said. "But as a leader, if somebody had broken those rules, then the government gets involved. That's too much. All of that by itself wasn't easy, but everybody followed the rules and did so well with that, not even knowing where we were going to go."

That's what made this even more difficult. The Blue Jays didn't know if they would receive approval from the federal government to host home games in Toronto, potentially with a modified quarantine system that kept opposing teams in a "bubble" of their own from the airport, into the hotel, and down into Rogers Centre.

There were layers and layers of restrictions. Summer camp was just the start of the strangest year in Blue Jays history.

* * *

The Blue Jays worked around the clock through summer camp, trying to find a way to satisfy the federal government and create a way to safely play Major League Baseball in Toronto.

Shapiro found the city of Toronto and province of Ontario to be "unbelievably supportive and communicative" throughout the process, sympathetic to what Canada's lone MLB club was dealing with. At the federal level, the stakes were higher.

"It was an education on Canadian politics," Shapiro said, thinking back. "I didn't know much, and I didn't understand parliamentary politics. I certainly didn't have a grasp of that [before]. I was dealing with the city, the province, and federal governments at different times. It was an incredible window into the political underpinnings of decision making and what the political stakeholders' interests were."

The Blue Jays had also begun to explore backup plans. They looked at sharing Baltimore's Camden Yards, where one potential plan involved them building a temporary clubhouse on the concourse. They explored Pittsburgh's PNC Park, where a left-field restaurant could have been converted to house another MLB club for a few months. Plenty of minor league facilities were explored along the way, but the Blue Jays, first and foremost, wanted to be in Toronto.

They just needed to convince the Canadian government that this could be done well, done right, and done safely.

"It didn't always feel like public health was the primary motive," Shapiro continued. "Public opinion was often the main driver. That would probably be the same with any politician. We were certainly dealing with boards of health more on the provincial and city level, and there was genuine interest and genuine desire there in regard to public health. That was more about logistics as we thought about constructing a bubble or opening up to fans."

"When it came to the border.... The border was one issue. Everything else was about public health, but the border didn't feel like a public health issue. The border felt like a political issue. There was a lot of avoidance from accountability and decision-making. No one wanted to make that decision. It was very much about being on the right side of that from a public opinion perspective. That's how it felt and that was my interpretation."

On July 18, the Blue Jays were denied approval by the Canadian government.

They were left to scramble again.

The Blue Jays had to find a solution almost immediately. Baltimore and Pittsburgh were still on the table, along with another plan to convert Buffalo's Sahlen Field on the fly.

The only clarity the Blue Jays had was that they would be starting their season in the United States. Amid the chaos, the Blue Jays had to keep a foot in reality. Which staff would move to the United States? Who would be comfortable doing so?

In the middle of it all, Starkman, along with her husband and a small group of Blue Jays staff, got in a vehicle and started to drive. Shapiro and Anuk Karunaratne, who had been working with the government on a day-to-day basis at this point, ran point from the stadium in Toronto.

"Mark and Anuk were in the office," Starkman remembered. "They were like, 'Get over the border. Call us when you get over the border and we'll tell you whether to keep driving to Baltimore, whether to head to Pittsburgh, or to stay in Buffalo.' We packed suit clothes for Baltimore and Pittsburgh, then sweats for Buffalo. I remember getting to the parking lot at Sahlen Field and Mark saying, 'We have to stay in Buffalo. This isn't going to work.' The governments were getting word that we were trying to stay there, and they were thinking that they didn't want a second team there with a second PR issue."

"What I remember most is having to get on the phone with employees and ask them if they were willing to move to Buffalo, then to Dunedin, to start to run this operation. That was hard. That involved people leaving their families. It also involved us, honestly, leaning on some of our younger staff who didn't have kids and families."

No one had time to catch their breath. Job titles became memories as the baseball and business sides of the organization blurred together, anything possible to prepare Buffalo for Major League Baseball. Health and safety was at the forefront of all of this, but the Blue Jays still had to keep a portion of their collective brain free for baseball. This was a 60-game season, and for a young, up-and-coming team like theirs, it could be the perfect opportunity.

"We had to deploy a ridiculous amount of resources just to understanding protocols and executing protocols," Ross Atkins said. "It took away, a little bit, from thinking about the things we normally think about, which is how to win baseball games."

The Blue Jays did just enough of that. After starting with 13 consecutive road games while the organization worked on Buffalo's Sahlen Field, the Blue Jays snuck into the postseason with a wild card spot, 32–28.

Their postseason dream still fell apart quickly against the Rays, but for a moment, there was joy. As Montoyo spoke over Zoom the night the Blue Jays clinched, still soaked in champagne, a young Vladimir Guerrero Jr. came crashing into the picture. "We did it!" he shouted into the camera, his arm around Montoyo.

It had been Montoyo's job to help these young kids develop as players, but the previous six months had changed that entirely. He knew that if he panicked, or let on that he was overwhelmed, a young team could quickly take his lead. A light post could have fallen on top of Montoyo that season in Buffalo and he would have shouted out from underneath it: "It's fine. We're fine."

"When things go bad, I say, 'Man, it could be worse,'" Montoyo said that night. "I have a kid who's had four open-heart surgeries, so I know it could be worse. That's why after tough losses, I could turn the page and say, 'Let's go. Let's get ready for the next game.'"

Those moments after the Blue Jays clinched their surprise postseason berth were some of Montoyo's finest as a manager. As the media watched the celebration through a Zoom screen, the joy was so evident on their faces.

"I just told them I was proud of them, everything they've gone through with not having a home and playing here. It's a great ride. This has been a great ride. Just enjoy it now and have fun. The pressure is off. Honestly, just go play and have fun. Enjoy this. That's what we're going to do. We're going to enjoy every minute of it. We know what's coming is not easy, but that's fine. It hasn't been easy the whole time."

Even after all this, it was about to get harder.

7

670 Days:
The Homecoming

THROUGH THE WINTER OF 2020 INTO 2021, IT BECAME CLEAR that the Blue Jays were not out of the woods yet. COVID-19 numbers were still high across Ontario and the Canada-U.S. border was still closed to all non-essential travel. Another year would need to begin on the road.

In early February, the Blue Jays announced they would begin the 2021 regular season in Dunedin, Florida, at their spring home, TD Ballpark. This came with its own new set of challenges, but compared to the mad scrambles of 2020, this plan gave the organization an opportunity to breathe. They would either move to Toronto by mid-summer, when they got approval to do so, or set up shop in Buffalo for a couple of months when the weather warmed.

Still, this involved flying back into the United States and back into Florida, where COVID-19 numbers were still high. Most members of the Blue Jays' staff had been able to spend their offseasons in Toronto, and while there were still serious day-to-day challenges at home, there was a sense of control. Now, they had to mobilize again.

The playbook mirrored the year prior. The Blue Jays organized a team charter plane to take down the first group of employees, which included Shapiro and Starkman.

"That first plane ride, I remember we got on the plane and Mark had his dog, Cleoh, with him," Starkman said. "I was fortunate, because of what my husband does, that he was with us. I remember seeing tears in staff's eyes, who knew the right thing to do was to come help us, but in the middle of a pandemic, it probably convinced their families that they were crazy. I remember looking at Mark and being like, 'What the hell are we doing and how are we going to keep doing this?'"

Even though there was confidence that they would return to Toronto at some point mid-summer, they were chasing something that didn't exist yet.

That spring training played out in front of mostly empty ballparks. Zoom call after Zoom call piled up. Speaking with reporters is not the highlight of a player's day even under the best circumstances, but there was something so heartless about hunching over a laptop each day.

Here's the thing, though...this team was good.

That 2021 squad had its flaws, mainly a bullpen that this organization will look back and wince at for years, but the Blue Jays suddenly had one of the best offences in this organization's history. They were dangerous, a little chaotic, and fun as hell to watch.

Vladimir Guerrero Jr., just 22 years old, was suddenly showing the world the prodigious power that had made him a generational prospect in the minor leagues. George Springer, who'd just signed the biggest contract in franchise history at six years, $150 million, looked like he was worth every penny. Bo Bichette was stepping into the spotlight. Teoscar Hernández was hot. Marcus Semien was putting together one of the best offensive seasons we've ever seen from a second baseman.

It was all coming together for the Blue Jays at the strangest possible time.

They hadn't quite hit their stride by the time it came to move to Buffalo on June 1—a better place to spend your days than the heat and rain of Florida through June and July—but the pieces were clearly there for a run.

The logistics were still most challenging. The jobs of the Blue Jays' coaching staff expanded again and again. Many of the Blue Jays' staff and players stayed down the road from Sahlen Field at a Marriott hotel, but it was hard to fill the days. Add boredom to the challenges.

"We were in the same hotel, eating pre-packaged meals that we had to pick up to go," Schneider remembers. "You get accustomed to big-league travel and those cities. There was not much to do. If summer camp was lonely, Buffalo was lonelier. You were allowed to go out, but there was nothing to do, nothing going on, nothing open. The good part of it—and I'm not trying to sound like a teacher's pet here—was that you had to dive into your work. We just dove into that, watched a shit-ton of video, and spent a lot of time together. Buffalo was...very dull, let's put it that way. Very dull."

For players with families, it was even more challenging, Charlie Montoyo remembers.

"They needed to find apartments. Everybody needs to find a place. People don't think about that," Montoyo said, thinking back. "In '21, we moved three times, right? It was spring training and now we're going to play in Dunedin. You had your spring training place, but you have to find an apartment now because we didn't know how long you were going to be in Dunedin. Then, from Dunedin to Buffalo. In Buffalo, it was almost August, and we were still playing well. That team and everybody involved deserves so much credit for not complaining."

"Anyone could have said, 'OK, we have an excuse.' We never used it. I said that from the beginning. Nobody gives a fuck. Let's do the best we can, and we did."

It was an easy narrative to build. The Blue Jays, after a year-plus spent on the road, unable to return to their own country, could go on a miracle run.

* * *

Let me tell you the story of my favourite day in baseball and the best play I'll ever cover.

It was a pop fly.

After covering the entirety of the 2020 season over Zoom, I was the lone reporter who traveled from Canada to Dunedin, Florida, for spring training in '21, making the 22-hour drive straight through.

Those thousands of Zoom calls feel like another lifetime. Each game day, the Blue Jays would offer one player and Charlie Montoyo on Zoom near 5:00 PM ET, then a couple of players along with Montoyo following the game. My work life existed in the five feet between my couch and the edge of my kitchen countertop, where I would prop up my laptop for Zoom calls atop a few thick books. Over the many Zooms, it's possible that others noticed my camera flicking on and off, on and off, just long enough to sneak a sip of bourbon.

The trip to spring training in '21 was physically jarring. I'd been living by myself at the time in Toronto, and looking back, that was a dangerous game for someone who already liked spending time alone. My world had shrunk, and in Toronto, public health guidelines were so much different than in Florida. Mask usage was so much different. Social distancing was so much different. It felt like reintegrating into society after years away, not months.

That camp was unlike anything I have or will ever cover. My access required regular testing, which I had to take seriously through my time in Florida and, eventually, in Buffalo. As tempting as it might have been to walk into a bar and have a beer, mask off and surrounded by other living, breathing human beings, it wasn't worth the risk. So much was at stake, and with the Blue Jays doing everything in their power to get back to Canada, I couldn't be the one to bring COVID-19 into their clubhouse and screw it all up.

It was a treat, that spring, when the Blue Jays would play the Yankees, who would come with four or five media members. I wasn't entirely alone on the Blue Jays beat, as Ben Wagner, then the radio voice of the Blue Jays, and Buck Martinez lived in the area, but the days were particularly sparse on company. Before doing radio or television appearances from my hotel in the evening, I'd do vocal acrobatics for a moment, suddenly aware that I hadn't spoken for eight hours and worried that my voice would crack on the air.

When games began, it was like covering baseball before the dawn of television. Some games were available, and the Blue Jays eventually made an effort to get some live streams up, but other times, fans were left to track box scores alone. There are still a few Vladimir Guerrero Jr. home runs from that spring that are lost to the world, the only records in existence being the videos on an old iPhone tucked away in my drawer.

Returning home from Dunedin at the end of camp, I faced the mandatory 14-day quarantine entering Canada. I'd stocked my bar before leaving and could have food delivered to the door. The concierge staff in my building would call up when it had been left at my door, and after waiting a minute for the hallway to clear, I'd reach a hand out to grab the bags before slamming the door shut. Twice, during my quarantine, a border officer came to check that I was complying. One officer, pressing for details, asked how I'd been getting rid of my garbage, hoping I'd reveal that I walked down the hallway to the garbage chute myself. When I cracked my door open wider to show him a couple of garbage bags, propped up next to three empty bottles of Four Roses, he silently nodded.

From my front door to the far corner of my condo and back was 35 steps, up the long hallway and back. I'd try to walk that for an hour straight with a game on the television, catching two seconds at a time. Those were strange days, but nothing more and nothing worse than strange.

Through April, May, and June, we continued to cover base-ball via Zoom. It was a solitary life, but given what millions of others in the world were dealing with, it was still a life of great privilege. This was the type of season a reporter would have loved to cover up close, in person. Not only did this team have incredible talent, it had personality. There was such a vibrant joy to that 2021 team, something that is so difficult to capture through a television and the laptop next to your couch.

When the Blue Jays finally moved to Buffalo, I was back on the road again. Their first home game at Sahlen Field would be on June 1, 2021, against the Marlins, which would be the first regular season game I'd covered in person since the end of 2019.

I stayed at the Marriott LECOM Harborcenter in Buffalo, the same hotel many of the Blue Jays' players and staff used. Those were the days of taxi squads in MLB, with players shuttling in and out. Half the mornings I'd walk down to the ground level of the hotel to go to Tim Horton's, I'd see a player sitting on a bench, waiting for a ride, or someone hauling a couple of Buffalo Bisons bags out of the back of a cab. At one point, I lost track of whether Trent Thornton was coming or going, so I just nodded as I passed.

Testing, at this point, remained extremely strict, as it should have been. As a writer, I needed either a daily rapid test or a full PCR test—the real brain-scratcher—which would cover me for a few days. Roughly three times a week, I would drive out to D'Youville University, which had an excellent testing centre, for a PCR test. I'd pay my $150 USD, drive back to the hotel, refresh my e-mail and wait for the word "negative," then walk up the hill to the ballpark.

I will never forget that first game in Sahlen Field. The Blue Jays had set up socially distanced desks along the concourse and upper sections of the bowl behind home plate. To the left, behind the Blue Jays' dugout, was open seating where people could sit next to one another. To the right, behind the visitors' dugout, was socially distanced seating. Looking left then right, left then right, the image was burned into my mind. I sat atop the line that had been drawn down the middle.

With 15 minutes to pitch, I shut my laptop, leaned back in the hard plastic seat, and looked around. For so long, we'd lost the gift of shared experience. We sing loud at a concert because those around us sing loud. We laugh freely in a movie theatre because those around us laugh, too.

I'd lost touch with the beauty of going to a ball game. It's why we still buy a ticket, pay to park, pay for a hot dog, and buy the $15 beer. There's something about that shared experience—your voice being dragged up into the collective roar of everyone around you—that just can't be replicated.

There was an incredible anxiety to that evening. Even masked and distanced from the 5,321 in attendance, it felt like we were all breaking the rules, so far from the reality in Toronto, which was still limiting large gatherings.

Robbie Ray started that night. He struck out Jazz Chisholm to open the top of the first, a beautiful, back-door slider that Chisholm swung right through. Ray did the same to the second batter, Starling Marte, who swung over the top of another slider as it snapped down and out of the zone.

Jesus Aguilar, the big DH, was next. Ray missed with his first fastball, but then got Aguilar to swing through a couple of heaters, both 98 mph. This was Ray at his absolute best, marching to a Cy Young season. He was pounding the top of the zone with his heater and telling Aguilar, "Here's my best shit. Try hitting it."

Then, the crowd started to build. The best pitcher in the American League had just blown two fastballs by Aguilar, and with a 1–2 count, Ray had a chance to strike out the side in the Blue Jays' first inning back in Buffalo.

Ray challenged Aguilar with another fastball, this one in on the hands, and Aguilar popped it into the air.

The rising cheer of the crowd dipped into a lull, but as the ball floated up the first-base line toward Vladimir Guerrero Jr., the sound started to swing back. All of these people, ready to experience something together again, erupted as the ball fell into Guerrero's mitt. It was as unthreatening a play as you'll ever see, Guerrero standing on the foul line just a few feet behind first base.

What had felt so far away was finally close again. I remember the chills I felt in that moment. There was a tear in my eye. I leaned back again, looking from left to right at the fans standing, cheering, yelling into the night air.

In that moment in Buffalo, I found again the love for baseball I'd lost track of. If my mind ever goes, I hope that moment stays.

* * *

Two months into their residency in Buffalo, it was finally time for the Blue Jays to come home. Walking into Rogers Centre that day on July 30, 2001, Blue Jays players and staff wore shirts that read, simply, "670".

It had been 670 days since the Blue Jays last played a home game at Rogers Centre, nearly two full calendar years.

The Blue Jays stormed through an opening in the wall in centre field that night, looking like a college football team running out to the roar of 100,000 fans. Their path from centre field to the infield was lined by hundreds of healthcare workers, lining each side, all waving Blue Jays flags. A sellout crowd of 13,466—the most allowed while complying with the city's COVID-19 guidelines—sounded like 50,000.

There was a long ceremony, complete with videos to thank Canada's healthcare workers and Toronto's fans for sticking with this club while they were gone. The Canadian flag that stretches across the outfield was unfurled as "O, Canada" rang out.

This was when it finally hit so many of the players and coaches on the field. The camera, panning from face to face, showed them wiping away tears. Some had to look down to the ground while others, wanting to feel every ounce of the moment, turned in their spot and scanned the stadium. The last time they'd played there, it was summer camp, all of them locked inside the makeshift bubble.

"I was looking at Vladdy, looking at Teo," Bo Bichette said that day. "Everybody was looking at each other like, 'Man, I've got the chills.' I'm holding back tears. It's hard to explain the feeling. We've been trying to pretend like we had a home. It's difficult to do for two years."

Marnie Starkman, who was beyond the centre field wall on a headset, coordinating the ceremony, remembers this as the moment she and so many on her staff could finally see where all of their work had gone.

"I remember looking at Bo, Vladdy, and guys who would normally be telling us, 'Why are we doing this?' They had tears in their eyes."

"What I didn't see until later that night was the guys on the field, watching videos from fans and watching their reaction. I was behind the wall. I think that was the moment where I thought, 'OK, this is why we do what we do.' Why play a game if you're not surrounded by fans? It was something we had taken for granted for so long."

The Blue Jays won that game, 6–4, over the Royals. It was a beautiful game. Teoscar Hernández's 441-foot home run nearly brought the building crashing down around everyone. In Dunedin, that ball would have sailed off the stadium property and into a vacant elementary school yard. In Buffalo, it would have cleared the netting and bounced onto a highway, maybe rolling into a ditch. Back in Toronto, it ricocheted back down to the fans, all of them wearing Blue Jays jerseys again.

The final out of the game was recorded by Santiago Espinal, racing backward into shallow left field to make a barehanded grab. It was perfect in every way.

Charlie Montoyo called it his best day in baseball.

From John Schneider to Montoyo, the coaches and players, this day still brings up real emotions years later. Looking back, there's also heartbreak.

"People ask me, 'How come you had tears in your eyes when we first came back to Toronto?'" Montoyo said. "It's because I knew we would have won 100 games there, easily, being in Toronto that year. With the way that team was built, the way we were playing."

The Blue Jays shot out of a cannon when they came home to Toronto, winning eight of their first nine games. This team arrived in Toronto 51–48 but finished the season 91–71, an incredible stretch run that could have carried into a postseason for the ages. Instead, the Blue Jays missed the final wild card spot by just one game. It felt so cruel, a 91-win team finishing fourth in the AL East behind the 100-win Rays and the Yankees and Red Sox, both of whom won 92.

Their season ended 30 minutes after the final out of Game 162. The Blue Jays needed the Nationals to beat the Red Sox, but Rafael Devers hit a two-run home run in the top of the ninth and the Red Sox won 7–5. It was over. Vladimir Guerrero Jr. sat alone in the dugout for ages, staring out at the empty field. He'd just put together an MVP-calibre season—48 home runs with a 1.002 OPS—and it still wasn't enough.

So much was lost that night. The most explosive offence in baseball, its 262 home runs leading the league comfortably, was done. If they'd just had one more win, one more bounce, one more game in Toronto, it could have been so different. That could have changed how we view this entire era of baseball in Toronto.

"Our team really came together, and we started to build a culture here," Semien said after that loss. "We had some fans to play in front of. We became, in my opinion, the best team in baseball, but it was just a tick too late."

The front office had spent two years trying to keep the thought out. Mark Shapiro's mind reached back to 2007, when six home games in Cleveland were lost to snow early in the season. His analytics team told him that would hurt them all year, as they played those games on the road instead, but that team went on to go 96–66.

As Shapiro puts it, the Blue Jays never allowed themselves the luxury of thinking about it. They didn't allow themselves the luxury of an excuse.

"Whether we would have won more if we were here? I don't know. Probably, yes. Probably enough to make the playoffs, for sure," Shapiro said. "Whether it's 100 wins, I don't know, but we had a good team. I'm proud of it. My biggest takeaway from the whole experience was immense pride in this organization, in people on the business side who went way outside of their jobs and their roles."

Looking back, Montoyo can't help but wonder. Perhaps wonder isn't even the word for it. He's certain the Blue Jays would have won more games if they'd played their full season in Toronto, and with how they finished, it's hard to argue with him. There's conviction in Montoyo's voice as he speaks about this, even years later. That year means so much to Montoyo.

"Just knowing what we'd been through the last year and a half—almost two years—and to have the record that we did, to make the playoffs [in 2020] and to still have a chance in August to make the playoffs again. I knew. That's why my tears came out. It felt so good to be home, but I knew that if we'd been there from the beginning, I'm telling you.... I don't care what anybody said, 'Oh, you can say that but you don't know what would have happened.' No. No. I do. If you went to Dunedin, then Buffalo, then did it two times, there's not many teams that could have done that. We did.

"I'm never going to forget that. That's why I am always proud of the job that I did in Toronto. I don't think there's ever been a manager who's had to go through that. No. Not a chance. To win 91 games in the American League East when four teams won 90 games? That's why, the more I talk to you, I want to remember everything."

Those teams share a bond others simply can't. They experienced two seasons unlike anything the Blue Jays' organization has ever seen and, hopefully, never will again.

That thought will always linger, though.

What if the Blue Jays had come home sooner? What if they'd jumped from Dunedin straight to Toronto in early June, skipping the Buffalo segment altogether? What if, on March 11, 2020, the sports world hadn't slammed to a stop? What if.... What if?

8

Shohei Ohtani

FOR A MOMENT, IT FELT LIKE ANYTHING WAS POSSIBLE.

The Toronto Blue Jays nearly signed Shohei Ohtani. It's a memory that can't just fade into a footnote on this organization's history.

As one era of Blue Jays baseball burns out and, someday, returns with new colours, this "what if" will hang over the franchise. Ohtani, the game's brightest star, would have changed everything in Toronto. Absolutely everything.

Instead, Ohtani's name is spoken with melancholy, those who were there wrestling with how to frame the pursuit in their own minds. There's a heartbreak involved in all of this, a relationship with a beautiful future that suddenly vanished. Some believe it's better to have loved and lost than to have never loved at all, framing this as only a positive for the Blue Jays to have gotten so close, while others are still haunted by what could have been. Besides, there's not another Shohei Ohtani. There may not be in the lifetimes of so many involved.

This was one of the greatest dramas baseball has seen, building slowly over the early days of the 2023 offseason before exploding into the strangest seven days in Blue Jays history. There were mystery, strategic deceit, tracking airplanes, and, at one point, belief that Ohtani had chosen to sign with the Blue Jays. It's the hope that kills you.

On April 26, 2024, Ohtani returned to Toronto with the Dodgers, his 10-year, $700 million contract in hand. It was the largest in the history of worldwide pro sports at the time, surpassing even international soccer superstar Lionel Messi. The coverage was the most unique media event we've seen in North American professional sports since LeBron James' "the Decision" in 2010.

When that day came, everyone smiled and said the right things.

Ohtani spoke kindly of Toronto, of Canada, and of the Blue Jays' organization. Then, he strolled to the plate and launched a home run in his very first at-bat.

In the fog of pregame niceties, John Schneider toed the line well, complimenting Ohtani's game and pointing the conversation forward. He couldn't rewrite the past six months either, as much as he'd like to, but near the end of the conversation, Schneider was asked if there was any animosity between the Blue Jays and Ohtani. There it was: the moment that comes after every relationship ends, when you have a choice to either wish the other party well or take a shot on the way out the door.

Schneider took the high road. The process, heartbreaking as it was, had left him with an even greater respect for Ohtani, but one detail slipped out.

"If anything, just tell him we want our Blue Jays hat back that he took with him after our meeting."

Well, Ohtani took more than just a hat that day in Dunedin.

* * *

The Blue Jays were reeling again. They were coming off another early exit in the postseason, which cemented their reputation across baseball as a paper tiger.

They were so talented on paper, and most of the time, it worked on the field, too. The Blue Jays had one of the best pitching staffs in baseball, one of their best bullpens in years, and enough big names in their lineup to support those two things. Then, in Minneapolis, it all fell apart.

Coming off an absolute meltdown in the 2022 wild card series against the Mariners in front of their own fans, the Blue Jays' loss in '23 was a gut punch. The decision to lift José Berríos after just three-plus innings for Yusei Kikuchi will always hang over that season, an aggressive, analytic-driven move to flip the Twins' lineup by bringing in Kikuchi, but it didn't matter if the Blue Jays brought in God from the bullpen. Nobody is winning when you score zero runs, and with that 2–0 loss, another disappointing season ended with a thud.

The Blue Jays needed to make a splash, needed to shake off the stench of the years.

Ohtani was, as he could be for years to come, the best player on the planet. Fresh off his second AL MVP Award, he'd just hit .304 with 44 home runs and a 1.066 OPS for the Angels the year prior, posting a 3.14 ERA over 132 innings at the same time. He was prime, 2021-era Vladimir Guerrero Jr. and prime Kevin Gausman all in one.

The Blue Jays needed a plan. Already pushing their highest payroll numbers in history, team president and CEO Mark Shapiro later referred to Ohtani as "a unique business case that would have taken us significantly beyond that." Shapiro and the Blue Jays' front office had presented this to Rogers ownership as just that—a "business case" complete with the revenue Ohtani would generate in Toronto from not only existing Blue Jays fans, but the incredible Japanese baseball market that follows every move Ohtani makes. Stars like Mookie Betts, Joey Votto, or Vladimir Guerrero Jr. are adored in their countries, but Ohtani's following in Japan is something completely different. It's not close. It doesn't even remotely compare.

One thing was clear from the outset. Ohtani and his agent, Nez Balelo of CAA, wanted total secrecy. Ohtani has long been a private person, but particularly in these negotiations, he didn't want anything to get out. Forget a leak; Ohtani didn't even want a drop.

While the Blue Jays began to build their entire offseason around this once-in-a-lifetime pursuit, early momentum began to build internally. The Blue Jays' front office believed fully that they would have the financial backing of ownership to go as high as they'd need to make this deal, and while they couldn't exactly pick up the city of Toronto and drop it on the West Coast, they could start their full-court press to convince Ohtani that Toronto was the right place to spend the next decade of his baseball life.

Behind the scenes, this built...and then came the MLB winter meetings in Nashville, where all hell broke loose.

* * *

The scene of those 2023 winter meetings matters.

These were held at the Gaylord Opryland Resort and Convention Centre, a complex that sprawls over three million square feet with nearly 3,000 rooms. This behemoth is its own small town, complete with towering atriums, indoor trees, restaurants, waterways with boats, and a spiderweb of the most confusing hallways you'll ever encounter. The moment you enter and take that first breath of thick, heavy air, you know you're somewhere that exists a few inches outside of sanity and reality. It's like a billionaire tried to turn Willy Wonka's Chocolate Factory into a convention centre.

The baseball world descended into collective madness there from December 3 to 6. It was, in the strangest of ways, the perfect backdrop for what was about to happen.

At the winter meetings, each team's general manager typically meets with their team's beat writers each day. For Ross Atkins, that meant our traveling media group of five to six writers along with Sportsnet's cameras. These meetings have lost steam over the years as clubs look to protect information and so much of the offseason action takes place outside of the winter meetings—typically later in the offseason—but they're a vital moment nonetheless.

On the afternoon of Thursday, December 4, Atkins was scheduled to meet with the media, but just over an hour prior to that happening, a message was sent out to Toronto media members in Nashville saying that Atkins had a "scheduling conflict" and would need to speak with us over Zoom. A group of reporters huddled together outside the doors of the ballroom that housed the media centre, all of us caught off guard, but given that speculation had begun to ramp up about Ohtani and the Blue Jays, it was easy to connect the dots. Atkins was, some way and somehow, on the trail of Shohei Ohtani.

But it raised the question: Where in the world was Ross Atkins?

Writers walked back to their hotel rooms to set up for the Zoom call, an old tradition we all hoped we'd left in the COVID-19 era of media coverage, and waited for Atkins' face to appear. What happened next was one of the strangest media moments in this club's history.

Atkins appeared, sitting in front of a blank white wall, wearing a crisp black suit jacket with a plain white dress shirt, one button undone at the top. He was lit by two overhead lights, just above the screen, but his camera shot was cropped intentionally tight. There was no artwork behind him, no office plants, no window. Even when you expanded the image of Atkins, there was no obvious light coming in through a window, no clue at all to pick apart in hopes of finding out which coast, which time zone, which country Atkins was in.

The Zoom began. I opened by asking Atkins the obvious:

Question: "Are you with us here in Nashville or has business brought you elsewhere?"

Atkins: "I just wanted to say thank you for the adjusted opportunity here. I wanted to ensure that I was with you today with the scheduled meeting that we had. Due to some scheduling conflicts, Zoom permitted us to have this meeting. I appreciate the adjustment."

Question: "Are you physically elsewhere today, in terms of speaking with other players away from Nashville?

Atkins: "Due to scheduling conflicts, I was able to be on this call, and I am grateful for your adjustment to be here with me today. I wanted to make sure that I was with you, and Zoom permitted that."

What language was this man speaking?

Atkins was doing exactly what he needed to do, but still, it was stunning to watch this play out.

On these media Zoom calls, a member of the Blue Jays' communication team leads the order of questions, calling upon reporters who click the "raise hand" button to keep some order. Just as Atkins finished his scripted answer, though, the Gaylord Opryland Asylum decided to have some fun with us. The Wi-Fi began to drop out for most people on the call, including the Blue Jays' PR team, which left Atkins in silence, his face up on the screen as the "speaker," waiting for the next question.

Atkins: "I guess you and I are just going to...stay together, Keegs?"

As the rest of the call finally played out, reporters and the Blue Jays' PR team scrambling to connect to Zoom on their cell phones, Atkins didn't budge. If we'd asked him for the colour of the wall behind him, he surely would have delivered a long, drawn-out answer about how he did not want to commit to calling the wall white. Besides, it could be eggshell white, seashell white, cloud white, cream white, any number of whites.

But it was obvious by then. Ross Atkins was somewhere in the world chasing the biggest prize in the history of the sport. He was in Dunedin, Florida, at the Blue Jays' player development complex.

That was the day Shohei Ohtani walked out of the spring clubhouse wearing a Toronto Blue Jays hat. Looking back, John Schneider remembers more than just the hat.

"It was the weirdest thing I've ever gone through."

* * *

White walls barely scratched the surface.

The Blue Jays wisely bent to shape themselves around every single one of Ohtani's requests for privacy. They were originally scheduled to fly to L.A. to meet with Ohtani and his representation, but once that leaked out, the plans changed.

Ohtani came to the Blue Jays' complex accompanied by his agent, Nez Balelo, and his interpreter at the time, Ippei Mizuhara. They were picked up in a black SUV by the Blue Jays' senior manager of security, Jason Weaving, and driven back to Dunedin.

John Schneider, Ross Atkins, Mark Shapiro, and Edward Rogers waited together in a room that overlooked the parking lot and complex.

Time has never moved slower.

They needed the complex empty. We're talking *completely empty.* The complex was a ghost town, 10 men standing on its 65 acres.

There are MLB players who live nearby and use that complex through the offseason who had a better feel for what was actually happening. For the rest of the minor league players and many staff, the Blue Jays told them there was an important "Rogers ownership meeting" and they'd have to stay away for the day.

"We're standing upstairs in the suite and Jason is texting us updates. We watched him get out of the car. I'm wearing a sport coat and we're all done up. It was like royalty was coming," Schneider said. "There was no one in the complex. It was bare.

"It was like the president was coming. Seriously."

The tour began. This small group had the whole place to themselves, all of the fields, weight rooms, and clubhouses sitting bare. Ohtani had just undergone elbow surgery at the end of the last season, so these resources mattered. Besides, he'd be spending his springs here for the next 10 years.

As the Blue Jays' group walked Ohtani through the complex, they eventually passed a TV screen. Ohtani, still desperate to keep these visits completely quiet, looked at the screen and saw two players throwing a ball back and forth. He looked back to the screen again, then turned and asked Schneider, Shapiro, and Atkins where those players were. Was that a live feed of the complex? Were there other people who could see them?

Thankfully, it was a live feed of TD Ballpark. The group explained to Ohtani that the field was a few miles across town, where they dreamed of him selling out spring training games, and the group continued to walk. On the screen, Jordan Romano and a teammate continued to throw the ball back and forth, back and forth, not knowing they'd just survived a scare in one of the biggest moments of their franchise's history.

In fact, some of the players were in on it. While younger minor league prospects who use the complex might not have been as aware, a handful of big-leaguers were able to put two and two together, so they knew exactly what was happening. They understood the gravity of it all, the importance. Some MLB players using the facilities that week agreed—and asked others to follow—that they would not even tell their own agents about what was happening. Agents talk. This could not get out.

Those there that day describe being so impressed with Ohtani and his attention to detail. If one wall was painted eggshell white and the next was plain old white, he'd probably want to know why. He wasn't staring off into the distance or checking his phone. He was in some ways still such a young man, but in others a businessman looking to close a deal worth over a half-billion dollars. The best demands the best.

"It was genuine, authentic engagement, which was demonstrated by an unbelievable attention span for downloading," Atkins remembers. "Elite performers are that for a reason."

The moment that sticks in the brains of those there that day came at the very end.

The visit had gone well. Ohtani was absolutely thrilled with the club's complex, now one of the best in baseball after renovations that went beyond $100 million. A centerpiece in those renovations was the major league clubhouse.

Inside the Blue Jays' clubhouse that day was a locker for Shohei Ohtani.

The Blue Jays' group had set up three lockers in the clubhouse along with Marnie Starkman, the club's executive vice president of business operations, who never misses a detail.

There it all was—the jerseys, the gear, the hats, all the bags and accessories. This was how it would look for Ohtani, his own locker with an additional space on either side, the extra real estate that comes with the biggest contract in baseball history. This is what it would look like. It was sitting right in front of Ohtani. He didn't have to imagine anything.

By now, the Blue Jays' group was standing in the player dining area, on the ground level just beneath the boardroom where big deals are brokered and signed. It's what they saw next that sticks.

Ohtani had packed up the lockers.

He walked out of the clubhouse, a Blue Jays hat on his head, carrying bags filled with Toronto Blue Jays gear. Alongside him was Mizuhara, decked out in Blue Jays gear of his own. The two were stopping to take photos together.

This wasn't even the Blue Jays' plan. They'd expected it to be another selling point along the tour, perhaps something to place the reality of playing for this organization deeper into the mind of Ohtani, but they never expected Ohtani to pack up some of that gear and take it with him.

Then, they saw something else.

It was Ohtani's dog, Decoy, running alongside him. Decoy was wearing the Canadian dog jacket the Blue Jays had bought for him.

* * *

On December 5, Ross Atkins was back in Nashville.

No one will ever try to convince you that dealing with the media is Atkins' strong suit, but if the assignment is to say a lot while revealing little? He was the man for that job. He's the Shohei Ohtani of secrecy.

But this was a whole operation. Even this group's return to the winter meetings in Nashville had to be coordinated.

"When we flew to Nashville, me, Mark, and Ross had to go into the hotel at three different times through three different entrances," Schneider said. "Media was all over it. I walked down the next morning, which was my first time in the lobby, and there were 12 cameras on me from Japanese media. I didn't say anything, but they almost followed me into the bathroom."

The crush of Japanese media was remarkable to watch. Even when Yusei Kikuchi was in Toronto or on the road, there could be anywhere from three to six dedicated reporters following him exclusively, and that number would spike in larger markets like New York or L.A., but Ohtani is a different game altogether. We're talking dozens of reporters whose sole job is to document every move this man makes. Whether he hits a grand slam or eats a different flavour of granola bar than he had the day before, it's a story in Japan, home to such a vibrant, passionate baseball culture.

Atkins tap danced his way through some early appearances on radio that day, joking about how reports had him in different cities, in different countries, on different planets. Anyone with half a clue knew by this point, though, after overnight reports of Ohtani's visit to Dunedin.

Across the convention centre, down the endless miles of soulless hallways and past the Irish pub that had been turned into a Christmas-themed bar for the month of December, Dodgers manager Dave Roberts took a completely different approach. He said, out loud in front of a million microphones, that the Dodgers had spoken with Ohtani and it went well. His phone quickly lit up, and immediately after, he was seen huddling with the Dodgers' staff. Whoops.

The winter meetings came and went, though, media and executives filing out slowly. It felt like people were nervous to leave a party just in case something happened at 2:00 AM. No one wanted to be the one who wasn't there for the big story.

That finally came a few days later.

* * *

December 8, 2023, chaos erupted.

By the time half of the country woke up, Blue Jays fans were already tracking flights, digging back through old information to determine the type of aircraft Ohtani would be flying on and which airport he'd used in the past. Overnight reports that Ohtani was nearing a decision whipped Blue Jays fans into a hysteria, and rightfully so. These images of flight trackers dominated social media throughout the day, and by the end, there were videos of people standing on their back porches, phones pointed up to the sky to capture a distant blur, the jet they were certain carried Ohtani.

Blue Jays fans thought this because, well, they'd been led to. It's the job of a fan to give a damn. It's the job of the media to get things right every time. Only one group held up their end of the bargain that day.

Late in the morning, a report came out of Los Angeles that Ohtani had made his decision. It wasn't the Dodgers. It wasn't the Giants. It was the Blue Jays. Ohtani was, reportedly, signing with Toronto.

While many in the industry immediately questioned the legitimacy of this report, it's not a fan's job to be that far "inside journalism." Even as some cold water was thrown on that report in the hours afterward, excitement built. Flight trackers set traffic records. Tickets were bought.

In the early afternoon, things kicked into overdrive following an inaccurate report that Ohtani was on that plane to Toronto. An hour and 10 minutes later, that report was shot down, and 20 minutes after that came another report that Ohtani was sitting at home in California, where he'd been all along.

What the hell was happening?

"I had people from the industry texting me and saying, 'It looks like Toronto,' remembers John Schneider. "I'd just send back the fingers-crossed emoji. When that story broke, I called Ross and he said that nothing was official, we haven't heard. Then, when the whole flight thing started, I had other managers texting me saying congratulations. They had heard that he was coming."

Later, we'd learn that the man on that plane being tracked by so many was Robert Herjavec, a Canadian businessman and investor famous for appearing on shows like *Shark Tank* and *Dragon's Den*. Just like the viral story on Twitter that day from a Canadian opera singer, who'd heard that Yusei Kikuchi had rented out a high-end sushi restaurant downtown, there was nothing to it. Only a story this strange, and a player this great, could draw such a crazy cast of characters into the narrative.

Let's take another step inside journalism here. Regardless of how these reports came and went through the day, it was clear that Ohtani was nearing his decision. While other clubs had been involved throughout, most notably the Giants, the industry consensus was that it was down to the Dodgers and the Blue Jays. It was time to prepare a story...just in case.

Knowing that if Ohtani signed in L.A., I'd have some time to write a story on the Blue Jays losing out, we chose to prepare a tentative story for Ohtani signing with the Blue Jays. This is regular practice—having the skeleton of a story built so that, if and when the time comes, you can drop in some details and deliver a full story right away. Think about this the next time you see a long, beautifully written obituary from a major news outlet just moments after the death of someone famous. That might have been written five years ago, but dusted off and updated in the moment. Hell, I've pre-written obituaries for people I still see or speak with regularly. They're sitting in a folder somewhere...just in case.

At noon on December 8, I sat down to write a story that I knew might never see the light of day, but again, we wanted to be prepared...just in case we needed to move quickly when the news broke. At 12:31 PM, a story sat, ready for publication, on the screen of my laptop. Here it is, the unedited copy:

TORONTO—The wildest dream is real. Shohei Ohtani is set to join the Toronto Blue Jays.

Ohtani and the Blue Jays agreed to terms on a [**XXXXX**] **on [DAY OF WEEK]**, a moment that immediately takes its place behind the World Series wins of 1992-'93 as one of the biggest in the 48-year history of the organization. The club has not confirmed the deal.

The pursuit of Ohtani was unlike any we've seen before. Shrouded in secrecy, this drama played out behind closed doors, leaving entranced Blue Jays fans to search through the shadows for clues, tracking private jets across North America with a level of hope rarely seen before in this market.

This time, there's no letdown, no heartbreak, no lingering weight of what could have been. The biggest star in baseball is coming to Canada.

Toronto's pursuit of the Japanese superstar cranked up at the recent MLB Winter Meetings in Nashville, Tenn., where the spy games truly took hold. On the first day of the Meetings, when general manager Ross Atkins was scheduled to meet with the media in person, his session was suddenly pivoted online, leaving reporters to squint for clues that weren't there as Atkins sat in front of a blank, white wall and refused to reveal his whereabouts. With Ohtani's camp valuing secrecy throughout this process, the Blue Jays committed in full.

Clarity crept in the next day, with news that Ohtani had been visiting the Blue Jays' new player development complex in Dunedin, Fla., which was a cornerstone of the organization's pitch to Ohtani. Not only will that complex play a major role in Ohtani's rehab process from his right elbow surgery, which will prevent him from pitching next season and limit him to hitting, but he'll be spending a significant portion of his life there over the next [**XXXXX**] years, preparing for what the Blue Jays hope are annual World Series runs.

As a player, Ohtani is a once-in-a-lifetime talent. En route to his second career MVP Award, the 29-year-old hit .304 with 44 home runs and a 1.066 OPS last season, all while posting a 3.14 ERA with 167 strikeouts over 132 innings. It's as if you combined the 2021 version of Vladimir Guerrero Jr.—who finished second in MVP voting to Ohtani—with the current version of Kevin Gausman, all in one player.

Ohtani enjoyed a breakout season in 2021, making history at every turn and capturing the attention of the sporting world at large with his unprecedented two-way success. He won his first AL MVP Award in unanimous fashion after producing 46 homers with a .965 OPS at the plate and a 3.18 ERA with 156 K's on the mound.

One player on the planet can do this, and he's coming to Toronto.

Ohtani is a cultural force that will ripple well beyond the playing field for the Blue Jays, who are midway through the second and final year of their $300 million renovations to Rogers Centre. Those have come with the hope of improving the fan experience, of course, and with today's news, the phones at the Rogers Centre box office might not stop ringing until Christmas morning.

Ohtani's arrival also brings a crush of media coverage along with it, with Ohtani's traveling media corps likely to outnumber the existing group of media who already covered the Blue Jays. It is impossible to overstate Ohtani's fame in his native Japan, home to a remarkable baseball culture which holds up its stars with such respect and adoration, and this is part of the reason Ohtani has chosen to remain so private over his years with the Angels.

Now, for the second time, Ohtani hoists the hopes of a country onto his shoulders.

There are miles to go from here—kilometers now—but after landing Ohtani, the Blue Jays will never know "impossible" again.

That story never saw the light of day, but according to sources with direct knowledge of the negotiations, it almost did.

The early stages of the Ohtani talks had progressed gradually as Ohtani's representatives wrangled the legitimate bidders and laid out how the process would work. This was not your standard free-agent bidding process. It quickly became clear that clubs would need to clear a half-billion dollars to land Ohtani, but as the field of bidders began to narrow and the price continued to climb, the idea of deferred money was introduced. The Blue Jays, Dodgers, Angels, and Giants were among the teams still fully involved at this point.

Sensing the interest and an opportunity to swing even bigger, Ohtani's camp circled back one last time and drew a line. If you met the 10-year, $700 million commitment, you got a seat at the table. The Blue Jays, following a similar structure to the Dodgers with extremely heavy deferrals on the back end, were all in.

The Blue Jays got a seat at the table. It was down to the Blue Jays, Dodgers, and Giants, then eventually the Dodgers and Blue Jays as finalists.

They waited for Ohtani to decide.

Thursday passed with no decision. Friday came, the day of the infamous flight that Shohei Ohtani wasn't on, and front offices began to grow more anxious, all stuck in silence and mystery while wondering if the other teams knew something they didn't.

Many Blue Jays players and staff started to receive the same congratulatory messages John Schneider had received. Some came from rival players or old coaches who had just caught a snippet of the same news cycle everyone else was watching, but not all. Amid all the fear, suspicion, and paranoia that came to a head that day, word began to circulate among players, coaches, and even some rival executives—including clubs involved in Ohtani's pursuit—that the Toronto Blue Jays had landed Shohei Ohtani.

* * *

It came in an Instagram post, 3:05 PM the next day.

Shohei Ohtani was signing with the Dodgers. The news came from where we should have known it would always come from...Ohtani himself. He wanted to control the message, and in the end, he did.

For Blue Jays fans, it was like opening Instagram to see the person of your dreams posing with someone else, an engagement ring sparkling in the foreground with a diamond the size of an orange. He was gone.

Other free-agent pursuits are easier to shake, even when there's heartbreak. Nearly every player in baseball has another version of themselves out there somewhere. It's easy for teams to pivot, but you can't pivot from an Ohtani. This is the type of miss that sticks to you. Even as this organization trudges forward into 2025, 2026, and beyond, there will be this nagging temptation to step back and wonder what it would all look like had Ohtani been on that plane.

"You feel like you're kind of linked to him forever," John Schneider said.

It's sensible for people like Schneider or Blue Jays players to have more of an emotional reaction to the news. They're not as directly involved in the dollars and cents of it all, the planning, the talks with ownership, or Ohtani's "revenue-generating profile," as Mark Shapiro later put it. That's how many in the Blue Jays' front office had approached this, as a business case, one that made the biggest contract in sports history worth every penny.

"We were committed. We were realistic. We understood that if you made a list, L.A. made much more sense, but it was clear that the interest was genuine. It was clear that we were authentically a player, and once that was the case, we couldn't just go in halfway. We were all in," said Mark Shapiro.

"In the event that L.A. blinks at all—whether they're uncertain about the magnitude of money with other players on their payroll or they're a little bit unsure of the player for some reason—whatever it is, if they blink, we'll be there. We'll get the guy."

L.A. didn't blink.

"It's only a positive for Toronto, for Canada and for the Blue Jays. We were legitimate contenders for him, and we controlled everything that we could possibly control. There were good, compelling reasons, including the team in L.A., for why he went there and his life being in the west, not in this direction."

The fallout was crushing. This organization has bounced in and out of being baseball's little brother over the years, but lately, it had been sitting at the adults' table. Despite their on-field frustrations, this organization had shelled out big money to build a pitching staff led by Kevin Gausman (5 years, $115 million), José Berríos (7 years, $131 million), Chris Bassitt (3 years, $63 million), and Yusei Kikuchi (3 years, 36 million). Hyun Hin Ryu's four-year, $80 million deal had just run its course.

Going back even further, the Blue Jays had just handed George Springer the biggest contract in the organization's history, a six-year, $150 million deal. In Springer's case, like Ryu's, the Blue Jays were willing to stretch on term along with spending big. This organization has always had money, but finally the Blue Jays were throwing it around.

Even though Ohtani would have cost them $700 million, those numbers made sense to the Blue Jays and, more importantly, made sense to ownership. Pair Ohtani with the still-ongoing renovations to Rogers Centre, which eventually pushed past $400 million, and the Blue Jays had a one-billion-plus-dollar path to making the Blue Jays the hottest ticket in the country. The math worked. The head and the heart agreed.

"That was extremely unique. From the business case on incremental revenue he would have brought in to the unbelievable performance projections that actually modeled to support a large portion of the contract," Shapiro explained. "From a talent perspective and from a very unique revenue-generating profile, that was a once-in-a-lifetime type of player. It wasn't a question of making a business case for that and pivoting that money somewhere else. No one else could justify, for us, a contract that large."

There it is again, that wording so many involved in this pursuit have used. Ohtani isn't a once-in-a-generation player. He's a player you only see once, and if you do, you're lucky to have been there. Beyond his two-way brilliance, Ohtani represents something so much greater. He is one of the biggest stars on the planet, a baseball genius and a god in Japan.

It's easy to look at this pursuit and see where the optimist's eyes go. There's no such thing as being "close" in the big leagues—there is one team that gets the guy and then the 29 others—but the Blue Jays were right there. In the years that come, they should have a seat at the table with any player they want, regardless of how rich the negotiations get.

The Blue Jays are left with only the story, though.

Ohtani was the great hope. Him signing with the Blue Jays would have fundamentally changed every conversation we had about this team for the next decade, period. It felt real.

It never felt closer than that day in December. Ohtani was right there, in every room of that complex, looking over every inch, imagining a future there.

As Ohtani left that day, carrying the bags he'd packed up from his own locker in that clubhouse, he turned to them one last time. Ohtani gave them a thumbs up, Blue Jays hat on his head, and climbed into the SUV.

PART 3

FACES OF THE BLUE JAYS

9

Dave Stieb

Author's note: Stretching across the facing of the 400 Level at Rogers Centre is the Blue Jays' Level of Excellence.

It's the ultimate honour in Toronto, and even though that ring of names still feels incomplete, these represent the best of the Blue Jays. The names listed are:

Roy Halladay
Dave Stieb
Cito Gaston
Paul Beeston
Pat Gillick
Joe Carter
Tony Fernández
George Bell
Carlos Delgado

José Bautista
Tom Cheek

This list once included Roberto Alomar. In 2021, the Blue Jays announced they were "severing all ties" with Alomar after Major League Baseball placed him on the ineligible list and terminated him as a consultant following an investigation into sexual misconduct. Alomar had previously held the title of special assistant with the Blue Jays and had been involved with youth baseball initiatives in both Puerto Rico and Canada, acting as the commissioner of Tournament 12, an annual amateur baseball tournament put on at Rogers Centre by the Blue Jays Baseball Academy. That tournament now lives on as the Canadian Futures Showcase.

Alomar's name has been scrubbed from Rogers Centre completely. His Hall of Fame banner was quickly removed and his No. 12 jersey, once retired by the organization, was put back into circulation. Now, only the No. 32 jersey of Roy Halladay is retired in Toronto, alongside the No. 42 jersey of Jackie Robinson, retired across Major League Baseball.

So many other players, seasons, and moments remain worthy of celebration in this organization, and the beauty of the Blue Jays growing to approach their 50th anniversary is the amount of history this club has created. To tell the story of every player and every moment would take volumes of books covering nearly a half-century of baseball.

Someday, another Hall of Fame banner will hang alongside Halladay's. Someday, another World Series banner will hang alongside the two that have watched over Rogers Centre for over 30 years. These are the stories of the players and moments— some of them, at least—that have made up the rich history of Toronto's team.

* * *

Dave Stieb is an enigma. The elusive superstar, so brash and brilliant on the mound, lives in stories like a local legend. There's almost a purity to it now.

The moment an old teammate hears Stieb's name, it's like they've been waiting for that opening to talk about him. Something about Stieb's greatness feels frozen in its era, a VHS tape of the greatest movie you've ever seen that was never transferred to DVD, never went digital.

Forget the Toronto Blue Jays for a moment. Stieb was one of the faces of pitching in Major League Baseball for the entire 1980s, but he wasn't just tossing slop and eating innings. Stieb was a pitcher ahead of his time, a pitcher who could be picked up, dropped into the 2025 MLB season, and fit right in. He was that good.

Let's start with the three men who had the best seat in the house for Stieb's career: his catchers.

"He's the best pitcher the Blue Jays ever had," Buck Martinez said the moment he heard Stieb's name.

"Dave Stieb is one of the most underrated pitchers that I've ever been around," Pat Borders said at a World Series anniversary event in 2022. "He was a devastatingly good pitcher and I feel like he deserves more credit for how good he was."

"He was definitely the best right-handed pitcher I ever caught," Ernie Whitt said. "He was nasty with the slider. His fastball never went straight."

The story of one of the greatest players in Blue Jays history began in the outfield. Stieb, a fifth-rounder out of Southern Illinois University in 1978, was drafted as an outfielder and briefly struggled as one in the minor leagues.

Pat Hentgen, who has become one of Stieb's closest friends over the years, loves telling this tale.

"When he was in A-ball, and this is a cool story...Dave said that when he played the outfield, he could throw the ball right to the third baseman all through college. When they let him play one year in the outfield here, it was the same thing. He'd run in, get the ball, and say, 'I can throw this right on the bag from all the way out there.' Dave said that, when they told him to pitch, 'I couldn't believe how close it was. Shit, I can throw it right there.'"

Hentgen still remembers how Stieb explained it to him, so nonchalantly.

"Throwing strikes is easy," Stieb said to him. "I was doing it from the outfield. Now it's just 60 feet."

That's how Stieb, the outfielder drafted in 1978, debuted as a pitcher in the big leagues just a year later. The era of Blue Jays baseball he was born into is important to all of this, especially when you begin to consider the place Stieb holds in baseball's history.

"Part of the reason he's not in the Hall of Fame is because he did play here," Paul Beeston said. "He did play for bad baseball teams. He came up in 1979 and his first year, he was 8–8, but we won 53 games and he wasn't even up in the beginning of the year. He was a force. He just got better and better and better, more and more competitive. All he wanted to do was win."

The Blue Jays won 53 games in Stieb's rookie year, then 67 the next. In the strike-shortened 1981 season, they were a dreadful 37–69. Stieb was already a two-time All-Star by that point, but his younger years were not spent chasing pennants. The Blue Jays' franchise was still in its infancy.

This organization had struck gold with Stieb in such a shocking way, but the rest of the team was still growing up around him.

"Had he been on stronger teams in his career, he would have become the Blue Jays' first 20-game winner, not Jack Morris in 1992," said Jerry Howarth, radio voice of the Blue Jays for much of Stieb's career. "Dave had all of the ingredients and everything going for him to win 20 games. There were just too many games where they didn't score runs for him, maybe an error or two behind him. He was unfortunate that way. For me, he was the first 20-game winner they had, even though he didn't win 20 games."

Even though it all came so naturally to Stieb, he could do things with the baseball that most other pitchers simply couldn't.

"He had great shit. He had such a feel for pitching," Martinez said. "He would throw what he called his dead fish. It was just a BP fastball. We didn't even have a sign for it, he just knew when to throw it and he had such a great feel for it. He used to just get off on that when he'd get some big slugger to hit a weak ground ball. He'd say, 'I fished him.'"

"The best slider I've ever seen, too. It was a sweeper before anybody ever talked about a sweeper," Martinez adds, swiping his hand through the air above the table. "It just kept breaking and breaking."

It wasn't until Stieb's seventh season, in 1985, that the Blue Jays finally made the postseason. We could view Stieb's career so differently today—and this applies to all of those teams in the '80s—if the current wild card structure had been in place. Perhaps Stieb could have chased a World Series earlier, dominated on the biggest stage in front of the U.S. television audiences that rarely saw him.

"When I first came up, I didn't know any better," Stieb said at the anniversary event in 2022. "They had just turned me into a pitcher, so I was just happy to be on the major-league team, which was quite a surprise as fast as it happened. Losing was not fun, because when I'd played the outfield on teams, we'd won. I was used to winning. It was tough to swallow. Then, being a pitcher and relying on them for my success was a hard thing to accept and get used to. That's probably why I had some bad raps early on."

* * *

Stieb battled what so many stars do. This isn't just about baseball, either. When you're the best—the very best—it can be difficult to deal with the talent of those around you.

"It was really tough for him to be a bystander," as Gord Ash put it.

"You don't find too many true competitors," Jerry Howarth said. "A lot of major leaguers, they compete, there's no question about that. Dave took it one degree further than he had to."

We've seen this with so many star players in Toronto since Stieb's time, and for as long as baseball is played here, it will keep happening. It's too often a byproduct of greatness.

"He was just a tremendous competitor. The problem was that we weren't as good as he was and he couldn't handle that," Martinez remembered. "He'd be thinking, 'I could play as good as you guys.' But he was a marvelous player, a great competitor. He had all of the moves, a great pickoff move, a great fielder. I don't think he ever won a Gold Glove, but he should have."

Ernie Whitt remembers that famous Stieb glare, too. There were times that he or a coach would pull Stieb aside for a moment. That shortstop wasn't trying to screw up, they'd tell him. The shortstop got the error, not you.

"Nobody ever got a hit off of him that was his fault," Beeston said with a laugh. "It was either the catcher's fault, the umpire's fault, it was somebody else's fault. It was never him. Hence, Stieb always had a little bit of a disconnect with his teammates and with everybody else, but he's changed, as we all have. He was just a hell of a competitor. He would do whatever was necessary to win. He thought he should throw a no-hitter every game."

Beeston's point is echoed by nearly everyone who speaks about Stieb. He has softened with time, some of those rough edges eroding with the years. We don't get to see this as often as we do from other Blue Jays alumni, given how rarely Stieb has appeared at public events over the years, but he's changed. One of the challenges of greatness is knowing when to turn it off. If a player like Stieb carried that same energy into the real world, it could drive them mad.

Stieb is remembered as being difficult for the media to work with. This has to be remembered when we discuss his Hall of Fame candidacy, which is voted on by baseball writers. Much of that reputation came for good reason in the early years, but there were moments along the way that showed more of Stieb.

In a 1985 interview with *Inside Sports*, a monthly magazine at the time with similarities to *Sports Illustrated*, Stieb opened up about how he'd handled the attention over the years.

"Maybe that's a recent thing because I just got too much exposure and got tired of talking about my private life. I bore myself. And it was like the Michael Jackson thing. You just heard enough about the guy—leave it alone, everybody's tired of him. I don't want to be isolated, but then again, I don't enjoy having everything I do viewed under a microscope. Maybe people don't realize how that can affect you."

Could Stieb express that, he was asked by interviewer Alan Steinberg.

"Well, my first few years in Toronto I pitched well, but I didn't get any notoriety. I didn't care at the time. I didn't want publicity. Then all of a sudden, it just came and came—and it got out of hand. After a while I began to feel I wasn't a person anymore."

That 1985 season was one of Stieb's finest, a 2.48 ERA over 264 innings. The next year wasn't nearly as kind, though, a rare misstep in a decade of Stieb's dominance.

Those struggles brought us another look into the mind of Stieb. His book, *Tomorrow I'll Be Perfect*, was coming out that season, written with Kevin Boland. The timing couldn't have been worse, though, with Stieb fighting his struggles through that summer.

He wrote a piece special to the *Toronto Star* on August 9, 1986. The book had already been sent off to the publisher by then, but this was Stieb's way of promoting its upcoming release while still addressing the season at hand. It's a fascinating artifact, a level of access and introspection that we'd never see from a player today.

"Have I lost it? Are my best days, as few as they might have been, already behind me?" Stieb wrote. "Am I done? No. No. And no again."

"These are the questions—and the right answers to them, I keep telling myself—that cloud every waking moment of every day in this long hot and most unsettled summer of my life."

Stieb wrote about what had gone wrong, how those days had weighed on him and how the public discourse of it all played out. He also, in the most interesting lines of the piece, looked the reader straight in the eye and addressed his own personality, the reputation he'd built in baseball that he couldn't shake. Had he lost his edge? Had he lost the attitude that had earned him that "bad rap"?

"Maybe it's true, after so much media fuss has been made of my tantrums on and off the mound, that I am much nicer to be near. Maybe too nice. Reggie Jackson of the Angels, for one, and a host of my concerned teammates have suggested this is so."

"They wonder whatever became of the ogre they knew and loved to hate—the evil eye ever in search of errant fielders, the scourge of blinking umpires, the only guy on the team who could strut sitting down."

"By popular demand, they want him back. Anything to oblige, I always say. Mothers be warned, henceforth, to keep the little ones far from the TV set when the camera zooms in on my pantomime after yet another seeing-eye, blooper, broken-bat, tweener falls in. Mr. Mean, as you might have noticed recently, is back at his old stand..."

The ogre. Mr. Mean.

It didn't matter if you liked him. For most of his career, Stieb didn't seem to give a damn.

* * *

Dave Stieb spent one year on the Hall of Fame ballot—2004—and immediately fell off the ballot after receiving just 1.4 percent of votes.

Whether Stieb belongs in the Hall of Fame still lives on as a fascinating debate, but regardless of where you fall on the broader conversation, the fact he lasted just one year on the ballot is criminal. Stieb would have benefited greatly from a few years on that ballot, opening up space to discuss his career and frame it within the context of how we now value players. That picture, itself, would have changed significantly in the years that followed 2004, as voters and fans became more comfortable with the analytics we now discuss so casually.

It's something Stieb himself has wrestled with over time.

"I've always said I don't deserve to because my stats don't warrant it," Stieb said in 2022. "It was based on wins, basically. That's how I've felt about it, but apparently they look at it differently now with the new analytics. I've had people tell me that, if you look at it that way, it might be justified. With that said, I guess there's a way to look at it and say I should be in there. I really don't give a whole lot of thought to it. I accept the fact that I'm not in it."

"I don't know. If it's something I thought I deserved a long time ago, then of course it would mean everything to me. When you accept the fact that you're not in it and you shouldn't be in it according to how it was judged back then, I'm OK with it. I've been OK with it for a long time. People bring stuff like that up and make me think about, 'Well, should I be in it?'"

Dave Stieb career (1979–1993, 1998)
176–137
2,895 ⅓ IP
3.44 ERA
7x All-Star

Stieb never finished higher than fourth in AL Cy Young Award voting, another crime to add to the list. Take the 1984 season as an example. Using modern metrics, Stieb's 5.6 WAR ranked him second in the AL that season. His ERA also ranked second among qualified starters and he threw the most innings of anyone. First and second place went to relievers—Willie Hernandez and Dan Quisenberry—while Stieb was stuck at the bottom with one vote. Jack Morris also received one vote despite Stieb's numbers being better in nearly every possible way.

"His sabermetrics, his WAR, all of that stuff. I've looked at it," Pat Hentgen said. "There are other pitchers who get in and I think to myself, 'Wow. How can they not talk about Stieb?' Every hitter in the league talked about how he was the best pitcher for so long. There were 13 full seasons of domination until he got hurt."

We still need to respect that these awards represent their era, but as you look back on Stieb's career through a modern lens, there are dozens of these openings. When it came to the Hall of Fame, Stieb's 176 wins without a Cy Young Award makes the initial conversation a difficult one.

"His win-loss record wasn't reflective of who he was as a pitcher," said Ed Sprague. "If you put him on the Yankees or whatever team was in their heyday, he was probably the best of the best. He had that nickname, 'Cy,' for a reason."

Had Stieb carried his peak for another few years, perhaps made another postseason run or two, the conversation could have changed. He's left with a career WAR of 43.8, certainly on the short side of what we typically consider a Hall of Fame pitcher, but we're talking about one of the very best pitchers of a decade. He had the peak, and while he didn't do this for 22 years, there's enough there to call it longevity.

His old teammates lean on the stories, not the numbers.

"I remember when Wade Boggs told me at the All-Star Game that Dave had the best slider he ever saw," Hentgen said. "I played with Molitor, too, and we were sitting on the bench together one time in 1993 or '94. Dave's name got brought up and he laughed. He said, 'Are you kidding me? Best breaking ball I ever saw.'"

"When you've got two Hall of Fame hitters telling you that, a right-hander and a left-hander who were maybe the best hitters in their era...you know?"

Buck Martinez starts to list some names of his own.

"Jim Rice. Dwight Evans. All of those guys were like, 'I've got no chance.'"

"In one of the All-Star Games, Darrell Porter was catching. He threw three balls right past him. He never even got a glove on them. But his fastball was just so alive. He loved his slider and we used to argue all the time."

Stieb, as much as almost any player on the edges of the Hall of Fame vote over the past few decades, would benefit from a broader public conversation. He played out so much of his career in Toronto in a time when the Blue Jays weren't a big story. That changed with some of their runs later in the '80s and, of course, the World Series wins in the early '90s, but the Blue Jays weren't on TV each night for someone in New York, in Boston, in L.A.

Stieb hasn't stayed in the public eye, either. If Stieb had pivoted to a life working in the media or made himself more visible over the years, would we have these conversations more often? Would they eventually snowball, building enough momentum to grow into something larger? We'll likely never know, though the Hall of Fame's era committees could be an interesting place for those conversations to begin again. Staying in the spotlight is no player's responsibility, particularly one who didn't seem to enjoy it in the first place, but there's a human element to all of this.

He was, in so many ways, a product of his era. He has, in so many ways, stayed in that era, Stieb's greatness preserved in the minds of those who saw him.

"Stieb was...", Martinez began, before pausing. "Everybody talks about Doc, and Doc was so good, but Stieb, if he'd played on those good teams in his prime, he would have won 30 games."

After a year with the White Sox in 1994, Stieb's career was seemingly finished. He'd won 175 games. He finished his career with 176.

* * *

There's one last great Dave Stieb story, maybe the best of them all.

"It was unbelievable," Pat Hentgen said, shaking his head 25 years later. "It was the coolest thing."

Stieb, after four years away from the game, was 40 years old and came to Blue Jays camp as a guest instructor. It's a common thing to see former players do, even today.

"He's throwing BP and he's sawing guys off," Hentgen said. "Guys are yelling at him. 'Throw it straight! Throw it straight!' And Dave is out there saying, 'I'm trying!'"

They had fun with it, but again, Stieb was 40. His career was over.

One day that spring, Hentgen saw Stieb walking his way. Stieb asked to borrow Hentgen's cleats. Hentgen stood there, dumbfounded, as Stieb told him that he was going to throw a side.

"We had the same size cleats, so he wore my spikes," Hentgen said. "Me and Roger Clemens, we couldn't wait to see what Darrin Fletcher was going to say. Fletcher comes back into the clubhouse and we asked him how Dave looked. He said,

'Dude, he's got a better breaking ball than both of you.' That's what he said. He was 40.'"

Hentgen tells this story with the excitement of someone trying to convince you that the story is real. It is, though. Stieb launched a comeback, dominated some kids in Triple A Syracuse for a few weeks, and made it back to the Blue Jays. When he made his return to an MLB mound on June 18, 1998, it had been 1,853 days since he last threw a pitch in the big leagues.

"In '98 when he came back, I wasn't here," Beeston remembers. "I was in New York, but Gordie brought him back and I said, "Are you fucking crazy? Stieb was finished in 1991!"

Instead, Stieb had one last ride in the tank.

"We'd all played with Dave and we loved him," said Ed Sprague, still there in 1998. "He had the passion, and he probably didn't end his career the way he'd like to, so he gave it one more shot. I just thought that was awesome. His history with us allowed that to happen. It was so cool having him around. I don't think Dave ever got his just due as a big-league pitcher, even though I think people close to the game get it, just maybe not to the average fan."

There he was again, one of the great competitors in Blue Jays history. He went down swinging, posting a 4.83 ERA over 50 ⅓ innings.

"When he decided to put that uniform back on, I was not surprised. You have to be who you are. You can't be somebody else," Jerry Howarth said. "You can't follow somebody else's path or dreams. When I saw that Dave wanted to compete again, I saw that competitive gene. You have to get to a point where, finally, you can say that you know you're finished. He hadn't gotten to that point yet. He tried one more time."

Stieb's accomplishments were all his own, but since leaving the game, it's felt like fans of the Toronto Blue Jays have carried the torch, keeping Stieb's greatness alive as his years fade further into the past.

We may not get much closer to understanding Dave Stieb— all of those sharp edges—but perhaps we don't need to. He's always wanted it that way.

10

Cito Gaston

CITO GASTON IS A GIANT IN TORONTO, THE STERN, STEADY presence over those World Series teams, the winningest manager in Blue Jays history.

Back in the day, from 1967 to '78, Gaston played parts of 11 seasons in the big leagues between Atlanta, San Diego, and Pittsburgh. Outside of an All-Star season in 1970, he was an unspectacular player, but the building blocks were being put in place all along. With the Braves, Gaston roomed with Hank Aaron, one of the greatest players to ever step on a ballfield. He's credited Aaron with teaching him everything from how to be a man to how to tie a tie.

In Gaston's last year with the Braves, 1978, Atlanta hired a new manager, some 36-year-old who'd just been the Yankees' first-base coach for their World Series championship in '77. That man, who overlapped with Gaston ever so briefly, was Bobby Cox, the Hall of Famer.

When Cox eventually signed with the Blue Jays to be their manager in 1982, he brought on Gaston as the hitting coach, a role Gaston held through the '80s and thrived in. That's who Gaston was for so many years to so many people, the hitting guru who was content being just that.

When the Blue Jays got out to a dreadful 12–24 start in 1989, then-manager Jimy Williams was fired, but Gaston didn't leap at the opportunity to take over the club. He eventually did take the job, and led the Blue Jays to a 77–49 finish that landed them in the American League Championship Series, but that wasn't Gaston's master plan all along. He was never the hitting coach who waited in the shadows for his manager to fall, but when Gaston stepped into the manager's office for the first time, the history of this organization shifted in a new direction.

Gaston won 849 career games in Toronto and led the Blue Jays to two World Series titles, the first Black manager in MLB history to do so.

Today, the job of a manager is so different, so sprawled out across departments and staffs and responsibilities. In Gaston's era, it was simpler. Cito was the boss. His voice was the final voice.

Handed a brilliant collection of talent, particularly as the Blue Jays loaded up for their run in 1992 and overhauled their roster to repeat in '93, Gaston leaned on one core principle. To a man, the players who played under Gaston say the same thing, over and over again. He let you play. He trusted you.

"I always say that I'll lose one game but win three games down the road by giving somebody some rest or not changing a pitcher, not changing this or that," Gaston said at an event celebrating the 25th anniversary of the 1993 World Series win. "These guys would run through a wall to beat you."

Gaston approached managing with the mind of a hitting coach, leading with a trust and belief in players who had earned it. Fall out of Gaston's good graces, and it was just as steep a hill to climb to get back to the other side.

Managing a young, up-and-coming team can be easier, in some ways. The expectations are lower. The players, still learning the ropes, respect you automatically. Managing a roster of established veterans, many of them stars in their own right, is a different job entirely. Gaston, like John Gibbons later had to learn with those 2015–16 rosters, knew when to stand in front of a player and when to get off the tracks.

"I can only give you what I did, but for me, you never stop teaching," Gaston said in 2018. "You still write the lineup out, you still teach, you still coach. The first year I managed, I was on the plane one day and it kind of hit me. I turned around, looked around the back of the plane, and thought, "I'm responsible for all these people." Not only them, but their families, the front office's, everyone else. It's a tough job. There wasn't a day I walked into my office and there wasn't a problem, but you get used to that, you get ready for that. Also, when we were winning, there wasn't a day I walked into my office and didn't have a present either, so I kind of liked those days, too."

* * *

When Gaston arrived in 1982 as a hitting coach, there was a new radio guy in town. Jerry Howarth, buzzing around the field with his notepad, had just been brought in to call games alongside Tom Cheek.

Howarth had a front-row seat to all of this, to the small conversations that Gaston would have with players before the games and the teaching moments. Later, he watched as Gaston moved into the manager's chair and earned the quiet, easy trust of his roster.

"It's important for you to know this. This is so important. I'd be on the field talking to hitters about Cito Gaston. They would say to me, 'Jerry, whenever I'm on deck and the situation is tense, late in the game and there's a lot going on, we never have to look over our shoulder into the dugout to see if Cito Gaston is going to pinch-hit for us.' That never came up because Cito had 100 percent faith in his hitters.

"Pitchers would say.... We never had to look back at the bullpen and see if somebody was warming up because we knew that Cito was right there with us to finish this inning or finish this game. That's what made Cito special. He let them be who they were. He let them finish innings, finish games. Those players knew he had their back. That's why they could focus 100 percent on what they were doing."

No player feels the glare of a manager more than a reliever.

Whether real or imagined, relievers have a sixth sense for these things. It's one of baseball's most uncomfortable moments, watching a reliever struggle to hold a lead in the eighth or ninth inning and they look over to the dugout. In some cases, that's broken confidence, cracking right through. A good manager eliminates that altogether, though, and few have done that better than Gaston.

"It was a situation where you didn't have to look over your shoulder and say, 'Gosh, I gave up a hit, here comes so-and-so behind me,'" said Duane Ward. "No. Not at all. He would let you battle out of it. Cito let you do what you were there to do. He didn't second-guess you. He definitely made it clear what everybody's role was. That, to me, made it easy. If the game was three runs or less, I knew I was going to come in for the sixth inning, seventh inning or the eighth, then Tom Henke was coming in for the ninth. Everybody had their role.

"He doesn't try to micromanage; he has coaches around him to handle that. He has the first-base coach, the third-base coach, the hitting and pitching coaches. Cito lets them do their job. All he asked of his players was to give him 100 percent. Just give him 100 percent."

It sounds simple, but that's the beauty of it.

Gaston wanted effort, commitment, and consistency. Some of that shone through immediately, but rookies on those old Blue Jays teams quickly learned that Gaston wasn't exactly looking for the next big thing.

Take Carlos Delgado, who in the early '90s was one of the best young hitters in the minor leagues, a prospect the calibre of which we've rarely seen in Toronto outside of Vladimir Guerrero Jr. Delgado had a cup of coffee with the Blue Jays in late 1993, then again in '94 and '95, but it took him some time to stick as Delgado transitioned to first base and adapted to big-league pitching. Looking back, Delgado remembers the hills he had to climb as a rookie, but time has changed how he feels about those years.

"Cito was very good to me. I had Cito twice as a manager and once as a hitting coach. I don't want to label Cito as a veteran player manager, but he was very good at taking care of his players, the older players. You appreciate that," Delgado said. "I don't say this in a bad way, I actually say it in a very good way. When your manager takes care of you and has that great communication, it's great. There's also something to be said about earning your stripes and putting in your time."

"I remember when I was young, in spring training I would look up at that list and I was on every single road trip. Then, when you get six or seven years in and you get your work done, you don't have to go to Fort Myers anymore, you don't go to Sarasota anymore. It's really nice that you get taken care of and it makes you feel appreciated for your effort, your years in. I will always hold Cito in a very high regard."

Eventually, Delgado grew into the star everyone dreamed of and when Gaston returned more than a decade later in 2008 for his second stint as manager, Delgado was still there, one of the greatest power hitters of his generation. By then, Delgado had earned those stripes from Gaston. It takes years.

The other group of players who truly get to sense how a manager works—outside of relievers—are players on the edges of a roster. It's easy for Joe Carter to stroll into the clubhouse each day, knowing he's the man who will be batting cleanup and driving in a few runs. It's harder to be the utility man or the backup catcher, unsure of when your next moment will come.

In '91 and '92, that was Ed Sprague, who bounced between Triple A Syracuse and the big leagues, where he worked to carry over his success from the minors and establish a more permanent role. Sprague had appeared in just 22 games in '92, batting .234 with a .620 OPS, but lives on as one of the heroes of that season, his pinch-hit, two-run home run in the ninth inning of Game 2 still standing as one of the great moments in Blue Jays history.

"I give Cito almost the entire credit for my entire career," Sprague said. "He and Bobby Mattick are the two guys who were instrumental in me even having a career. Cito stuck with me. He saw something in me and believed in me. He gave me a chance.... Even after the home run, he gave me a chance to work through some struggles in 1994 and gave me the chance to play every day.

"It's not easy. It takes time, and I was given that time thanks to Cito."

Player after player comes back to that same message, that same appreciation for Gaston. That year's World Series MVP, catcher Pat Borders, spoke at that same World Series anniversary celebration about his appreciation for his old manager, his people skills, and the trust he felt from him.

"He was really good at conveying one message, 'I have your back and I'm going to help you as much as I can.'"

* * *

Between 1997 and his return to the Blue Jays in 2008, Gaston was shortlisted for several managerial jobs across baseball but never chosen. It felt like an injustice then, which has only grown with the passing of time.

Gaston was so respected by the people who matter most, which are the players. He had two rings, and while it's easy to point at those and say that Gaston just had to write out a lineup card of All-Stars each night, baseball has hundreds of examples of star-studded rosters that disappointed. There was an incredible skill to what Gaston did in his first stint with the Blue Jays, even if it was more subtle than, say, the manager who dragged a scrappy, 70-win team up to 82 wins.

Gaston's case for the Hall of Fame deserves more space, too. He's beloved in Canada, held up as this organization's greatest manager, but that respect hasn't carried over into these conversations often enough. Gaston was on the ballot for the Hall of Fame's 2023 contemporary era committee for managers, executives, and umpires, which eventually elected Jim Leyland. While Leyland received 15 of the 16 votes—clearing the bar of 12 for election—Gaston received fewer than five.

We can't put a stat on managers. We can count wins, rings, and ejections, but in a sport obsessed with quantifying the value of each breath, the way we remember managers still relies so heavily on the stories we tell, the ways we frame them in our conversations.

Gaston's return to the Blue Jays from 2008 to 2010 is part of that story, a new generation of players experiencing the old-school skipper, colouring in the stories of those players from the '90s.

Gaston took over for John Gibbons midway through the '08 season, and in '09, Ricky Romero arrived. Romero represented the next great hope for the Blue Jays' rotation as the sixth overall pick in the 2005 MLB Draft, and coming up behind Roy Halladay, Romero was positioned so well to learn from the legendary manager and pitcher. What a room for a rookie to walk into.

"From Day 1, you understand that he doesn't like pitchers," said Ricky Romero, breaking into a laugh. "You just kind of understood it. Coming from the era that he came from, he was used to bulldogs, guys who took the ball and went nine innings. He had Doc Halladay, then all of the young guys after that. From Day 1, I think the one thing I appreciated about Cito is that he always let me pitch, man. He'd come out to the mound sometimes, but he'd just ask, 'How do you feel?' You'd think you were out of the game, but he'd just stand there and ask, 'How do you feel?' You almost had to earn that respect with him and earn that right. There were a lot of times when I'd tell him, 'I feel great,' and boom, he'd turn right back around."

Nothing had changed. Nearly 30 years after Gaston first walked through the doors of Exhibition Stadium as the Blue Jays' hitting coach, there he was managing Romero—a player who hadn't even been born yet in 1982—the same way he had all along.

"I think that's what Cito did so well. He gave you a chance," Romero said. "He wanted you to go out there and be you, but when he jumps your ass, you better be ready. I think he wanted to see the response from his players. I've heard José Bautista and Edwin Encarnación say nothing but great things, too. He just gave these guys an opportunity and a belief in them. When you have a manager who believes in you and is going to jump your ass when he has to, that makes for a great combination. I always appreciated Cito because of that."

There's one story Romero will always remember, though. It takes him a minute to even start the story. He's already laughing.

It was June 16, 2009, and the Blue Jays were facing Cole Hamels and the Phillies. It was Romero's first Interleague game against a loaded lineup, and it didn't start well.

"Jimmy Rollins led off with a double, then Chase Utley hit a single. It's first and third, just a few pitches in, and Cito bolts out of the dugout."

The rookie hadn't even recorded an out yet.

Romero stood frozen on the mound, watching the great Cito Gaston stride toward him while Rod Barajas jogged out to join them. What the hell was happening?

"We all meet at the mound and Cito said, 'If you don't throw your fucking curveball right now, you're out of this game.' Then he walked away. That's what he said. I looked at Rod Barajas and his eyeballs could have popped out. I don't think he'd ever seen that either.

"I will never forget it. We were like three pitches into the game, three fastballs. People hadn't even gotten to their seats yet. People were just walking in, and this guy is already motherfucking me. I thought it was so great."

"It was so funny, because I was pitching so well. My first three career at-bats were against Cole Hamels, and I think for all three, I had runners in scoring position. In the third at-bat, I looked back, because I was wondering if I was getting pinch-hit for or not. But I was pitching so well, so when I looked back at Cito, he looked back at me and he said, 'Oh, just fucking go.' He had it out for me that game, but it was hilarious."

Romero loves telling this story. It's one of those first moments that the rookie could really feel it, that respect coming across from his great manager. Romero, after he finally threw his fucking curveball, gave the Blue Jays seven strong innings that day and struck out nine batters in an 8–3 win.

Years later, Romero ran into Gaston at a golf tournament and told him the story again.

"Well, did it work?" Gaston asked. "You went seven innings, right? You're welcome."

11

Joe Carter

THE MOMENT JOE CARTER TURNED ON THAT 2–2 FASTBALL from Mitch Williams on October 23, 1993, a man became a moment.

Only two men have done it in the game's history, Carter and Bill Mazeroski, who won the 1960 World Series for the Pirates with a walk-off home run.

It was, and may forever be, the greatest moment in the history of this organization. Carter, already known as a productive cleanup hitter since coming over from the Padres in a deal that also netted the Blue Jays Roberto Alomar, took his permanent place in Blue Jays lore that night. As envious a position as that might be, it's not one that comes easily to all who earn it.

Moments like these can swallow a man whole, a 16-year career—an entire life, even—remembered for one moment. How often do you think Carter is asked about coming up with the Cubs or the six years he spent with Cleveland earlier in his career? Instead, there's a beauty to how Carter has embraced this.

At charity events and anniversary celebrations, Carter moves through the room in a way that almost looks like a choreographed dance. It's so fluid, so joyful, how he bounces from fan to fan, old teammate to old teammate, his smile just as bright in 2024 as it was in 1993. For Carter, it's the 5,000th time he's been asked about that home run, but for the wide-eyed Blue Jays fan asking him, it's the first. He meets them exactly where they are, just as eager to relive the moments that ball cleared the left-field wall as they are.

He listens to the stories, over and over again, of where people were that night in 1993. Younger fans now come up to Carter, telling him they weren't even alive then. Maybe they were only three years old, and while they don't remember the home run themselves, their mother tells the story all the time about how they were plopped right in front of that TV, watching history. It's a moment that people's lives orbit around. Everyone knows where they were.

Carter can still celebrate this. At the endless streams of dinners, galas, golf tournaments, and meet-and-greets, he celebrates it. He'll never get tired of talking about that home run.

"Which one?" Carter joked at the 25th anniversary of the 1993 World Series. "Of course not. Are you kidding me? All we have left are our memories. Once you retire from the game, you look back on your memories and how you played the game, how successful you were. You look back and see what you accomplished. To accomplish back-to-back world championships, it doesn't happen that often. We got to do it. I still think about it, and it still feels good."

By now, you've watched the video and heard Tom Cheek's call hundreds of times, "Touch 'em all, Joe!"

It's part of the welcome kit to being a fan of the Blue Jays. The moment you watch your first game or slide on your first jersey, someone sits you down and teaches you a history lesson that begins with Carter. With Rickey Henderson on second and Paul Molitor on first, the Blue Jays down 6–5 in the bottom of the ninth, the Blue Jays were at risk of going to a Game 7 against the Phillies. Champions for the first time just a year ago, the "back-to-back" of it all hung in the balance.

The narrative came together so perfectly behind Henderson, who the Blue Jays had acquired for moments just like this, and Molitor, brought over in '93 as the Blue Jays tried to capture that magic one more time. The big cleanup hitter was at the plate.

Cito Gaston, remembering the Joe Carter the rest of baseball knew before he became the walk-off hero, is still amazed it happened at all.

"You know what's amazing about that?" Gaston remembered at the anniversary event. "When Joe Carter played for Cleveland, we'd hide in the dugout because Joe would pull the ball so far foul. To this day, I'm very surprised he kept that ball fair. He talks about it, too. He said that the only reason he kept it fair is because he was looking for it.... Most of the time, he would pull that ball foul."

Stepping in, though, Carter wasn't trying to play hero. He looked at Henderson, looked at Molitor, and thought about finding a gap, maybe tying the game with one swing. That's what Gaston had pounded into his head in those years: Have a plan.

"The last thing on my mind was a home run," Carter remembered. "Once I got to two strikes, I thought, 'Sit back, wait, put the ball in play.' I looked for a breaking ball because on the pitch before, but he came with a fastball down and in.

That's my happy zone. That's the 'beware' zone. I was able to keep it fair, and as they say, the rest is history. Great history."

Carter has called keeping that ball fair "the biggest accomplishment I have." He's had to watch that highlight more times than he can count, and each time, something different jumps off the screen to him.

In the moment, it was all such a blur. Now, Carter will watch the home run and see his first-base coach, Bob Bailor, as he rounds first base, leaping into the air. He sees Alfredo Griffin leaping into the air and the Blue Jays' equipment manager, Jeff Ross, in the mob of celebration. He sees John Olerud running onto the field. At one point, someone sticks their hand in front of the camera in the middle of it all and for years, Joe Carter thought that was Al Leiter. Eventually, he realized it was a fan who'd rushed the field and just so happened to look like Leiter. There are so many of these details to comb through, even for the man who authored the moment.

Like most Blue Jays fans, Carter can still hear Tom Cheek's famous call:

"Here's the pitch on the way. A swing and a belt. Left field! Way back! Blue Jays win it! The Blue Jays are World Series champions as Joe Carter hits a three-run home run in the ninth inning and the Blue Jays have repeated as World Series champions. Touch 'em all, Joe, you'll never hit a bigger home run in your life!"

It's so rare to create something like this in sports. This isn't a record for the most home runs or the most hits. Those, even if they're never broken, can be bent with time as we talk about the changing eras of a game. Sure, Wayne Gretzky's NHL-record 2,857 points will never fall, but what if he played with the current rules? There's always a "but" in those conversations, even when we talk about once-in-a-lifetime players.

Carter created a moment that exists outside all of that. Perhaps it can be matched someday, just like Carter matched Mazeroski, but it will never be topped. It can't be.

Now, we're left to find each generation's version of what Joe Carter did. José Bautista's bat flip didn't carry nearly the same weight, given that it happened in the seventh inning of Game 5 of the ALDS, but for a fan who was 10, 18, or 29 years old, it holds the same place in their heart that Carter's held in their parents'.

"At the end of the day, we're trying to create happy, long-lasting memories, right?" José Bautista said, remembering his own incredible moment. "That's a big one when it comes to this franchise. Hopefully, it's in the top three or top five moments of the organization. Nothing is ever—well, I can't say 'ever'—but it's going to be hard to top Joe's. In all of baseball."

Carter's greatest accomplishment in all of this—besides keeping that ball fair—may be how he's come to frame this in his own mind.

Carter loves the moment, but he also understands the moment and everything it's become, not only to him, but to the millions of people who remember it.

What happened that night in 1993 only happens once.

"When I was six or seven years old, I started playing baseball and that's what you do in the backyard," Carter said. "Bases loaded, bottom of the ninth, Game 7 of the World Series. If you're a basketball player, it's 3–2–1 for the last shot to win a world championship. You live those dreams. Dreams come true, because I'd thought about that since I was seven years old. It happened.

"That's something you can't go back and do over again."

12

Carlos Delgado

Carlos Delgado exists in the middle of it all.

The big catcher from Puerto Rico made his MLB debut on the third-to-last day of the 1993 season. The Blue Jays were down 6–1 to the Orioles in the sixth inning and had already clinched the East comfortably, so out came the regulars. Joe Carter, Devon White, Rickey Henderson, Ed Sprague, and catcher Randy Knorr sat for the final few innings, opening the door for Delgado to come in and catch Woody Williams.

Delgado was a monster in the minor leagues that season. Fresh off hitting 30 home runs with 100 RBI the year prior in High A Dunedin, Delgado hit 25 home runs with 102 RBI in 1993 for Double A Knoxville, just a remarkably productive two-year run. In two big-league games to end the '93 season, Delgado strolled to the plate twice, a walk and a pop out.

These early years of Delgado's career were no grand unveiling. The Blue Jays were about to make a run to back-to-back

World Series championships. Delgado was the new kid on the block, representing a "tomorrow" that the Blue Jays weren't ready to turn to yet. This was a roster stacked with veteran stars and the man behind the plate, Pat Borders, was a newly minted hero in Toronto, MVP of the 1992 World Series win over Atlanta.

Sure, the organization would find time for Delgado, but what was the rush?

"It was Joe Carter, Robbie Alomar, Paul Molitor…I walked into the room and I was like, 'Wow, what am I doing here?'" Delgado remembers. "You start wondering if you even belong or not. Right in the middle of a pennant race, too. You could feel the energy, you could feel the tension. Obviously, Robbie Alomar, being Puerto Rican, was very good to me. Joe Carter, he was good to me. It was one of those things where I stepped back and got out of the way so they could play."

The next two seasons came slowly, too, with the strike interrupting Delgado's rise from the next big thing to a big-league star. He didn't exactly hit the ground running, though, and by the end of 1995, Delgado had hit just .194 with 12 home runs and a .678 OPS over 82 games.

For the next decade, though, Delgado showed Toronto what greatness looked like. After touching that 1993 team, Delgado's entire career in Toronto existed in the early half of the 22-year postseason drought, none of which can be placed on his shoulders. For so many years, Roy Halladay gave Blue Jays fans a reason to turn on the ball game every fifth night. In between, they watched Delgado.

There was an elegance to Delgado's swing, the arch of a left-handed stroke met with the raw power of one of the game's great sluggers. Delgado existed as a 24-year-old DH for much of the 1996 season as he rebranded himself as a first baseman, his power numbers climbing and climbing in a full-time role. First he hit 25 home runs, then 30, then 38, then 44 in 1999.

The kid who had debuted at 21 years old was gone, but he'd carried the memories of those World Series teams with him.

"It was an experience that, when you're young, you are so scared," Delgado said. "You have butterflies, all of that stuff, but it made me mature quicker. When I looked back, I thought, 'Wow, this is what it takes.' I saw how those guys went about their business and it was fantastic. A few years later, I had a better grasp for the intensity of what goes on there. It was a nice way to get my feet wet."

To this day—and for any day to come—Delgado will stand as one of the greatest players in Blue Jays history. He still stands atop so many of the biggest offensive categories in this franchise's history, including:

Home runs: 336 (1)
RBI: 1,058 (1)
Slugging: .556 (1)
Walks: 827 (1)
Runs: 889 (1)
Plate appearances: 6,018 (1)

Only the great Tony Fernández has worn the Blue Jays jersey more times than Delgado, appearing in 27 more games. Only Fernández and Vernon Wells have more hits.

Delgado was not only one of the most talented players this organization has seen, but he stuck around, playing parts of 12 MLB seasons with the Blue Jays, the club that signed and developed him out of Puerto Rico. He was, in every way, a face of this franchise.

That should be enough, but another conversation has always hung over Delgado's name—one concerning the Baseball Hall of Fame.

These conversations don't go away now, either. Delgado was a one-and-done candidate in 2015, receiving just 3.8 percent of the votes and falling below the threshold of 5 percent to stay on the ballot. We live in a time of era committees, though, like the Contemporary Baseball Era Players Committee that elected former Blue Jays outfielder Fred McGriff to the Hall of Fame in 2023. The door may close, but it doesn't lock.

That's why it never feels like a conversation about Carlos Delgado's career can stop at saying he was a great baseball player, a truly exceptional hitter for 17 years.

"When you're in the game as long as I've been in it, you're around a lot of really good hitters. He would be in the top five hitters I've ever seen," said JP Ricciardi, who came to the Blue Jays when Delgado was in his prime. "He had power to all fields, he walked, he had a very good idea of what the strike zone was and what he wanted to do. He hit good pitching and he hit bad pitching. I, personally, think Carlos should be considered for the Hall of Fame. I think his numbers are pretty close to a lot of people who have gotten in."

Delgado is so close. He may forever be so close, and how you view Delgado's candidacy for the Hall of Fame depends so much on how you view both.

* * *

The Baseball Hall of Fame is elected by the Baseball Writers Association of America, votes given to members who have maintained 10 consecutive years of membership. It is, in ways you see in each year's voting, an imperfect system.

Players are elected based on their stats and personal achievements, but we'd be fools not to admit that the stories we tell about a player have their role in it all. Do we frame a player as a gifted athlete who cashed in on their talent or a scrappy, hard-nosed ballplayer who had to fight for every hit they got? These stories lean on truth, but they're still stories.

All of this matters for Carlos Delgado. His era matters, too.

Delgado played through the height of the steroid era, which colours his candidacy in two ways. While other sluggers were putting up eye-popping numbers around him, Delgado's accolades were limited to two All-Star Games and three Silver Slugger Awards, totals that feel downright disrespectful for a player of his caliber. Playing in that era also carries the risk of voter suspicion, too, unfair as that is. This is all voted on by human beings with their own biases and theories, but Delgado, unlike so many stars of his era, has no links to PED use. That immediately puts Delgado in a different conversation than so many of the players he was chasing during his prime.

To a man, Delgado's former teammates and executives who worked with him stand behind that, all coming back to a similar example—Delgado was a big, hulking slugger when he was 19 and he was a big, hulking slugger when he was 29. Nothing changed. You can't say the same about many other sluggers from that era.

The ballot Delgado landed on was like reading the lineup at Woodstock, too.

Randy Johnson, Pedro Martinez, John Smoltz, and Craig Biggio were elected that year. Future Hall of Famers on the ballot that year included Mike Piazza, Tim Raines, Jeff Bagwell, Lee Smith, Edgar Martinez, Alan Trammell, Mike Mussina, and Fred McGriff. Even Larry Walker, who was eventually elected in 2020, ranked all the way down at No. 17 in voting that year with just 11.8 percent of the vote.

Between all those names, you can add in others like Barry Bonds, Mark McGwire, and Sammy Sosa, who received their own share of votes but fell short while voters wrestled with how to handle candidates with such glaring ties to PED use.

Lost in the mess of it all, No. 23 in voting with just 3.8 percent, was Delgado. He was just below the line, just behind Nomar Garciaparra, who survived with 5.5 percent. No one will make the argument that Delgado should have been a first-ballot Hall of Famer—of course not—but he's a prime example of a player who could have benefitted from sticking around on the ballot for a few years. He's the type of player we would have debated, and from that debate, some votes could have slowly swung from one side to the other.

Delgado, a decade later, still remembers that feeling…3.8 percent.

"I will be completely candid with you. When I first got the news that I didn't make it to stay on the ballot, I was upset. But when I look back on my career, I gave everything that I had. I put in my time. I think I did well. I had a lot of support calls from colleagues who said, 'I can't believe this happened.' In a way, that made me feel better."

Let's start with what matters most: Delgado's baseline numbers.

17 seasons—2,038 career games
Home runs: 473
Hits: 2,038
WAR: 44.1 (FanGraphs)
wRC+: 135

Delgado is 27 home runs away from the magic No. 500, which surely would have kept him on the ballot—and in those conversations—for at least a few years longer. What if Delgado had broken through sooner and played more regularly from 1993 to 1995? What if that hip injury hadn't ended his career a couple of years earlier than he'd planned? We can't play god, because there are just as many "what ifs" that could have dragged Delgado's career in the other direction, but it's forever tempting to do so.

Still, these are not numbers that immediately demand a place in the Hall of Fame, particularly when you consider that Delgado was a first baseman. If he'd been a corner outfielder with a moderate amount of defensive value, perhaps that WAR number is in the 50s, creeping closer to the threshold voters look for.

In these cases, we reach for players to compare. If Player X is in the Hall of Fame and has similar numbers to Delgado, why can't Delgado have a seat at the table? It's a flawed way to evaluate the Hall of Fame, but the Hall of Fame is flawed, itself.

Kirby Puckett is an easy Hall of Famer to draw comparisons to, given his similar WAR at 44.9, but Puckett did that over fewer seasons and as an outfielder who went to 10 All-Star Games and won six Gold Glove Awards. He picked up a batting title along the way, hit .318 for his career, and won six Silver Slugger Awards.

Andre Dawson is another outfielder to whom we can compare Delgado, even as a first baseman. The Expos great, worth 59.5 career WAR, had fewer home runs than Delgado and a lower wRC+, but he was a better base runner and defender, winning eight Gold Glove Awards with eight All-Star nods. He was also the 1987 NL MVP when he hit 49 home runs with 137 RBI.

Perhaps Vladimir Guerrero is a useful example, his 54.5 career WAR held back by his regressing defensive value later in his career. With 449 home runs and a 136 wRC+, Guerrero and Delgado live in the same neighbourhood when it comes to power numbers, but again, we come back to accolades. Guerrero went to nine All-Star Games, won eight Silver Slugger Awards, and was named AL MVP in 2004, even if modern metrics would have resulted in a much different ballot.

When we reach the DH and first-base types, fellow Puerto Rican Orlando Cepeda might be the best Hall of Fame case to discuss Delgado alongside, but you find names like Dave Winfield or David Ortiz. While Delgado can go toe-to-toe with these greats in some offensive categories, they have the accolades to back up the numbers. Ortiz in particular has the career of a Hall of Fame player but also the aura, an icon in Boston who became so representative of that city and those teams.

That matters. The stories matter and how we talk about these players matters, particularly for players who slowly crawl up the ballot over eight or 10 years to be elected. Their numbers don't change, but the way we look at those numbers and the people who produced them still can.

"I feel like at some point, maybe with the players' committee or one of those committees, I will have a second chance and I really look forward to it, to any chance. I am not trying to minimize the Hall of Fame, but I am saying that I can't get another hit, I can't get another home run," Delgado said.

Without the numbers to command a place in the Hall of Fame at first glance, it will be these conversations that will have to reignite Delgado's candidacy. It's when we enter this part of a player's candidacy that we see the disadvantages Delgado had along the way.

First things first, he played for the Toronto Blue Jays—that team up in Canada—when they weren't making the playoffs.

"I don't think this is as much the case anymore, whether that's a social media revelation or what it is, but at that time, if you weren't on the national TV broadcasts, you weren't getting much exposure and we weren't on those all that often," said former Blue Jays GM Gord Ash.

Near the end of Delgado's tenure, the Blue Jays were also running into some financial constraints and no longer sitting at the adults' table in free agency or on the trade market, which had been the case through the late 1980s and early 1990s.

"The only bad part of Carlos Delgado for me was that I could not surround him, financially, with other players that could help him get the Blue Jays to another level because of the restrictions we had in Toronto," said JP Ricciardi. "Carlos made up 33 percent of my payroll, which was $50 million. It just really hamstrung me as a general manager to be able to bring other players in and around Carlos. That's not his fault, either. He got the contract before I got there, and I don't blame him. He deserved every dime he got, and he was worth every dime he got. I just felt bad that I could never surround him with three or four other guys in that lineup because of the financial restrictions that we were under when I was the general manager."

A couple of postseason runs may have put Delgado more squarely in the consciousness of U.S. baseball fans—and Hall of Fame voters—but this was the late 1990s and early 2000s. It was still possible to be quietly dominant. While something like Delgado's incredible, four-homer game would make headlines across the league, his year-to-year greatness wasn't as big a story. This isn't a conspiracy theory about American media ignoring Canadian baseball, but instead just a reality of the times. The Blue Jays weren't on prime-time television much in the United States because they simply weren't much of a draw in those years. Without his clips circulating on Twitter or Instagram each night, baseball fans weren't exposed to him nearly as much as they would have been if his prime years had come in New York or Boston.

This is what so many people who knew Delgado point to when the Hall of Fame discussion comes up. If only he'd had a bigger profile. If only he'd had some help.

"Carlos should have gotten more consideration and been on the ballot longer because of everything he's done as an offensive player," Ricciardi said. "I mean, what more could you want? He hits home runs. He hits for average. He walks. He's a complete player offensively. I loved having him in our lineup. My biggest disappointment was not being able to surround him with guys who could help us have a more formidable lineup."

That's one of the tragedies lost in this. Delgado could have been an even bigger star if the right era and right market had aligned better. He was brilliantly talented, handsome, and charming, and embraced the fame that came along with his talent.

Delgado also used his platform to stand behind what he believed in, which has to be part of this story.

* * *

When you ask an old teammate or coach about Carlos Delgado, they don't jump to describe his broad shoulders or powerful arms. They don't start rattling off stats or describing the flight of his home run balls into the right-field bleachers.

The first words spoken about Delgado are typically about his intelligence, his thoughtfulness.

Delgado wore No. 21 for the great Roberto Clemente—first in 1996 with the Blue Jays and later with the Mets—to honour his fellow Puerto Rican who is known just as much for the man he was off the field as on it. Delgado, like Clemente, was unafraid to stand behind the human rights or social issues he believed in.

"I tried to learn from Clemente, but I always said that as much as I admired Clemente, I tried to be the best version of Carlos Delgado. I'm not trying to copy anybody. Any time you have an opportunity to learn from someone's career or legacy and you can incorporate it into yours, that's great, but I always say that you have to feel what you do, so it becomes a genuine act. I'm never going to say, 'I'll do this because so-and-so is doing it.' At the end of the day, people will see right through that."

Throughout Delgado's career, he was openly against the United States Navy using the island of Vieques—an island just off the coast of his native Puerto Rico—as a bombing practice site. In 2001, Delgado, along with a group of other Puerto Rican celebrities including singer Ricky Martin, took out a full-page ad in the *New York Times* and *Washington Post,* asking the U.S. Navy to cease bombing near Vieques, which at the time had a decimated economy and the highest cancer rate in Puerto Rico.

In 2004, Delgado chose to stay in the dugout instead of standing for "God Bless America," typically played between the seventh innings at American stadiums, as he protested the ongoing wars in Iraq and Afghanistan. This drew widespread media attention, particularly in New York.

The terrorist attacks of September 11, 2001, were still so fresh at that time, and the coverage of Delgado struggled—or often failed completely—to explore his beliefs and why he was doing this. Delgado was against the ongoing war itself. He was protesting those wars and those decisions, not the United States of America on a grand scale, as it was too often portrayed.

Remember, this was 2004. Athletes had been speaking on social and political issues for as long as they've had a platform to do so, but we weren't nearly as comfortable with those conversations as we are now—and *comfortable* may still not be the word for it. These moments were not as common in 2004, and coming from a Puerto Rican player who played for the Canadian team? The reaction was not exactly warm.

It's when Delgado reflects on these moments that you can hear the voice that so many former teammates and coaches respected so deeply.

When Delgado said something, he had a reason to. He'd thought about it not just on a surface level but from all different angles. He wasn't sitting there re-sharing an Instagram story to get behind the social movement of the day; he was putting his heart and reputation behind things that he truly believed in.

"I was brought up this way. For us, in our family, values were important. Justice was important. Fairness was important. Just because I'm a baseball player, that doesn't mean that I don't live in this world, that I'm not connected to this community. Actually, it's the other way around," Delgado said. "You have a platform. These days, it's much, much stronger, but I had a platform where my voice could be heard. There were some social issues and some responsibilities that you can address respectfully, and I thought that I did. You have to be prepared, too. Your voice is going to be heard because you're the guy who is on TV every single night and the reporters are calling. For me, it was important because it was something I believed in. What I said, when I said it, it was because it was near to my heart, because that's the way I represent. I look for justice. Those were my values coming through, it's the way I was brought up since I was a little kid. I have no regrets."

We want to measure every inch of a Hall of Fame candidacy, but this is one we can't. Were there some old Hall of Fame voters kicking around who just plain didn't like that Delgado guy? That guy who wouldn't come out to stand for "God Bless America" in New York City, the greatest city in the greatest country in the world, according to people who haven't been to many others?

It's impossible to measure, but it's part of Delgado's story, and the story matters.

It's how we talk about Delgado now that will determine whether he's considered again for the Hall of Fame.

The next Contemporary Baseball Era Players Committee will meet in December 2025, for induction in 2026. Arguments will be made and votes will be cast, just as they were for Fred McGriff, who was sent to the Hall of Fame by that same committee in 2003.

At the end of it all, we also need to ask ourselves how much the Hall of Fame matters and to whom. Delgado deserved better than to fall off the ballot in one year, but whether he receives that call or not, it doesn't change what he meant to the Blue Jays or the city of Toronto. Delgado was the main attraction for so many years, the headliner at a festival thin on other acts. He mattered when the Blue Jays didn't, and while that's enough for him after the door was closed, it's still so hard to lock that door forever.

"If I don't get in, I don't get in. If I do get in via those committees, it would be fantastic, but I look back on my career and I have nothing to be ashamed of," Delgado said. "I am proud. I am really proud. That's what is important to me."

13

Roy Halladay

ONE OF THE WORST SEASONS IN BLUE JAYS HISTORY WAS ONE of the most important.

It still feels surreal, looking at the 10.64 ERA next to Roy Halladay's name in 2000. Fresh off a 1999 season that backed up all the prospect hype Halladay arrived in the big leagues with, the sudden spiral this 23-year-old fell into was stunning.

In all of Major League Baseball's history, pitchers have thrown 50 or more innings in a single season more than 27,000 times. None of them have posted an ERA as bad as Halladay's 10.64. It wasn't just bad; it was historically bad.

Something needed to change, and the next spring in Dunedin, Florida, one of the greatest tales in Blue Jays lore was born.

Buck Martinez was the Blue Jays' new manager that year, tasked with taking over a team that had been hovering just over .500 in an era that lacked the second and third wild card spots. If the Blue Jays stood a chance against the mighty Red Sox and Yankees, Halladay had to be part of it. Martinez can still remember the day, exactly where he was sitting in the dugout in Dunedin at what we now call TD Ballpark. Next to him was Mark Connor, the Blue Jays' pitching coach. They watched Halladay as he laboured through a spring outing, fighting himself as much as he fought the hitters.

"Mark and I are sitting next to one another and [Halladay is] getting his ass kicked. He's throwing the shit out of it. I turned to Mark and I said, 'What are we going to do with this guy?' He was too good just to cast away. We had to come up with something to take advantage of that talent, because that talent doesn't come around very often."

"Mark was awesome. Mark loved Doc," Martinez remembered. There's emotion in his voice, thinking back to those years with Halladay. "He loved him."

The organization was so invested in the towering, young right-hander. He and Chris Carpenter were the duo big-league clubs dream of developing. Halladay was the club's first-round pick, No. 17 overall, out of high school in 1995. He was homegrown, the future ace of the Blue Jays who had suddenly fallen apart.

"He was our No. 1 draft choice and with that comes a lot of expectation," said Gord Ash, the Blue Jays' GM at the time. "He was a workmanlike guy, very dedicated and very hardworking.... There was always some concern about his delivery. He went right over the top. That eventually got to him, and he struggled with his delivery until he took that new approach."

"He really struggled, but this guy was too determined. I couldn't give up on him. It then became a conversation of what the best way was to fix this. I really thought the best way to fix it was to get Roy out of the limelight and put him in a situation where he could move at his own pace, maybe get some of the veteran pitching coaches in the minor leagues to help him out. Then, well, we all know the story of Mel Queen."

There's that magic name.

Martinez remembers the day, too, when he called Halladay into his office to tell him their plan. They loved Halladay as a pitcher, as a person—everything about him. They just needed to help him, even if that meant hurting him first.

"He was not happy," Martinez said. "No. He was not happy."

Halladay was sent all the way down to Single A. This wasn't a quick breather in Triple A Syracuse, it was something more serious, something that required higher patience and lower stakes.

Halladay threw a "straight, four-seam fastball" at the time and his knuckle-curve wasn't effective, rarely landing for strikes. If hitters sat on his fastball, it would whiz back past Halladay's head quicker than he'd thrown it. The Blue Jays needed to fundamentally change how this young man threw a baseball.

Enter Mel Queen, quietly one of the most important figures this organization has known. Queen was a roving pitching instructor in those years who loved to play with trial and error. Try this. No, try this. OK, how about this, instead?

First, Queen had to understand Halladay. Then, he could help him.

"Everybody was trying to get Doc to throw from three quarters," Martinez said. "It just never registered; he never could feel what that was like. Finally, Mel Queen said, 'Doc, throw sidearm.' He ended up out here," Martinez said, holding his arm out at a three-quarter angle, "and that was sidearm to Doc. The ball started to move. He started to throw a slider and a cutter instead of a curveball. He started throwing a split. He had pitches that went in both directions on both sides of the plate."

In Dunedin, Halladay pitched in shorter bursts as he worked on his mechanics, spreading 22⅔ innings over just 13 appearances. He stretched out to start in Double A, throwing 34 innings over five excellent starts, then made two starts in Triple A. The hard part was over, but the Blue Jays still didn't know what would happen when Halladay returned. The last time they'd seen him on a big-league mound, he was setting the wrong kinds of records.

He got rocked.

In his return to the big leagues on July 2, 2001, Halladay allowed six runs over just 2⅓ innings to the Red Sox. The Blue Jays lost 16–4. Halladay just had one more clunker to get out of his system.

From that moment on, greatness began. Halladay pitched to a 2.71 ERA the rest of the way and ended the season with a complete game shutout against Cleveland. He allowed just two hits and threw only 83 pitches, a stat line that sounds made up by modern standards.

Halladay's teammates saw the same big, strong right-hander atop the mound. They saw the same talent. Sure, his arm angle was a little different, but something else in Halladay had shifted.

Carlos Delgado was in his prime at the time, one of the game's finest hitters. This was the beginning of an era in Toronto where Delgado and Halladay were the main attractions, two of baseball's brightest stars. There's still such a sense of pride, of admiration, in Delgado's voice when he talks about his old teammate.

"Well, there is Roy Halladay, then there is Roy Halladay 2.0," Delgado said.

"I had the privilege to watch him at his best and at his worst. I remember Roy Halladay and Chris Carpenter, they were both high picks who came in, these tall right-handers who threw hard with a lot of potential. I saw Roy struggle for a little bit, but he went down all the way to Dunedin with Mel Queen to rebuild himself. It takes a lot of humility. It takes a lot of pride to go from the big leagues all the way down to change your mechanics, change your mindset, and trust Mel Queen. He was such a great instructor. God bless him."

Halladay, once again, had announced himself to the rest of baseball. He'd been the next big thing in Toronto and one of the league's great curiosities, all in one year. Of the many ways in which Halladay's name will forever live on in Toronto, the story of his shocking fall and incredible rise will always be one we reach for.

He was, for a moment, the worst pitcher in Major League Baseball. He was, for a lifetime, one of the best.

"We called him back up in 2001 and he's pitching in Yankee Stadium," Martinez said, a smile coming back to his face as he knew there was one more story to tell. "We had Todd Greene with us as a catcher in spring training, so he had caught Doc, then he hit against Doc when he came back with the Yankees. I'll never forget this. Todd came up the next day and said, 'What the fuck did you do with Doc?'"

14

José Bautista

José Bautista was better than you. He knew it, but that wasn't always enough. He wanted you to know it, too.

Bautista is beloved in Toronto for who he is as much as what he did. If, after hitting that go-ahead home run in Game 5 of the 2015 ALDS against the Rangers, Bautista had simply dropped his head and rounded the bases, we wouldn't talk about that moment in the same ways we do now.

That wouldn't fit Bautista. Instead, Bautista watched his ball soar into the left-field bleachers, then shot a quick glare back at Sam Dyson on the mound. He wanted to make sure the pitcher was watching, too, glancing back as if to say, "Look at what I just did to you."

Then, Bautista flung the bat from his left hand, high in the air toward the Rangers' dugout. As Bautista ran out of the frame, Ryan Goins came down the third-base line, screaming into the air above him. It's one of the great images from this generation of Blue Jays baseball. The camera was shaking not only because of the moment, but because of the man. José Bautista, the heart and soul and middle finger of the Toronto Blue Jays, had just done it.

Bautista owned this city for a decade, capturing Canadian baseball fans who had suffered through the postseason lull of the late '90s and early 2000s. He was as beloved in Toronto as nearly any professional athlete in North America at his peak, and that peak hasn't exactly dipped, even long after his playing career.

"I watched José become a god for that city," remembered Edwin Encarnación. "They love José in Toronto. They love him. He deserves it. He earned it. He worked for it. What I see in Toronto, with the way they love José, it is something very special. There is something very special there, in that love for José. They will never forget José in Toronto. What he did for that city, that organization, he changed a lot of lives in Toronto. He changed people's lives. The fans will always love José."

Bautista had an incredible rise in Toronto. He arrived as a bit of a journeyman—maybe "utilityman" would be more kind— who hadn't quite established himself in the big leagues, and the clock was ticking. He exploded with 54 home runs in 2010, remained the face of the franchise through some disappointing years, and then had his moment in the sun in '15 and '16, leading a roster that had then added enough attitude to fill 50 lineups.

He was, in every way, the perfect face of baseball's resurgence in Toronto. This city finally had the one player the rest of baseball wished it did. Even with a personality and talent that towered above everyone around him, Blue Jays fans could look at this man and claim him as their own.

"You can't say Toronto Blue Jays without saying José Bautista's name," said Kevin Pillar. "They're synonymous with each other. Maybe this is me talking as a 35-year-old who isn't a Canadian and isn't a lifelong Blue Jays fan, but when I think about the Toronto Blue Jays, I think about José Bautista and what he was able to do even before the bat flip. He was the face of the franchise. He put Blue Jays baseball back on the map."

"I think about him representing the Blue Jays in the All-Star Game and the Home Run Derby, for a franchise that might have been forgotten a little bit since their World Series runs. He put them back on the map. He made the Toronto Blue Jays cool again."

There it is. None of the words we write or stories we tell about Bautista capture him as well as what Pillar said—he made the Blue Jays cool again.

Baseball has long straddled that line, particularly in Toronto and particularly when the Blue Jays aren't making postseason runs. In an average 81–81 season, are the Blue Jays cool? Are they a social destination? For years, the answer was an exhausted "no." That started to change as Bautista grew into one of the game's most feared players.

The other reason Blue Jays fans fell in love with Bautista? Everyone else hated him.

In the years since the World Series runs of '92 and '93, the Blue Jays still had their stars. Roy Halladay, Carlos Delgado, Vernon Wells, and others—all beloved players in their own right—had their entire Blue Jays careers play out in that gap, but the Blue Jays weren't enough of a threat around baseball to create many rivalries. Halladay wasn't screaming at hitters and challenging them; his intensity pointed inward. Delgado was widely respected, and the charismatic Puerto Rican slugger didn't create much tension with his personality on the field.

Bautista, on the other hand?

"He sure made some enemies on the opposing side," John Gibbons said, laughing at the memories.

"With José's personality, he wasn't well-liked in the league. For one, he burned them all so many times. Number two, he was volatile. He wore his emotions on his sleeve. He complained to the umpires all the time, but most of the time he was right. He was a marked man in that way."

Great rivalries need some stakes, some true bad blood between teams and players. Think back to the benches-clearing brawl against the Rangers involving Rougned Odor, who was booed each time he stepped to the plate in Toronto for years to come, despite the fact that him coming to the plate was never all that threatening. Think back to the battles with Darren O'Day, the Baltimore Orioles' dominant reliever in those years who always seemed to draw Bautista. It was a dream rivalry, each player poking the other, but Bautista claimed its brightest moments.

Bautista was pulled to these moments. He couldn't resist them if he tried, but he never tried to. Early in his career, these emotions got the best of him at times, but he developed them like the muscle they are. When Bautista struck up a new rivalry, whether it be for a night or a few years, he knew that he had a mentality the other man couldn't match. He was, on top of everything else, tough as hell.

"I tell people this all the time. José was No. 1—he and Kevin Pillar, the guys who showed up to play every single night," Gibbons said. "You couldn't get him out of the lineup. You knew you could count on him every day because he was going to get everything he could out of his career. He also understood that people came to watch him play, and that's important. It was rare if you did. He'd have to be really banged up. That's what I admired about José most. Even if I tried to give him a day off, he didn't want it. He had the perfect personality."

Russell Martin, his old junior college teammate reunited all those years later, finally saw the fully realized version of Bautista on the game's biggest stage.

"Intense. He was intense," Martin said, chuckling at his own understatement. "He expected to have success every time he stepped in the batter's box. If he didn't, he's pissed. That was his attitude. That's how high of a standard he held himself to. He was just super intense. You have to be a little bit crazy to have that attitude, but that's what separates the guys who have a bit of success from the guys who have more. He was hungry. He expected to be a force. He willed himself into that."

Everyone wants to talk about the bat flip, though. Still today, and for years, it's what people want to talk about when they hear Bautista's name. It doesn't matter if they're a casual fan or an All-Star.

Bautista understands the value of the moment, too. He's a businessman. He understands how this game works.

"We're coming up on 10 years," Bautista said the moment it was mentioned, looking out at an empty, quiet Rogers Centre to bring back the memory.

Bautista's edge is still there today. It's an inch under the surface, but sharp as ever. He hasn't aged a day since that home run, still in playing shape, still going through rigorous stretching routines before he takes a swing in the cages. He's still Joey Bats.

"I was lucky enough to be the guy at the plate at the moment, to have that chance, but the build-up of that whole series and that game, the environment and the atmosphere here, to be able to do something that I know a lot of people will remember for a long time in a positive way was amazing. I was lucky to be in that moment.

"I definitely blacked out. I just remember the guys jumping out of the dugout, mainly Dioner Navarro and Russ Martin. They were going bananas. I remember them."

The hearts of those batting orders in Bautista's prime were horrifying. He'd have Josh Donaldson on one side and Edwin Encarnación on the other, a one-two-three punch that rivaled any team in baseball. It was a nightmare for opposing pitchers.

Bautista and Encarnación grew particularly close and still are, the two Dominican sluggers who pummeled the AL East together for years.

"José is a great man, a great person," Encarnación said. "He helped me a lot. When I got traded to Toronto, he was there already, and he showed me how to move around the city. When you come to a new team, you don't know what you are going to see. He was a great teammate for me, and we are very close. Always, we would have a scouting report together. We would watch the video together, the pitcher we were going to face. Always, we would sit together in the dugout talking about the pitcher, what we saw. Those were the great moments. We helped each other. We knew we could do damage."

Bautista's personality was on full display when the cameras came on. Bautista's relationship with the media was fascinating. It's where you could really see that Bautista was not just a great baseball player, but smart as hell. He understood what to say and when to say it.

Sometimes, that meant a jab, either playfully or with some force behind it. Other times, he used those microphones pointed in his face to make a statement.

Entering the final year of his contract in 2016, fresh off an incredible season that had ended the organization's 22-year postseason drought, Bautista stepped in front of the assembled media on one of the first days of spring training and set his sights on the stock price of ownership, Rogers Communications.

"In a publicly traded company, everybody can track their performance fairly easy. It's not a secret. It's out in the public," Bautista told reporters when camp opened in 2016. "Stock prices are monitored very closely by the whole financial world, and I think there is a direct correlation with the success of their earnings-per-share after we start experiencing success.

"Are they going to put it out in the media and say because of the Jays, we made all this money? No. But everybody can read between the lines."

This wasn't just your usual contract negotiation with an athlete. This was José Bautista.

Other times, Bautista would have fun with the media. There's a story reporters still love to tell about a day when Bautista was surprised by the number of media members surrounding his locker, and this is where it's important to state plainly that Bautista was in full command of every social interaction he ever participated in.

Bautista turned to see the reporters approaching his locker and surveyed them slowly.

"One..." he began, pointing at the first reporter.

"Two...three..." he continued slowly, pointing and pointing.

All the way through the mob, Bautista went, his own not-so-subtle way of making a point.

Many veteran writers came to love covering Bautista—or better put, the daily game of covering Bautista. He could be difficult to pin down and was always thinking, his mind always churning to find a hole in your question before it had fully left your mouth. If you lost Bautista with a premise he disagreed with, you might as well throw the rest of your question out the window. He was fascinating as an interview subject.

In my own early days covering the Blue Jays, it was decided that an assignment to interview Bautista would be my initiation. I just didn't know it at the time.

The Blue Jays had opened 2017 with a 1–5 road trip through Tampa and Baltimore, so by the time they returned home for a nine-game homestand, it was time for my first assignment on the beat. I was an associate reporter at the time for MLB.com—a fancy word for "intern"—working under Gregor Chisholm, who is now the baseball columnist for the *Toronto Star*. Still clean-shaven with a dress shirt tucked into dress pants, I was entirely too eager when this first assignment came down—interview José Bautista and ask him about why the Blue Jays are hitting off a curveball machine.

Frantically, I pulled up research from the early games of the season, convincing myself that it represented any sort of useful sample size. Bautista, like the rest of the Blue Jays' lineup that year, was off to a slow start and not hitting breaking pitches well.

So there I stood, in front of the Blue Jays' dugout at 4:00 PM, waiting for José Bautista to run in from the outfield, where he was shagging fly balls. I waited, waited, and waited until finally, he jogged past and I asked him for a moment of his time.

There was no "yes," no "sure," no "whatcha got?"

Bautista just stopped and stared, his version of accepting the interview.

When I asked Bautista about hitting off the curveball machine, he was immediately confused. So proud of the information I'd gathered about the Blue Jays' inability to hit a breaking ball for one whole week, I began rattling off data, a flustered fool vomiting up numbers to one of the best hitters in baseball. The point I finally reached, at the end of the long road, was that the Blue Jays weren't good at hitting breaking balls.

Bautista paused and—mercifully—thought better of lighting up the new reporter.

"...There is no way of knowing that," he said, and there he went, down the dugout tunnel.

When I turned to glance up at the press box before leaving the field, I saw a handful of the beat's veteran reporters huddled together, waving. I can still hear them laughing when I walked back into the press box.

There was no curveball machine.

This is why it's difficult to capture Bautista, the person. There are so few others to compare him to.

Others have hit iconic home runs. A handful have hit 54 in a season. To do all of this with Bautista's edge, his intelligence, and his taste for revenge is rare. When Bautista's old teammates think back to those years, they tend to stray quickly from the field. Everyone saw what he was capable of with a bat in his hands, but it's everything else that made him more than just another slugger.

"He was huge for this organization, this city, this country," said Marcus Stroman. "That homer was special, but just his overall contributions to the game while he was here was pretty incredible with how many All-Stars he made. He was a perennial All-Star who wasn't expected to be that guy. He had a weird come-up in the big leagues. He wasn't a high-profile or high-round guy. To turn into what he did, I think it's just a testament to the work that he put in."

"He's always been someone who's tried to maximize in life, which I try to do. We're baseball players and we train, yes. I don't think anyone will outwork me, but we also have hobbies and stuff that allows us to have an outlet from the game. He's always had that passion to explore and better himself away from the field."

Now, he lives among the greats. His name was added to the Blue Jays' Level of Excellence in an emotional ceremony in late 2023.

For years, the standard was set by hitters like Tony Fernández, George Bell, Jesse Barfield, Joe Carter, and others. The next generation saw Carlos Delgado and Vernon Wells, but for years to come, hitters who put on the Blue Jays uniform will be chasing Bautista, the man who became so much more than a baseball player in Toronto.

José Bautista was, above all else, an original.

There will never be another. There can't be.

15

John Gibbons

JOHN GIBBONS WAS TORONTO'S LAST COWBOY, ITS LAST OLD-school manager gifted with an ability to shape the old around the new.

Gibbons was one of the game's great rarities, a manager as beloved in Toronto as some of the names he wrote on the lineup card each night. It wasn't always that way, of course—his first tenure with the Blue Jays led to his firing midway through the 2008 season—but in most ways, Gibbons was the right man for the Blue Jays. It was just about finding the right version of the Blue Jays for John Gibbons.

In 2015 and '16—those postseason runs with those unforgettable teams—it all came together.

Those teams were built to be managed by this man, whose greatest talent was knowing when to stand his ground and when to get the hell off the tracks.

We're talking about rosters stacked with José Bautista, Josh Donaldson, Russell Martin, Troy Tulowitzki, Marcus Stroman, David Price, Edwin Encarnación, R.A. Dickey, Mark Buehrle, Marco Estrada, Aaron Sanchez, Jason Grilli, and so many more. At any given time, those teams had 10 different players who would have been the biggest personality—or maybe the most difficult one—in your average major league clubhouse, but here they all were in one room, and it was Gibbons' job to be the rancher, wrangling them all together.

"I had fun with them too, but when you needed to put your foot down a little bit, you did it," Gibbons said. "There's a lot of guys out there who micromanage everything and try to control everything, but that wasn't going to work for that group. In a lot of ways, they policed themselves. When game time came, just like that '86 Mets team, they played to beat you. That's the most important thing."

Gibbons keeps coming back to that comparison to the '86 Mets team he played eight games for as a 24-year-old, baseball's bad boys who won the World Series with both middle fingers up.

The beauty of Gibbons' managing was so subtle with these Blue Jays teams. It's taken years—and a few more managers sitting in that chair—to appreciate just how well he handled those clubhouses. It was in the moments that Gibbons needed to stand his ground, maybe even bark back a bit, that we saw him at his best.

There's no better example than Josh Donaldson, the baseball equivalent of dropping a lion right into the middle of an MLB clubhouse. Donaldson wasn't afraid to call out teammates, coaches, even members of the front office. We're not talking about veiled shots through the media; we're talking about face-to-face, nose-to-nose conversations that might both begin and end with a "fuck you." It's part of what made Donaldson the player he is, but also part of what made Gibbons the perfect manager to tame him.

The perfect snapshot came in 2016 in New York.

Gibbons, as a manager, had the gift of a great comedian: timing.

"He's going to tell you a different story, but here's what happened," Gibbons began, already chuckling. "I tried to give him a day off in New York because CC Sabathia was pitching and Sabathia was tough on him his whole career for whatever reason. Josh said, 'No, I'm good' and whatever else, blah blah blah. I said I'd DH him instead to give him half a day off. In his first at-bat, he goes up there and Sabathia strikes him out. As soon as Josh turns around, he's walking back to the dugout and he's looking right at me in the dugout. I liked to sit in that corner right by the stairs where he comes in, so he was pissing and moaning. Next at-bat? Same thing. It was a mismatch, which was hard because that didn't happen to Josh too often. Here he comes again and he's looking right at me. He's walking over and I was standing there, and he took his bat and hit it against this pole that lined the stairs up to the field, right next to where I was standing. Naturally, I thought, 'That ain't gonna work.' So I went down there to the bat rack and sure enough, ol' Tulowitzki shows up. Tulo was the peacemaker for everything, man. Any time there was any tension, Tulo would step right up, it was beautiful."

Donaldson was the reigning AL MVP. The game was in New York. The Blue Jays were one of the biggest, boldest stories in baseball. Of course, any level of dust-up between the star player and the manager was going to be news.

After the game, reporters and cameras circled Donaldson's locker and asked the star third baseman what had happened between him and Gibbons.

"Gibby asked me what kind of cologne I was wearing, and I said it was this new cologne called Tom Ford. I just got it," Donaldson said at the time. "He got pretty close to me, so I guess he got a good whiff of it. I was like, 'Hey, man, back up. I'll give you some after the game.'"

It was the perfect answer to defuse the situation, and by the time Gibbons was asked about it again, there he was, the comedian who'd just had a ball put on the tee by his own player.

"I saw that, and I said, 'Tom Ford? He shops at Wal-Mart, man. He ain't getting no Tom Ford.'"

This was Gibbons' genius. Even though he hid it so well behind the image of a country boy, he knew how to leave you laughing. He knew when to wink at the camera, catch you off-guard, and cut through the tension of a room, leaving everyone else in it relieved.

The players on those 2015 and '16 teams experienced that, day in and day out, but they felt so much more for Gibbons. They loved him—still do—and speak of Gibbons in a voice you so rarely hear in the game of baseball.

* * *

Russell Martin was the Blue Jays' big splash coming into 2015, the Canadian catcher who had been to the postseason in seven of his first nine years in the big leagues. He brought a toughness to that clubhouse, perfectly complementing the chaotic collection of talent already there.

When Martin sat down one afternoon in mid-2024 to relive the glory days, pulling his stool up to a table in a new club lounge at Rogers Centre that would open days later, he looked so refreshed. Everything about him felt lighter, five years removed from the daily beatings that baseball brings a catcher. When asked about Gibbons, Martin pauses to think for a moment. He smiles, his eyes bright, and shakes his head before giving his old manager four words of the finest praise you'll ever hear in baseball.

"He feels like home."

Over and over again, when Gibbons' name is mentioned to members of those 2015 and '16 teams, his former players don't even wait for the rest of the question to come out.

Martin continued, moments later calling Gibbons the "dad" of those teams. Player after player calls him a father figure, especially the younger crowd from those teams. He was, Martin said, "the glue" that kept that beautiful mess together.

"Everybody loved Gibby," Martin said. "There's not one guy that didn't like Gibby. That's honest. One-hundred percent honesty, everybody would say the same thing, how much they like and they appreciate Gibby."

Well, Martin was right.

The description of a father figure is so fitting. These players speak of him like someone speaks of their parents once they've moved out, grown up, and come to appreciate what they did for them. There's always a loving "but" involved.

"I loved Gibby because he wasn't afraid to speak his mind," Josh Donaldson said. "That got him in trouble sometimes, but at the end of the day, we knew that he had our best interests in mind. Sometimes, yeah, he'd need to put his foot in my ass and say, 'Hey, let's go.' He knew how to spark each individual to get us to play at a certain level, but he was also vulnerable enough to let you know that he cared about you. He wanted the best for me."

Players who have gone on to play for other organizations after playing under Gibbons, in particular, see how unique a manager he was.

Baseball still has room for the old-school managers, with greats like Bruce Bochy, Dusty Baker, and Ron Washington, but the game has drifted away from Gibbons' style of managing people over process.

"I love him. I think he should still have a managing job," said Marcus Stroman. "I just saw him with the Mets. His personality is rare. He's truly unwavering. He truly doesn't care about the highs and lows; he just cares about his guys. He's so personable, being able to come up and talk to you and get a real read on how you're feeling. He could bring different personalities together, too, he kind of neutralizes that.

"Gibby's the man, bro. We all had a lot of respect for Gibby. We also knew that he had our back. He would argue for us. Kind of like [Aaron] Boone, there's not a lot of managers in the league who really have your back. Gibby always felt like that."

Managing requires trust. It's easy for a player of Donaldson's or Bautista's caliber to know that they'll be in the lineup every single day, but for someone lower on the roster, they need to be able to trust that their manager has their back...that what they're saying is true, day in and day out.

In too many of these relationships, players can grow nervous that the front office is standing over the manager's shoulder, whispering in their ear every word to say. The moment a manager drifts from the side of the players in the clubhouse to the side of the executives in the front office, it can all unravel.

"He's just not a bullshitter. He'll tell you exactly how it fucking is," Russell Martin said. "If he's not happy, he'll tell you. I feel like nowadays, there's a bit of a lack of trust in what you're getting relayed from a manager or a higher-up. It's not the same as it used to be. He's one of the last legit, old-school managers. When you look up the definition of a manager, Gibby, that's what you see. Kind of like the movie *Major League*, he's that iconic character. When you think of a manager, Gibby is who you think of."

Ryan Goins feels like a fine example of a player on the other side of this. Goins was a regular for the Blue Jays in those years, a defensive whiz who was never really an everyday starter but was so reliable that he'd always find his way into the lineup card around injuries and off days. In 2015, he appeared in 128 games, but he struggled in '16 and his playing time fell dramatically.

"I've said before and I'll say it forever. There's not an easier manager to play for," Ryan Goins said. "All he asks you to do is go out there and play hard. If you're in the lineup, go out there and play hard. Do the right things and play the game the right way. He cared about us. He cared for every single one of us, always asking how we were doing. He was so easy to get along with, but if things were going bad, he wasn't afraid to let you know. He was always honest and never beat around the bush, he just let you know. He's just a great human. He's someone who, any time I'm around him, I appreciate him. I appreciate what he did for me, for our team. Just the human that he is, he was unbelievable to play for. He was my favourite manager that I ever had."

There's a reason these types of players had career years under Gibbons.

Take Justin Smoak as another example. Smoak was supposed to be the next great hitting prospect, but had struggled in his early years, went from Texas to Seattle, and eventually landed with a thud on the waiver wire, where the Blue Jays found him. His next four seasons, all in Toronto, were the best days of his MLB career. He felt so free again as a hitter.

"I didn't really feel like there was that pressure. Other places I've been, I felt like there was that pressure to have success," Smoak said. "Here, when you have so many guys having success at one time, it was easy to fit right in. Gibby's a big part of that because he allows it to happen."

These are the many reasons—all this praise raining down—that John Gibbons got a second crack at managing the Blue Jays.

He even survived regime changes when Alex Anthopoulos left town and the duo of Mark Shapiro and Ross Atkins landed. While Anthopoulos and Gibbons seemed a great fit, Shapiro and Atkins barely even spoke the same language as Gibbons. The ol' manager did what he always does, though. He endeared himself. He showed the value of managing people, not just numbers and potential outcomes.

Having the stars in your corner doesn't hurt, either.

Even José Bautista, famous for his dead-serious approach to the game and the scowl he shot at umpires and opponents, lights up at the mention of Gibbons' name.

"He's a straight shooter," Bautista said. "He keeps it light. He keeps it fun. He goes straight to the point. You get what you see with him. He embraced us. He let us be who we were. He didn't try to force everybody into a mold. He played to our personalities, our strengths and our weaknesses. It was a tough job for him, obviously, when you have all of those personalities and a lot of established names in the game making good money, those rooms can be hard to manage. He was perfect for what we needed. He knew when to kick your behind, but he also knew when to put his arm around you. He was really good at handling that balance."

This is what made John Gibbons, well, "Gibby."

He became beloved in Toronto. A handful of times each season, you'll still see a No. 5 GIBBONS jersey in the crowd at Rogers Centre.

Gibbons wasn't trying to sound smarter than you. He was the everyman to whom fans felt a genuine connection. At times, he was an entertainer, and some of his finest moments came with the cameras on.

* * *

The media meets with the manager twice a day, before the game and after. This happens all spring and all season long, covering hundreds of sessions and thousands of questions each year.

Stepping into Gibbons' office before a Blue Jays game was an experience unlike any other. By the time writers poured into his office near 4:00 PM each game day, Gibbons would already be leaned back in his chair at a dangerous angle, his feet up on the desk. He had a deep closet of T-shirts that had been free giveaways at Blue Jays games over the years, many of them sporting the faces of players long gone. His favourite look, though, may have been a white Taco Del Mar shirt with the sleeves cut off.

It didn't look like he'd taken that thing to a tailor, either. The slashes from the scissors were clear.

Gibbons had a way of subtly but effectively keeping order.

In my early days covering the team, beginning in 2017, there were still several veteran writers on the beat, Richard Griffin of the *Toronto Star* and John Lott of The Athletic among them. Gibbons' office was always open to surprise guests from years past, too, often in the form of Dave Perkins, who had covered the team for the *Toronto Star* when Gibbons first came to town.

As the vets filled the couches or took their positions in the square room—all of which had been quietly agreed to over the years and respected as law since—I would tuck into the far corner, clean-shaven, shirt tucked in, looking like I'd gotten lost on my way to a job interview. Gibbons fielded questions for

10 or 20 minutes, subtly showing through his answers that he knew who the veterans were and knew who the regulars were. If he started giving you better answers or using your name in his replies, you knew you were starting to do something right.

Gibbons had such subtle, effective ways of sparring with the media, too. Whether he wanted to show you some respect, take a playful jab, or tell you to get the hell out of his office, he found ways to do it that left everyone in the room laughing along together.

Once, a reporter was asking Gibbons about a struggling pitcher with troubling home-and-road splits. Just as the reporter started to reference those numbers, Gibbons interjected with "OK, Statmaster." With the wrong delivery, you'd mistake him for an asshole. With Gibbons' wry smile and timing, it landed so perfectly.

In my second season covering Gibbons, I made the drive from Toronto to Dunedin, Florida, in one long, sleepless blur and stumbled into the stadium just in time for his first media availability of the new season. Gibbons looked me up and down, a smile spreading across his face and said, "Shit. Look at you, Keegs. They just dig you up, or what?"

Before I'd even asked my first questions of the season, he'd landed his first jab.

There were so many Gibby Classics over the years, too.

In 2014, after one of his 53 career ejections, he told reporters, "Maybe I got tired of looking at bunts not getting put down, so I said, 'I'll go have a beer.'"

In 2016, after a struggling Troy Tulowitzki had a big game, he said, "For all the Tulo haters out there, suck on that one tonight, will ya?"

In 2017, he famously called into the post-game show on Sportsnet 590 The FAN, *Blue Jays Talk*, hosted by Mike Wilner.

He identified himself as "John from the Bronx," but by the time he got his next sentence out, Wilner and anyone listening knew exactly which John this was. Ryan Goins had been picked as the player of the game on the post-game show, but Gibbons had his own thoughts on the matter.

"I think it was great on Gibbons' part to catch Maile," said John from the Bronx. "I thought that Maile did a great job. I heard you before the game and what an expert you are. I'm glad you were wrong once again."

After asking if the show was giving away any free tickets, Gibbons asked Wilner what kind of ratings this show got. Who was listening? "Is it the same bozos every night?" he asked.

There he was, the manager of the Toronto Blue Jays, leaned back in his chair making a prank call.

Gibbons' pregame meetings with the media were like stepping into another world. More often than not, we'd walk out 10, 20, or 30 minutes later all wondering the same thing: *How the hell did we get to that topic?*

Over the course of these hundreds of sessions spanning a full camp and 162 games, you tend to touch on just about everything.

One day, after a player had changed the walkup song they'd been using for years, someone asked Gibbons in the room a quick, off-hand question: What would your walk-up song be if you were back in the big leagues today?

Gibbons took out his iPhone and, after fumbling around for a moment, played us Billy Ray Cyrus' 1992 hit "Some Gave All." He didn't just play a clip, though. He played all four minutes and four seconds of this Billy Ray Cyrus song.

All gave some, some gave all
Some stood through for the red, white, and blue
And some had to fall

And if you ever think of me
Think of all your liberties and recall
Some gave all

As the chorus played for the second time, Gibbons held his fist up in the air and pumped along to Billy Ray's vocals as if he were sitting on the couch among us, strumming his guitar.

Above the two couches in Gibbons' office in those years were two big televisions. These days, the manager has those tuned to MLB Network or a live shot of the field at Rogers Centre to track what's happening. Gibbons' TVs were different. We'd typically walk in to find CNN on each.

On a slow news day, there would always come a point where the momentum of the group's questions started to trail off. These days, there's a sharp PR person in the room to cut off the availability and get the manager off to their many, many meetings, but Gibbons tended to run the room. As the questions slowed, you'd see his eyes drifting above our heads to whatever was playing out on CNN that day.

Suddenly, Gibbons would be asking for our opinions on the United States' relations with Russia. Did we see what happened with the satellite launch on Tuesday? Who was the next Democratic nominee going to be? Did you see what happened at the Republican convention? Have you heard what's going on with the Supreme Court nomination? The midterm elections are coming up. There's a hurricane forming in the Atlantic and they're saying it could reach Category 3 by the time it hits land.

Some of these would just be Gibbons' passing curiosities, complete with a smile and a joke, but it was all another lesson on the fine balance of John Gibbons.

His exterior, that good ol' boy with his feet up on the desk and sleeves cut off, is what endeared him to people. It's what made people feel immediately at ease, like they were on his team and he was on theirs. This all hid the part of Gibbons that was thoughtful, caring, and intelligent. That's the side of Gibbons that made the whole thing work.

John Gibbons gave a damn. He just plain cared, and when you handle your business the right way, it's how much he cares about his players that is left for them to remember.

Even on his way out, in a 2018 season that everyone involved knew would be his last, there were no shots on the way out the door, no anonymous quotes or whispered comments.

"I love Gibby," Troy Tulowitzki said late in that season. "Without a doubt, I hope Gibby's back, but I also want Gibby to be happy, so whatever he wants to do, I stand by him. That's what friends do."

That's the story of Gibbons and those teams of 2015 and '16. John Gibbons was more than just their manager.

"He was a father figure to a lot of us," said Kevin Pillar. "It was just the right blend of personality that we needed at the time. I think about so many instances on the field where he was a father figure. He could belittle me and make me feel tiny, and rightfully so, for doing something stupid on the field. Then, I think about times we'd have an off day. I'd be at a concert with my wife and the boys and Gibby would be there. He'd have a couple pops and we'd put our arms around one another, singing country music. It wasn't weird, it was just normal. Then, we'd show up to the field the next day, have a laugh about the night before, and we'd go to work. He always had our back. He supported us. He loved us. We would run through a wall for him."

16

Vladimir Guerrero Jr., the Prospect

Vladimir Guerrero Jr. allowed us to mythologize him. It all happened at just the right time.

The Blue Jays signed Guerrero, the prodigy with the famous father, in July 2015 for $3.9 million. This organization was about to launch itself into two incredible postseason runs, though. It wasn't time to dream about prospects just yet.

By the time 2017 rolled around and it quickly became clear that this organization needed to turn an eye to the future, Guerrero was coming over the horizon. Guerrero reached High A Dunedin that season, dominating pitching that was older and more experienced than him, and the Blue Jays had a decision to make the next spring.

John Schneider had been Guerrero's manager in Dunedin in 2017. He'd watched an 18-year-old kid hit .333 with more walks (36) than strikeouts (28) over a couple of months of base-ball, showing power that no one around had seen from a player that age. Schneider was headed to Double A New Hampshire in 2018 to manage, but the organization was debating, internally, how they should handle Vladdy and Bo Bichette, the two faces of their future.

The organization was open to the idea of starting both back in High A Dunedin. It wouldn't raise any eyebrows, given their ages, and each could earn a promotion in a couple of months to spend most of their 2018 seasons in Double A.

Schneider didn't agree. He'd seen these two up close. He knew what Vladdy was capable of—what he could be capable of—so he walked into the Blue Jays' player development complex one day and found Gil Kim, who was then the director of player development.

"I walked to his office and I said, 'Send them with me. I will not fuck this up.'"

The Blue Jays listened. It worked.

What Guerrero did in those 61 Double A games needs to be frozen in time. At just 19 years old, he hit .402 with a 1.120 OPS and 14 home runs. He became the best prospect in baseball, evaluators stretching to grasp what they were seeing, struggling to find players from the past to compare him to.

"My first 'holy shit' moment with him was in Double A," Schneider remembered. "He was hitting home runs off of a tee on top of the plate on MLB Network. That whole year in Manchester, there were probably 10 'holy shit' moments.

"There was the home run off of the hotel. One time, he hit a home run off someone in Trenton and it was about 23 degrees Fahrenheit. He hit it so hard that it sounded like a gunshot went off. I said to him, 'Vladdy, how the hell did you hit that?' He said that he knew the pitcher threw his fastball up here, so he told himself he was going to swing up on top of it. I thought, 'Dude. You're 18.'

"I always tried to take a step back once a week with him. He was not a normal No. 1 prospect. Watching him take BP, listening to him talk about hitting, you could just tell. It was so weird because I had him and Bo together...and they were just better than everyone else. They were just better. What Vladdy could do with the bat, I realized that's something you only see once every 20 years. It was just different than anything I'd ever seen."

It was different from anything that *any of us* had ever seen.

There was something so pure about those prospect years, tracking Guerrero through the minor leagues. He was a dream prospect, as exciting to the most casual fan as he was to the savant. His power was devastating, his feel for hitting unlike anything we'd seen from a teenager.

Had Guerrero's prospect rise come today, it would have landed in a new era of accessible data. Most minor league parks are rigged for Statcast data now, the number growing by the year. We can reach down to Single A or Double A to find exactly how hard a pitcher throws, a runner's speed on the bases, or the exit velocity of a home run.

In most ways, this information is incredibly useful. It's helped fans better understand players, and as more organizations use social media to promote their own prospects—all clubs should; it's marketing—the stars of tomorrow feel closer than they ever have. It's all been demystified.

Vladdy arrived on the last train, still some mystique trailing behind him.

From Single A Lansing, grainy videos would come of Guerrero turning another pitcher into a highlight reel. By the time he reached Double A, the public appetite was insatiable, but it was more about what we all saw, not the numbers and data of it all. You could tell, just by watching those incredible clips, that the young star had nearly broken the baseball in half. The number 113.7 would not have broadened your experience.

The future of the Blue Jays was all right there in one place, Double A New Hampshire. As the 2018 Blue Jays went 73–89, fans needed something to cling to, a hope to hold.

It was right there, and it wasn't just Guerrero.

"Our team was like a boy band," Schneider said. "It was the Vladdy and Bo show with Cavan Biggio as the chaperone, the old guy. We were taking trips up and down I-95 into the middle of nowhere. We'd arrive at 3:00 AM and there would be 50 people at our hotel. I remember one day in Harrisburg we were leaving the hotel and about 20 people ran after the bus to try to get it to stop. Then, on the way to the field, there was this humongous digital billboard that said, SENATORS VS. FISHER CATS, VLAD JR. IS COMING. I remember thinking to myself, 'Wow. OK. This is not normal.'"

In any other organization, Bo Bichette would have been the singular face of the future. When Vladdy was topping every prospect list on the planet, Bichette was always close behind, on the edge of being a top-10 prospect in the sport. He and Guerrero balanced one another so well.

"What I learned about Bo in those years is what an intense competitor he was," Schneider remembers. "He was solely focused on being the best player on the field every single day. He wanted to kick your ass in ping pong. I think he gets over-shadowed because he was quieter and not as outgoing as Vlad, but that was another situation where I had to step back and go, 'OK, I've got two of these guys on my team? This is fucking crazy.' If it was just one of them, it would be crazy, but two?"

The pressure on Guerrero was immeasurable, but he's always handled that so casually. Growing up around the game with his father, Vladimir Guerrero, had taken the glitter off everything for Vladdy. As he climbed from level to level, nothing was new. His eyes had no need to be wide. He'd been in better clubhouses before.

The Blue Jays needed to manage this as much as Guerrero's development on the field. It was unlike anything that any other prospect in baseball had to go through. The Blue Jays were absolutely flooded with media requests for Guerrero from the United States, Canada, and the Dominican Republic. Everyone wanted a piece of the next big thing.

What rounded out the aura of Guerrero, though, was his joy. This kid was not a robot.

The pipeline of elite youth sports in Canada and the United States can have side effects, stripping some joy from the game at a young age. We see pros in the NBA, NFL, NHL, and MLB now who have trained from a young age. It's the age of first-round picks who have never been to McDonald's.

Guerrero was a showman, though, even as a teenager. He lit up the game, lit up the screen. He carried the incredible Dominican baseball culture in him. His game was a celebration of its own talents.

"I think it's how he was raised and how he connected with the game at a very early age," Ross Atkins said. "I've played with players like that in the minor leagues and I've been around a lot of players who, in my opinion, end up playing a lot longer because of it. Marco Scutaro was a player who really, immediately resonated with me as a young minor league player who had that joy and love he played with. Vladdy's joy, it's not something you can ask someone to have. It's actually something that coaches say all the time. 'Hey, make sure you enjoy it. Make sure you have fun.' Me, as a player, I would always say, 'OK, how do I do that? I would love to.'"

It all came so naturally to Guerrero, every corner of the game.

All through the minor leagues, before the balls and strikes of it all mattered to the Blue Jays' record, fans felt so free to enjoy Guerrero. They knew that times would come—and they sure have—when Guerrero would frustrate or underperform, but those were still in the distance. The Blue Jays had baseball's next big thing. He was an incandescent talent.

Naturally, the years that come will colour how we remember Guerrero in his entirety. Whether he goes on to have the legendary career that was once prophesied or he lands in the realm of "very good," that doesn't matter for this conversation. We need to carve out Guerrero's prospect years and hold them by themselves. They're the type of thing that may not happen again for decades, if ever.

The rest of baseball certainly took notice.

Ask Ross Atkins if another GM ever tried to pry Guerrero away from the Blue Jays and he breaks into a laugh.

"Oh, yeah. Especially in my first year here. It was every fourth phone call. There was one team in particular, which I certainly won't mention...but we had a good laugh about them internally and still do."

"It's funny. At GM meetings or the winter meetings, you always see it, especially if it's a younger new GM. There's a line of other executives waiting to find them at the cocktail hour... or preferably two hours after the cocktail hour."

Vladdy wasn't going anywhere, no matter what you offered the Blue Jays. Charlie Montoyo had been brought in at this point to lead a young Blue Jays team through its rebuild, which Guerrero Jr. would be the face of.

The 2019 season finally came. The calls to promote Guerrero persisted, as they had through all of '18. A minor injury delayed Guerrero slightly to open the season, but by the time he got back to Triple A Buffalo, he made a mockery of it again. Vladdy put together 11 hits with three home runs over his eight games there and the Blue Jays couldn't wait any longer.

Back in Toronto, the Blue Jays were off to a slow start. On April 25, a Wednesday, they lost 4–0 to the Giants, an unspectacular night in an unspectacular season. Media filed into the press conference room following the game and Montoyo took the podium, but leaned in to speak before taking his first question.

"I have an announcement to make. We're planning to call Vlad Guerrero up for Friday's game."

PART 4

STORIES OF THE SEASONS

17

Vladdy

Two years into Vladimir Guerrero Jr.'s career, it was still difficult to get a feel for what the Blue Jays were dealing with.

Between his 2019 debut and the COVID-shortened 2020 season, Guerrero had posted a .778 OPS with 24 home runs over 183 games. These were not the gaudy, eye-popping numbers everyone had become accustomed to from the minor leagues, but he did this as a 20- and 21-year-old.

Something clicked in 2021.

Looking back, Charlie Montoyo doesn't point to a swing change or a grand moment where the lightbulb went on for Guerrero. He's always had the talent, always had the exact swing he needed to win MVP awards. It's always been about getting Guerrero to that place consistently, which is about something so much simpler.

"He was happy," Montoyo said plainly. "He was always happy. He had friends. He could speak if he had a problem. He was happy."

That 2021 season, as the Blue Jays dragged their suitcases from Dunedin to Buffalo to Toronto, everything aligned for Guerrero. For the first time, we saw in the big leagues what we'd once seen in the minor leagues.

Vladimir Guerrero Jr. (2021)

.311 / .401 / .601

1.002 OPS

48 Home Runs

123 RBI

6.3 WAR (FanGraphs)

That 6.3 WAR ranks Guerrero's season only 13th among Blue Jays hitters all-time, but above him, you'll find players whose defensive value was far greater than Vladdy's. Narrow this to Guerrero's offense, and he stands alongside the best years we've seen from José Bautista and Carlos Delgado, two names Guerrero's could someday rest alongside.

To understand how Guerrero got to 2021, though, Montoyo has to go back to the start.

When Montoyo was hired as the Blue Jays' manager, he flew to the Dominican Republic and spent time with Guerrero and his family. Yes, the visit even included meals at the table of Guerrero's grandmother, Altagracia Alvino, whose legendary cooking has drawn the love of Latin baseball stars for decades now.

Montoyo has been a baseball man all his life. His cup of coffee in the big leagues came with Expos in 1993, just a few years before Vlad Sr. burst onto the scene. He knew the Guerreros and everything that comes with that name—a name that carries so much weight in the Dominican Republic—but seeing it up close was a different experience entirely.

"Oh my god, this is not fair," Montoyo remembered. "It was like the World Series, everybody there for this one kid. That first day that he got called up, I thought this isn't fair to that kid. One thing that he has is a level head, a good family, good friends. The group that we had helped a lot with Teoscar, Lourdes, and all of those guys. They became brothers. It was fun. That's what we had. Anyone who played us in 2021 said, 'They win, but they also have fun. This team has fun. They're different.'"

Guerrero, Hernández, and Gurriel were inseparable, a comedy act without someone playing the straight man to keep it all together. All three had fantastic seasons in 2021 by their own standards, too. It all came together and worked wonderfully.

"If you look at the videos from 2021, he was always smiling," Montoyo said. "He was always smiling because he had friends. If something went wrong, he had friends telling him, 'Hey, man, you'll be all right. Do this. Do that.' Him being happy, himself, that was a big part of that year.

"One thing I always wanted him to do—which he did— between him and me I would always say, 'Talk shit. When you talk shit, you're good.' Most big-league players, if they say they're going to crush a guy, they're usually the best players and usually they're good. Mentally, that's in your brain and you're positive instead of saying, 'Oh, no, this guy....' That never came out of his mouth. He'd talk shit."

Montoyo is onto something here. The 2021 season saw Guerrero coming into himself as a man and a baseball player. Gone were the prospect days. Gone was the COVID season of 2020 and the vagabond season of 2021. Guerrero, like the Blue

Jays, had his feet under himself again. We saw this same thing play out again in 2024, Guerrero taking another noticeable step in his maturation as a leader and a person, which coincided with another excellent season offensively.

Vladdy had tasted disappointment. For prospects as gifted as Guerrero, that often doesn't come until they reach the big leagues. It can break some players, but Guerrero responded to it.

"I don't want to forget about 2020 because that's when he went home and he gained all of that weight," Montoyo said, reaching back to highlight the lessons Guerrero learned. "We had to deal with that. When one of your best players gains a lot of weight, you have to deal with that on top of COVID. Our star, one of the best players in baseball, just gained a lot of weight. We had to be careful because we didn't want him to get hurt, but that's one thing he learned that year, personally. After that, you can see his workouts in the offseason are great and that's never going to happen again. It was a good lesson for him."

There are so many ways we can measure Guerrero's 2021 season. Like his prospect rise, it's something that needs to be cut out and appreciated all on its own.

Guerrero finished second in AL MVP voting that season, but he might have needed to break the single-season home run record to change that.

Shohei Ohtani hit 46 home runs with a .965 OPS, 100 RBI, and 26 stolen bases...all while posting a 3.18 ERA with 156 strikeouts over 130⅓ innings. It's one of the most remarkable seasons we'll ever see, so given that Guerrero's season has to exist with that as its backdrop, let's settle on calling Guerrero's 2021 "MVP calibre."

He felt inevitable that year. It's this special ability only a handful of hitters can possess at a time. It felt like, when a big moment came around in the game, Guerrero could leapfrog spots in the lineup to be the next man at the dish. The big moments found him, over and over.

The Blue Jays were good, too. Damn good.

"We were winning and having fun, and he was part of it," Montoyo said. "It seemed like those guys just wanted to play the best teams all the time. That was like a gauge for them to know who they were. They loved playing against the Yankees, against the Rays. I remember in 2021, I think Aaron Boone said this, which was a great compliment back then, that he'd rather play in Boston than play the Jays."

"At the beginning, people would say he's too cocky. That's not cocky, he's just having fun. It's a game. That's what I saw from the beginning. He didn't do it to show up the other team. He was just having so much fun and he wanted to win. For a guy that young...wow."

Guerrero's career seems to have settled into an unintentional rhythm. Two good years, then a great year. Two good years, then a great year.

In 2022, the .818 OPS and 32 home runs that would have been a career year for most of the league felt like a letdown from Guerrero. His 2023 season was a step back from even that, but he rediscovered himself in 2024.

It feels like he's always chasing something on one side, while on the other side, he's trapped in the shadow of something that was.

"Vlad, since he's been 18, because of his name and his dad there has always been some unfair expectations put on him, I think," John Schneider said early in the 2024 season, when Guerrero was still struggling. "Having the year he had in 2021 made a lot of people say, 'Holy shit.' It's tough to live up to that. That was a remarkable season."

As Guerrero has shown us again, though, he is still capable of greatness. His mid-season renaissance in 2024 has reignited the imagination again.

When you watch Guerrero at his best—his very, very best—nothing seems impossible. You're drawn back to his prospect days, when Guerrero was this franchise's next great hope, the big kid you'd watch in grainy videos from Lansing, from Dunedin, from New Hampshire, from Buffalo.

When he's at his best, you see that joy again. It spills out of Guerrero, that luminescent smile lighting up the field.

It's fair to pose the question of the chicken or the egg. Sure, Guerrero's joy brings out the best of him, but isn't it easier to feel that joy when everything is going your way?

Vladdy has the ability to make it all snowball, growing bigger and bolder by the day. He can tempt you—with a swing, with a week, or with a season—to dream.

18

Perfect Moments: Roy Halladay

THOSE WHO KNEW ROY HALLADAY—REALLY KNEW HIM— want to tell stories.

It's their way of keeping Halladay's memory alive, for themselves as much as the person they're telling stories to.

Halladay is a Hall of Fame pitcher, one of the greatest of his generation and one of the faces of the Blue Jays' organization forever. This was the legacy he left, one that all who come after him in Toronto will reach for.

After Halladay's incredible rebuild, climbing from Dunedin all the way back to the big leagues, he spent a decade atop the baseball world. From 2001 through 2011, Halladay's peak, no pitcher in baseball was worth more than his 62.9 WAR (FanGraphs). Only CC Sabathia, edging Halladay by a single game, had more wins. Only Sabathia, Liván Hernández, and Mark Buehrle threw more innings.

He was everything a pitcher wanted to be.

"Oh, I could talk all day about him," Pat Hentgen said.

"I remember Chris Carpenter and Roy Halladay coming up to spring training for the first time. You'd just see two big dudes that wanted to learn, wanted to work, and they couldn't wait to compete. I think Doc would have made it just fine pitching over the top. I know a lot of people think I'm crazy, but I just think he's that good and he would have figured it out. To go down and revamp your whole delivery like that is a real credit to him. It's not easy to do."

"He and Carp, they'd walk in, and it was the twin towers. They were just just 6'5", 6'6", these two big guys who would follow me and Clemens around. I tried to make them better because I wanted to win. I was doing everything I could to make Doc and Carp better. I think Clemens and all of us tried that back then. We all knew they were coming. We all knew they were good."

No season captured the scope of Halladay in Toronto like 2003, when Halladay won the AL Cy Young Award, beating out Esteban Loaiza and Pedro Martinez, who had a brilliant season for the Red Sox.

Halladay threw a career-high 266 innings that season, one of eight times he crossed the 200-inning mark. Unless Major League Baseball expands its schedule to 262 games, he'll likely be the last Blue Jays pitcher to cross 200 innings that many times.

He made 36 starts and threw nine complete games, two other numbers that feel so detached from the modern game despite being just over two decades old. Five of his six starts in September were complete games. On September 6, he pitched a

10-inning shutout against the Tigers on just 99 pitches. Could you imagine that in today's game?

"We're headed to extra innings here at SkyDome, tied 0–0, and still...no movement in the Blue Jays' bullpen."

That season captures Halladay so well, lugging a 3.25 ERA like a workhorse across all those innings.

Halladay was must-see TV in a time the Blue Jays weren't always that. JP Ricciardi, the Blue Jays' GM at the time, would sit back and tell his managers just one thing: Make sure John McDonald is at shortstop when Doc is on the mound.

"I had the best pitcher in baseball for eight years. Not even a doubt," Ricciardi said. "I knew every time that Doc went to the mound—and you can ask the guys in Toronto—I used to plan out the calendar like this. I would say, 'Monday is Doc, Tuesday, Wednesday, Thursday, Friday, Saturday is Doc... Sunday, Monday, Tuesday, Wednesday, Thursday is Doc....'

"I knew every fifth day that we had a chance to win, because we had the best pitcher in baseball. If Halladay didn't pitch in the American League East, he would have won 300 games. He was beating the Red Sox and the Yankees. Both of those teams were scoring 1,000 runs a year. It was the height of the steroid era, and he was beating them on a regular basis. If he was in a different division with less powerful lineups, he would have won four Cy Youngs and he would have won 300 games. Not only did he post. Not only did he give you innings. Not only was he a legit No. 1. He beat the best teams in baseball."

It's difficult to capture Halladay, the person. Where did the pitcher end and the person begin?

He was at the absolute height of his powers in 2003. The Cy Young Award removed any veil that had been over Halladay, who was hidden on the other side of the border when the Blue Jays weren't often on national TV. As other stars joined the

Blue Jays' organization over the years, they recognized the moment they walked in the door that this was Halladay's house. What he said goes, and if he said nothing at all, don't be surprised.

"His intensity, his work ethic and determination. Wow," José Bautista said. "This guy was a bulldog who came in every day ready to take on whoever, whether that was who he was pitching against that day or just his own work. Even when he wasn't pitching, you could see the intensity there. He would show up and have such a strict regimen."

"Roy was one of the first guys that I saw and thought, 'OK, this guy has a plan from once he walks through the doors until he leaves.' There was not a minute wasted in his day playing cards or chit-chatting. He had a structure to his day. I learned a lot from him."

To spend even a day around Halladay was a lesson on what greatness demanded.

"He became a machine. He worked harder than anybody else," Carlos Delgado said. "He was at the spring training facility earlier than anybody else. He studied hitters harder than anybody else. Next thing you know, he became a Cy Young Award winner. I had a lot of appreciation for Roy. I feel so bad that his life ended so short. Every time he took the mound, he was going to compete. He did not want to leave the game."

* * *

Halladay spanned eras in Toronto. He was the young guy coming up in the shadow of those World Series teams, watching those veterans each spring.

By the time Halladay was nearing the end of his tenure in Toronto, a new wave had arrived. Bautista was in Toronto, moments away from breaking out as one of the biggest stars in baseball, launching a new era of Blue Jays baseball alongside him.

Ricky Romero was the new kid in the rotation that year. Just as Halladay had watched pitchers like Hentgen or Clemens while he came up as a prospect, Romero watched Halladay. Romero had, as he always said, front-row tickets to greatness.

Romero, the Blue Jays' first-round pick in 2005, shared the rotation with Halladay for just one year in '09. His memories of Halladay run parallel to his experiences pitching under Cito Gaston early on, another Blue Jays legend he rubbed up against so briefly, but in such a meaningful way. Romero's relationship with Halladay was not an immediate friendship. This was not the veteran quarterback taking the rookie out for a steak dinner. It took time.

"Doc, it was one of those things where he really had to warm up to you," Romero said. "He wasn't going to be the guy who was going to come to you, approach you and guide you. I always tell this story, but we were finishing up this series in Oakland and I had gotten the win. He always used to sit in the front seat, and I was walking in. He taps me and he said, 'Hey, Ricky. I just want to congratulate you on your 10th win. Double digits as a rookie is a big deal. Congratulations. I'm so happy for you.' I was like, whoa, that's the most words he's said to me all year right there. He wasn't a man of many words, but when he told me that, I was like a little kid. I said thank you, but I remember going to sit down and just thinking, wow, that was really, really cool.

"Doc usually sat next to Brad Arnsberg, the pitching coach, during games. From time to time, I'd go sit next to him and ask him questions. I'd think, 'You know what? Hell no. I'm from East LA, man! He's not going to intimidate me!' I'd sit there and ask him questions and he would answer them. I think people wanted to build this persona of Doc, that you had to leave him alone, but no, man. He's a human being. He just wanted to be approached the right way. Don't ask him dumb questions now. Don't come and say something stupid. But he would always take the time. Then there was…I remember the last conversation I had with him. I'll never forget it."

This is when Romero's voice shifts. He's stumbled back across the memory he always wants to hold onto. It's another one of those stories these players tell, their own act of remembering.

This came years later. Halladay's Phillies were in New York to play the Mets and Romero's Blue Jays were in town to play the Yankees, but the two teams were staying at the same hotel.

"He called my room. We were both struggling at this time. It was 2012…. I was shocked. I was shocked that he called. He said to me, 'Hey, Rick, got a minute? Come to my room.'

"I went to Doc's room and, no joke, we sat there and talked for two hours. We talked about life, about the season. Doc, at this time, he was hurting. You could tell he was hurting. I felt like I was seeing my hero, the guy I used to watch, who worked so hard, who was unbeatable. Talk to any fan in the city of Toronto, when he pitched people were excited. They loved it. Two hours, complete game, no shenanigans. We had a conversation that night about everything. If I knew that would be the last time I'd ever talk to him…. I wish I'd had a recorder that night. It got deep. The stuff we said to each other, at times, I kind of black out about what we talked about. I was so in that moment. But I remember him telling me, 'Keep fighting. You're so young. I admire you and the way you've gone about it.' I thought that was pretty cool. That conversation went so deep, and to be able to have that with the one guy I look up to in the organization..."

This is what still lingers over so many who knew Halladay, the man who once looked unbreakable.

Halladay died on November 7, 2017, when the small aircraft he was flying crashed into the Gulf of Florida, just north of Tampa. An autopsy report later revealed evidence of an amphetamine, morphine, and an insomnia drug in Halladay's system. That day in November is still burned into the minds of so many, from former teammates who knew Halladay to fans who only watched from a distance. Early reports spread on social media. The tail number traced back to Halladay's plane. The announcement was made. It was Roy Halladay.

"I loved him as a person. I spoke at his funeral and delivered one of his eulogies which was very sad," Ricciardi said. "He died way too young. He left us too young. We had a great personal relationship. I look at Doc and that's a hard one even to this day. I loved him as a professional, but I loved him even more as a person. He left us too soon."

As the years stretch on, it doesn't feel any further away.

"He leaves incredible statistics, an incredible person off the field, a great, silent leader who led by example," Hentgen said. "He was an incredible worker, a good teammate, a good dad. He was everything. He checked all the boxes, brother. It's a sad, sad thing, but his name will live forever."

Halladay's wife, Brandy, along with his sons, Braden and Ryan, have carried on his legacy. Brandy Halladay has continued the work that she and Roy started together in his playing days. The Halladays were involved with local charities in his playing days, including "Doc's Box," where the Halladays would host kids and families from SickKids. Now, at Roy Halladay Field, an accessible ball diamond in Scarborough that the organization's charitable arm, Jays Care, named in his honour, one of the dugouts has a sign reading "Doc's Box."

"You're stuck with us, like it or not," Brandy Halladay joked on the day that field was opened in 2022.

"It validates that what he did matters," she said. "It really matters."

When Roy Halladay was inducted into the Baseball Hall of Fame in 2019, it was Brandy who spoke in his place. She spoke about how Roy would feel in that moment, about his competitiveness, his love for his teammates. It was beautiful and heartbreaking, and ended with one of the finest moments we will ever see on that stage.

"I think that Roy would want everyone to know that people are not perfect. We are all imperfect and flawed in one way or another. We all struggle, but with hard work, humility, and dedication, imperfect people can still have perfect moments. Roy was blessed, in his life and his career, to have some perfect moments."

19

"This Isn't the Try League": Josh Donaldson

THERE'S ONLY ONE JOSH DONALDSON, WHICH IS PROBABLY for the best. If there were two, there would be a brawl.

Donaldson's peak in Toronto, that three-year flash from 2015 to 2017, was some of the best baseball we've ever seen in this market. His MVP year in '15, right after Donaldson was brought north by a stroke of brilliance from Alex Anthopoulos and the Blue Jays' front office, stands as one of the greatest individual seasons from a Blue Jays hitter in franchise history.

No hitter has matched the 8.7 WAR Donaldson put up that season, his sharp defence at third base buoying his dominant offensive numbers. Donaldson hit .297 with 41 home runs,

123 RBI, and a .939 OPS that season. It was enough to even keep peak Mike Trout at bay for the AL MVP Award, just the second in Blue Jays history.

Ask an old coach or teammate for a Josh Donaldson story, though, and the conversation does not leap to baseball. It doesn't go to his remarkable 2015 season or the postseason run in '16, his mad dash home to win the ALDS against the Rangers, a play that captured the chaotic brilliance of Donaldson's game so perfectly.

John Gibbons calls Donaldson one of his "all-time favourites." The two were the perfect pairing, the unpredictable superstar and the old-school manager who knew when to throw a jab or sling his arm around him.

"Oh, he had his moments," Gibbons said, laughing already. "There was no telling what he was going to say, and he was probably going to piss somebody off, but he rose to the occasion. He helped unite guys in his own way. Of course, that year he was the MVP of the league, too. He did incredible things on the field.

"We had our moments, too. Being the manager of the team, I still had to keep things under control. He was one of our top players and he was a volatile guy. He had a big personality and I loved it."

Donaldson was a rarity in baseball, an aggressor by every definition of the word. Baseball doesn't typically lend itself to that. You take turns and tally up the score at the end.

Instead, Donaldson brought an intensity and energy that quickly became the identity of those Blue Jays teams in 2015 and '16. They were the teams that Canada loved, and the United States hated. Right atop the list, alongside the defiant and dominant José Bautista, was Donaldson. He didn't just want to score the first run, he wanted to land the first punch.

"We were coming to get you," Donaldson said. "That's what we were about. We knew that we were good. We knew we had the offensive capability as a team to really do damage."

Kevin Pillar calls Donaldson the "emotional and spiritual leader" of those teams.

"As talented and as important as José was to the city, Josh was equally talented and equally intense," Pillar said. "He really changed the mindset and the belief and the mentality of the entire organization."

"He just brought a new level of intensity and held everyone to that standard. Talent was starting to get in place in 2014 as I was there and then in 2015, the talent was brought to another level, but JD brought the intensity, he brought the mentality, he brought the mindset, he brought the 'fuck you' to that clubhouse and the field every single day."

Those teams weren't lacking personality by any means. Bautista was already the face of it, but adding Russell Martin took it to another level. He brought the toughness to it all, a postseason veteran with a winning reputation. The younger wave of players on that roster, led by starter Marcus Stroman, dripped with energy and personality. It all came together in such a dense, crowded clubhouse.

"Donaldson kind of changed the culture," Stroman said. "He was such a confident guy, someone who was never scared to ruffle some feathers. He was always super confident. When he stepped on that field, there was no one more confident than him…. Donaldson was special during those years, man. The confidence, then just being able to go out there and do it like he did, day after day, everyone fed off that."

Donaldson is the ultimate example of the player you love to have on your team but hate to play against. In baseball circles, it stands among the highest forms of praise.

Martin had seen Donaldson from the other side for years. Donaldson actually came up as a catcher with Oakland, which is so difficult to envision now. He'd put together a couple of very nice seasons with the A's in 2013 and '14, but the Blue Jays saw another level to unlock. They saw another late-blooming superstar who could slide in alongside two others—José Bautista and Edwin Encarnación—to form one of the most feared sections of a lineup we've ever seen in Toronto.

"JD, he's a friend. If he would have never been my teammate, I never would have thought he'd be my friend," Martin said. "He's the guy who, if you're on the other team, you don't like that guy. You just don't like him. Then you play with him, and he just grows on you. There's a lot of good in JD. He's another guy who, in the league, is definitely misunderstood. You only really understand it when you're with him every day.

"He's an absolute warrior. He will run through a wall for you. He wants you to be successful, as well. In baseball, you kind of have to be selfish, but at the same time if you want to be good for your teammates, you have to be willing to share your information. You have to be selfish and take the time to make yourself better, like batting cage time and the weight room, you have to be selfish. If you want to win as a team, though, you have to make sure you're impacting everybody else around you in a positive way. He would do that. He would challenge you. Let's say you were struggling a little bit, and instead of feeling down, he would challenge you and that would send you into a different headspace.

"And he was all-time. He was in his MVP season. The swag was just through the roof. You get a confident JD and he's going to be loud, he's going to be obnoxious...in a funny way and a good way...but he wouldn't be afraid to call you out. He didn't just want to play good baseball, he wanted to play good and for the team to win. That's important. Some people don't care."

This comes up in nearly any conversation about Donaldson's career.

"He wasn't afraid to call someone out, but..."

There's always a but. Teammates saw Donaldson challenge other players, coaches, and members of the front office. We're not talking about veiled shots and jabs muttered under his breath; we're talking face-to-face, nose-to-nose, don't blink first.

Had Donaldson been a .210 hitter with a .670 OPS, he might have caught a fist in return. Being the calibre of player he was in Toronto, though, Donaldson's teammates respected what he did because they saw it work.

"Not everyone agreed with his leadership style, but somehow he was able to motivate and get the best out of everyone every single day," Pillar said. "Sometimes, that came with saying things you didn't necessarily agree with or like. He would challenge you to take your game to a different level. He got the best out of every single person, every day."

Ryan Goins remembers getting a taste of that, himself.

"He was not afraid to challenge anyone on the team, no matter who you were," Goins said. "He was going to challenge you and try to make you better. Some people want to call him crazy, but he had that ability to make guys uncomfortable and call you out. I remember me and him had a conversation before a game one time and he was like, "I think you're just happy to be here." We were in each other's faces. We were going at it, but that brought out the best in me. He wasn't afraid to challenge guys and make them elevate their game to another level."

This didn't work on everyone. For every handful of teammates who look back with appreciation on Donaldson's tactics, there's someone he rubbed the wrong way and understandably so. Donaldson was one of the faces of those teams that were, as John Gibbons once called them, "a bunch of renegades."

Donaldson didn't just want to beat you. He wanted to kick your ass, to make sure you remembered it. Those playoff teams will always be remembered more for how they felt than for the finer details of it all. Donaldson was out in front of all of it, the player that Toronto and his teammates loved—for the most part—because the rest of baseball couldn't stand him.

20

MVP and Heartbreak: George Bell

MENTION THE 1987 SEASON TO A BLUE JAYS FAN WHO WAS the right age at the wrong time, and you'll get a physical response.

It was the great heartbreak.

The Blue Jays had a 3.5-game lead on the Detroit Tigers with seven games left in the season and lost all seven, including a sweep to end the season in Detroit. If only we could freeze time and go back to the night of Saturday, September 26.

Yes, the Blue Jays were reeling after losing their great shortstop, Tony Fernández, to a broken elbow two days prior after the Tigers' Bill Madlock took him out on a slide into second base. They'd won that game, though, and the next two, sweeping the Tigers at Exhibition Stadium. That's the part often left out of the retelling of 1987. Before the Blue Jays lost seven in a row, they won seven in a row. It only adds to the pain.

The Blue Jays had just walked off the Tigers on back-to-back nights, the 25th and 26th of September. They were 96–59, standing on the doorstep of a season that could have been remembered for something completely different. If they could go 4–3 or better over their final seven games, they'd eclipse their 99 wins from 1985 to become the first 100-win team in Blue Jays history.

That never happened. It all fell apart.

This was an era of Major League Baseball without the wild card. Forget one, two, or three wild card spots like we see today, allowing teams shy of 90 wins to sneak into the postseason. This was a time when only truly great teams advanced. The bar feels so high in hindsight, but 96 wins wasn't enough.

So much was lost in the fire of 1987. Mention the season and that's all it is remembered for now. Rightfully so—the fan's only job is to give a damn—but the tragedy of it all lies in how many great seasons died along with the Blue Jays' postseason hopes on that day in Detroit.

George Bell won the American League MVP Award that season as a power hitter who had fully come into his prime alongside a team that seemed to be doing the same. After finishing eighth and fourth in MVP voting the two years prior, Bell hit 47 home runs in 1987, a number that's only been topped by José Bautista and Vladimir Guerrero Jr. since. He drove in 134 runs, a number that's only been topped by Carlos Delgado. He beat out Detroit's Alan Trammell by four first-place votes in MVP voting, 16 to 12.

This vote is an example of one that would have gone differently today, with voters valuing what we now do, but each MVP and Cy Young winner represents the best of their era.

Bell was worth 5.3 WAR that season, tied with New York's Don Mattingly for fourth in the American League. Wade Boggs led the AL in WAR that year at 8.9, followed by Trammell at 7.7. Bell's power numbers were undeniable, though, the best hitter on what looked like the best team in the American league until they weren't.

Looking back on that year, even with the wins that followed in the days immediately after, it's the injury to Tony Fernández that feels like the turning point.

Fernández was coming into his prime, 25 years old with a .322 batting average. He was in Year 5 of 12 seasons he'd eventually spend in Toronto, spread out across four different stints. A gifted shortstop, Fernández had a generation of Blue Jays fans trying to throw like him in the backyard, those picturesque sidearm plays back across his body that always seemed to land.

It was in the top of the third on September 24 that Madlock singled. Then, Kirk Gibson hit a ground ball to Nelson Liriano at second base. Fernández, taking the throw at second, was taken out by Madlock's slide and came down on his elbow.

The '87 season was Buck Martinez's first year in retirement. He'd started work for TSN, beginning a new life in the media, but still remembers the moment so well at Exhibition Stadium, the old ballpark that played its own role in the injury.

"It was a patchwork job, for sure. It was turf," Martinez begins. "Tony broke his elbow when Bill Madlock took him out at second base. When Tony came down, there were two-by-fours wrapped in Astroturf around the dirt sliding pits. There was a seam between them. It was kind of like there was a ledge there and he came down and broke his elbow on that."

"It's the only time I ever missed playing. That was my first year not playing. I was doing the game in Detroit and I thought, 'I should be playing.'"

So many of the teammates Martinez had left in that clubhouse were playing some of the best baseball of their careers. While Dave Stieb didn't have his finest year, posting a 4.09 ERA over 185 innings, Jimmy Key was downright dominant with a 2.76 ERA over 261 innings. Key won 17 games that season and finished second in Cy Young Award voting to only Roger Clemens.

Around Bell in that Blue Jays lineup, Lloyd Moseby, one of the most gifted athletes to play for this organization, hit 26 home runs with 39 stolen bases. Jesse Barfield belted 28 home runs. Fred McGriff, the new kid on the block at 23, hit 20 home runs with an .881 OPS over just 107 games. Ernie Whitt, then 35, put up one of the best offensive seasons of his career.

The Blue Jays had everything they needed that season, led by Bell, the MVP of the league the Blue Jays let slip through their fingers.

It's the type of season that makes you reach back through every week, every game, to find one pitch or one bounce that could have gone the other way. There's no way to shake the legacy that 1987 Blue Jays team is left with, though, and the seven losses that brought with them the biggest letdown in Blue Jays history.

21

The Unlikely Rise of José Bautista

Trumpets did not sound the day the Toronto Blue Jays traded for José Bautista.

Forget the front page; Bautista barely made the newspaper.

The morning after Bautista was dealt to the Blue Jays—August 22, 2008—his name was buried in the bottom right corner of the box score page in the *Toronto Star*.

Under a misspelled header, AMERICNA LEAGUE, it read, "TORONTO—Acquired INF José Bautista from Pittsburgh for a player to be named."

No one knew what would come next. How could you?

A few days later, the trade was completed when catcher Robinzon Díaz was sent to the Pirates. Díaz was a minor league catcher putting up modest stats, by no means a top prospect.

The trade was depth for depth, the Blue Jays hoping they could squeeze a little value out of this Bautista guy, a 27-year-old who'd spent the past few years bouncing around baseball.

Of all the paths to stardom, we may never see another like Bautista's in Toronto:

June 2000: Drafted by the Pirates in the 20th round, No. 599 overall

December 2003: Selected by the Orioles in the Rule 5 Draft

April 2004: MLB debut with the Orioles

June 2004: Selected off waivers by the Rays

June 2004: Purchased from the Rays by the Royals

July 2004: Traded to the Mets

July 2004: Traded to the Pirates

August 2008: Traded to the Blue Jays

Forget being a No. 1 prospect; José Bautista was a late bloomer who stretches even that definition. He had just enough talent that each of these teams wanted to take a shot on him, but it wasn't coming together. He couldn't stick.

Coming into that 2008 season with Pittsburgh, Bautista was a career .240 hitter with a .724 OPS. He'd hit just 31 home runs in 334 games. He was, quite frankly, just another role player bouncing around the league. Scott Rolen was hurt at the time and the Blue Jays needed someone to take some reps at third base, maybe slide out to the outfield a few times. There wasn't anything more to it than that.

"When I debuted, he was my third baseman," Ricky Romero remembered. "People forget he was a third baseman. I remember sitting in the dugout one day and I forget who was next to me, but I looked at him and I said, 'Man, if this guy can get regular playing time, this guy is going to hit a lot of home runs.'

"To watch his growth, nobody could have seen that from a mile away. Nobody."

Bautista, of course, remembers every little detail.

"I was coming from a shaky situation in Pittsburgh," Bautista said. "In '08, new management came to Pittsburgh, and you could tell that most of us weren't part of the plan moving forward. It was a quick reset. Back then, some of the GMs or presidents who came in, they would change things very quickly. They started offloading guys in spring training and things were changing quickly. I was definitely excited about a new beginning somewhere else. It didn't really matter where. That's how my situation was.

"Once I found out that I was going to Toronto, it was…I got really excited to be in the AL East. At the time and still to this day, this is the toughest division in baseball. Other divisions have gotten stronger since, but I think this is still where the best ball is played by some of the teams with the biggest budgets. They're signing the best players; they have the best front offices. It's very competitive.

"I came from…no offence to anybody, but it is what it is. Pittsburgh is a middle of the pack or bottom of the pack franchise when it comes to spending and the way that team was constructed was with a couple of guys on their way out who were on their last deals and a bunch of rookies. It was a different mix of bodies. Here, there were a couple of big-time players with Alex Rios, Vernon Wells, Roy Halladay, may he rest in peace, and a bunch of others. B.J. Ryan, at the time, was one of the top closers in the game. I got inserted into a team with a completely different makeup. The roster composition was completely different. That got me really excited.

"I could tell the difference the moment I walked in the door, coming from a low-budget team in Pittsburgh to being in the AL East with all of these guys in the room. It brought my game up to a different level. The focus, the determination every single day, I felt like those guys would bring it every single day. When I was in Pittsburgh, it was more lackadaisical, and people were fighting for their jobs. Here, it was about winning. Let's win the division. It was a different culture. I was super excited once I got here."

Soon after arriving, Bautista began to work with Cito Gaston, the new manager…and the old hitting coach. The Blue Jays' actual hitting coach at the time, Dwayne Murphy, was also instrumental in this. Bautista was behind on pitches and not starting his motion early enough, which left him exposed to certain pitches and too often forced him to rush through his mechanics. By getting started earlier, Bautista could suddenly swing with a more controlled aggression and attack the baseball. It wasn't much, but Bautista didn't need much.

"You know what, man, he was determined. He had a chip on his shoulder," John Gibbons remembered. "He never got an opportunity early on in his career because he was a journeyman, a utility guy, he bounced around. Then, it all came together for him in Toronto. He got with Cito, and they cleaned up his hitting. That's where it all took off."

Finally, it was working.

There's a reason Bautista never stuck elsewhere…but there's also a reason he got all those opportunities. Teams could see above-average power, when you see that in a player who can handle themselves defensively, it's attractive.

This is why we'll forever dream on upside. For every 99 players who come, go, and are forgotten, there's one like Bautista. A few years down the road, those postseason teams of 2015 and '16 were built on these late bloomers. It became an unintentional identity of the Blue Jays, creating the mystique of magic in Toronto.

"What was so cool was that Bautista, Edwin, and myself, it wasn't like, 'Oh, here's the golden child of MLB coming,'" Josh Donaldson said. "We had guys who came up, got humbled, and had to revamp their games. We were playing with a chip on our shoulder to prove it. Even when we were at our peak, we felt like we had more to prove."

Donaldson, like Bautista, didn't really establish himself in the big leagues until he was 27. Edwin Encarnación, who dominated the AL East alongside Bautista for years, had exciting power upside earlier in his career but was a defensive liability and never truly found his footing until he was 29.

They see so much of themselves in Bautista. It's like its own secret club, the superstars who were never supposed to be.

"This is why I tell young players that you have to work," Encarnación said. "No matter how you've been doing or what happened to you the season before, you have to keep going, keep looking forward. What can you learn from other players? That's what José did. He always tried to figure something out. He always worked. He always tried to get better. That's why he found it, and when he found it, he didn't lose it. He never stopped working. That's why I tell players to keep going, keep working. Never quit. Never put your head down. Keep your head up and work hard. Someday, some time, you will find it. That's what happened to José."

"It's God's plan. When God has his plan, you have to keep going. Someday, it is going to happen. When you keep working, it is going to come. Sooner or later, it is going to come. I remember when I came from Cincinnati and he came from the Pirates, we'd been together playing in the same division. Then, we got to be superstars in the league. It's almost something you don't believe. But I believed in myself. I knew we could do this."

Even in Toronto, though, it took some time.

In Bautista's first full season, 2009, he put up a .757 OPS with 13 home runs over 113 games. Those were fine numbers, but still painted the picture of a player reaching for their potential. It was the next year, in 2010, that the King of Toronto was born.

Bautista launched 54 home runs, still a franchise record in Toronto, with a .995 OPS. He finished fourth in AL MVP Award voting that year behind only Josh Hamilton, Miguel Cabrera, and Robinson Cano.

He was even better the next year, finishing third in MVP voting with a 1.056 OPS and 43 homers, kicking off his reign of dominance in Toronto that stretched through 2015.

From 2010 to 2015, no player in Major League Baseball hit more home runs (227). Only Mike Trout, Miguel Cabrera, Andrew McCutchen, Buster Posey, and Adrian Beltre generated more Wins Above Replacement (FanGraphs) than Bautista's 33.2 in that span.

All of this from a player the Blue Jays expected so little from. Like the lone newspaper clipping said, "Acquired INF José Bautista from Pittsburgh for a player to be named."

If there's one man who knew that 2010 season was coming all along, though, it was Russell Martin.

Long before the two were reunited as teammates in Toronto, Martin and Bautista had played baseball together at Chipola College in Florida.

"I knew how talented this guy was because he was my junior college teammate," Martin said. "I saw what he could do at the amateur level. He was so much better than everybody else around. If there was anybody I thought would just come in and have an impact, it was him…but he didn't. He struggled for a while. He bounced around, then finally found a home. Finally, you got to see the actual talent. He flourished late. He grinded for I don't know how long, for years. Then, we saw the guy."

"For some people, it was out of nowhere. For me, it was like, 'Damn; about time, José! It's about time you showed up, dude.'"

22

The First Cy: Pat Hentgen

I𝚃 𝚃OOK 𝚃HE B𝚕UE JA𝚢S 20 𝚈EARS 𝚃O WIN 𝚃HE ORGANIZA𝚃ION'S first AL Cy Young Award. Then they won three in a row.

Pat Hentgen was one of this organization's great development success stories, a high schooler plucked out of Michigan in the fifth round of the 1986 draft. The day he was drafted, Hentgen's father, Pat Sr., said, "You went on the first day!" The first five rounds were held on Day 1 back then. He was thrilled.

Hentgen built up as a starter in the minor leagues for years. What a snapshot of how pitching development has changed. As an 18-year-old in Single A Myrtle Beach, Hentgen threw 188 innings. In each of his five full years in the minors, he topped 150 innings. He'd thrown 855 innings before his big-league debut.

Hentgen came up in late 1991 as a reliever and, after the Blue Jays signed Jack Morris in 1992, was bumped into a long relief role. When Dave Stewart was injured early in the '93 season, Hentgen slid into the rotation where he belonged.

In the middle of it all, from the role changes to trying to find his footing in a clubhouse stacked with veteran stars, Hentgen had all of the talent he needed. What he needed was a mental shift, a nudge to change how he viewed himself.

"That was really when it happened for me. We were in the outfield one day and Pat Borders and I were shagging," Hentgen remembers. "We were talking about fastball command, and I was coming off a five-year minor league career and I'd walked 90 guys down in Triple A ball. I could be buckshot and spray it around with the best of them, but I remember standing there, shagging balls with Pat. He looked at me and he said, 'Fastball command? You might be the best fastball command guy on the team.' I just didn't realize where I ranked. Even though I may have ranked ninth, he told me I ranked No. 1 and I think it may have had an impact as a young player. Almost like a sports psychologist. I really think that was a turning point for me. He believed in me, and it forced me to have more confidence."

Hentgen hit a speed bump with an ugly 1995 season—a 5.11 ERA over 200⅔ innings—but when he came back to camp, he leaned on some of the veteran pitchers. Hentgen said he learned to have a good memory...but also a bad one, shaking what had gone wrong to move to the next pitch.

He'd tasted enough success and enough failure. He was 27 at this point. It was the perfect storm of talent, physical maturity, and mental strength.

"You know what, I think that in 1994, I had better stuff. My stuff played better then, it was more electric, and my ball had more bite on it. In '96, though, everything came together, it all came together as a player. Your mindset, your confidence, your mentality, your work habits, and your routine, then I was in my prime physically. Everything just hit perfectly. I look back at the 700 innings I pitched in the minor leagues and how I learned to overcome some things. I learned how to self-coach. That helped me."

The Blue Jays had also signed catcher Charlie O'Brien that year, fresh off two years in Atlanta catching Greg Maddux.

"I remember telling Ed Sprague and my teammates, 'I'm going to be all over this dude.' I loved Maddux and I knew he'd caught Maddux the year before," Hentgen said. "I clung to Charlie right away and he got me throwing some pitches that I wouldn't have thrown. He was another great catcher who could really instill confidence into a pitcher, like Pat did in my rookie season."

O'Brien got Hentgen to throw his fastball up and in more often, challenging hitters like Dave Stieb, who Hentgen had grown close to. Mel Queen was involved, too, and had taught Hentgen to throw a cutter effectively. These small adjustments on top of all of his talent, all of his work, were enough.

Sprague, who played with Hentgen for years in Toronto and calls him one of his closest friends in baseball, saw "the ultimate competitor" come out in those years. He also echoes what others say about Hentgen—we don't talk about his stuff enough. He didn't light up the radar gun like some other top-end pitchers at the time, but if you hooked Hentgen up to all of the cameras and computers of today, Sprague is certain you'd see a fastball with excellent extension and an extremely high spin rate.

"I was talking to Wally Joyner a few years ago and I asked him who he thought the hardest thrower was back when he played," Sprague said. "He said, 'I thought Hentgen's fastball was the hardest to hit.' I thought, really? Pat threw 92–95, but he had this explosiveness. He could pitch at the top of the zone with his fastball that would complement his breaking ball, then he threw that cutter down and away later in his career."

Looking back through old awards, baseball's history books are littered with votes that are very much…of their era. Pitcher wins, for example, still carried a weight in 1996 that they no longer do.

"I barely won that award, by the way. I won my 20th game on the last day of the year," Hentgen is quick to say.

Hentgen beat out Andy Pettitte of the Yankees by a hair, earning 16 first-place votes to Pettitte's 11. Modern metrics back up Hentgen's award, though. This is one that still holds water, regardless of which year you look back from. Hentgen was valued at 6.0 WAR that season, well above Pettitte's 4.6. Only Roger Clemens of the Red Sox and Kevin Appier of the Royals ranked above Hentgen, but Clemens was surely held back by his 10–13 record, receiving zero votes, while Hentgen had each beat in ERA and led Major League Baseball with 265⅔ innings pitched.

The Blue Jays' first Cy Young Award is a sturdy one. It always will be.

"I credit the Blue Jays for the way I was developed and not rushed," Hentgen said. "That helped me overcome a lot of adversity in the minor leagues. I didn't have my first ass-kicking in the big leagues. You have to learn how to overcome that stuff. It's going to happen, and it sucks when it doesn't happen until you get to the show."

That's what allowed Hentgen to bounce back in '96, those five full seasons plugging away as a workhorse in the minor leagues.

Hentgen is a special assistant with the Blue Jays now and works with young pitchers in the organization, his passion for the craft still buzzing out of him. The beehive of young pitching prospects at the Blue Jays' complex in Dunedin will take such dramatically different paths to the big leagues than Hentgen did, but they're all still chasing him, the homegrown righty who once did what no Blue Jays pitcher had ever done.

23

The Rocket: Roger Clemens

THE TWO SEASONS ROGER CLEMENS PITCHED IN TORONTO are locked away like a family secret.

We have stories, but not the full story. We tell those stories, but with hushed voices.

"Jays land The Rocket" read the sports page of the *Toronto Star* on December 14, 1996. It was a stunning move from the Blue Jays, aggressively trying to reclaim their place atop baseball as the World Series runs of 1992–93—and the many stars that powered them—began to fade.

Clemens, at 33, was already a three-time Cy Young Award winner and AL MVP with the Red Sox. He was, by every measure of the '80s, '90s, and today, one of the best pitchers on the planet, his dominance only rivaled by his consistency. What he did in Toronto has never been matched. Pitchers in this city may chase those numbers forever.

1997
21–7 (264 IP)
2.05 ERA
10.7 WAR (FanGraphs)
1998
20–6 (234 ⅔ IP)
2.65 ERA
8.2 WAR

These two seasons stand above all others in Blue Jays history. Roy Halladay and Dave Stieb have not touched them. In MLB's live-ball era, which brings us back to 1920, only three pitchers have had a better season than Clemens' 1997, measured by WAR: Bert Blyleven in 1973, Steve Carlton in 1972, and Pedro Martinez in 1999.

Clemens ran away with the AL Cy Young Award each season, winning unanimously in 1998.

One of the first calls Clemens made after landing a rich, four-year deal with the Blue Jays was to a young Carlos Delgado. He'd just established himself with his first full season in the big leagues and Delgado had just switched to wearing No. 21. Well, that's the number the Rocket had worn in Boston for 13 years. Delgado's phone rang.

"When I got called up to the big leagues, they gave me No. 6," Delgado remembers. "When you're a rookie, you take what they give you. Once I had an opportunity to settle into the big leagues, I requested No. 21 in honour of Roberto Clemente. It was in 1997 when Roger Clemens came over as a free agent and I'd never met him before. I'd only played against him when he was in Boston, but he called, and he asked. He didn't say 'I want,' he said, 'Would you give me...?' For me, a guy that has those numbers taking the time to pick up the phone? I said, 'Roger Clemens, no problem at all. It would be an honour to play with you.' And you know what? An honour, indeed, it was. I got to watch back-to-back Cy Youngs."

"The story also goes that I got a watch out of the deal... which I did," Delgado added, laughing. "I didn't ask for it, but I thought that it was a very classy move. And it still works."

Pat Hentgen was just coming off his own Cy Young Award in 1996 and firmly in his prime. The rest of the Blue Jays' rotation was still a patchwork in those years as a young Chris Carpenter broke in. Woody Williams was giving the Blue Jays solid innings in those years, too, but this was all about Clemens and Hentgen.

For those two years, Hentgen was Clemens' throwing partner.

"He was a guy who had an incredible ability to block things out and focus," Hentgen said. "His focus was on the next level. It was his focus when he worked, his focus on side days. I have stolen so many of his lines and passed it on to these kids here for the last 20 years."

Hentgen remembers a phone call he got at some point during the 1997 season from Dave Stieb, the great Blue Jays pitcher who was then retired but hadn't yet launched his surprise comeback in '98. Hentgen remembers it like this:

Stieb: Man, you guys signed Clemens, what's he like?

Hentgen: Dave, it's like the rest of us have shit on the ball compared to his stuff.

Stieb: What are you talking about? You just won the Cy Young.

Hentgen: Dave. Listen. You asked me how it feels and I'm telling you. His stuff is so much better than everyone else's.
Stieb: No, you're shitting me.

Soon enough, Stieb had a chance to see for himself.

"In '98, he made the team. Remember how he came to
camp as a guest coach, Dave Stieb?" Hentgen said, continuing
his story. "Stieb makes the team and by June, they call him up.
He had one month of watching Clemens and I remember one
night, Dave and I were on the road together and he said to me,
'Yup. I know what you mean now.' His stuff was just better
than everybody else's. On top of that, you add his command?
He has the best stuff and that command?"

In a bubble, it was brilliance on display. Those who have
been around the organization for the many years before and
since Clemens' tenure still struggle with how to frame these
seasons, though, great as they may have been.

"In his two years with the Blue Jays, I have never seen anyone
in my career—with the Blue Jays or any other team in Major
League Baseball—dominate hitters the way he did for six straight
months," said Jerry Howarth, the longtime radio voice of the Blue
Jays, who saw all the greats. "It was just unbelievable. There was
no question that he was one of the best pitchers I'd ever seen."

In the same breath, Howarth has to consider everything
that came later.

"That's when you have to question how he did it, what he
did, why did he rise above everybody else?"

You already know the "but" to all of this. You know the
reason why fans don't often talk about Clemens' brief flash of
greatness in Toronto.

Clemens was named in the Mitchell Report, released in late
2007, the result of a lengthy, independent investigation into

the use of steroids and other performance-enhancing drugs in Major League Baseball. Clemens was accused by former trainer Brian McNamee of using PEDs. In the years that followed, Clemens testified before Congress and was involved in a lengthy defamation suit against McNamee, which was eventually settled. Clemens has denied using PEDs in his MLB career.

This is a conversation that baseball has grappled with on a large scale coming out of the steroid era, particularly when it comes to the Hall of Fame cases of players like Clemens or Barry Bonds. Clemens is, by every imaginable metric we can look at, a first-ballot Hall of Fame pitcher, one of the greatest to ever do it.

The 2022 Hall of Fame voting cycle was the 10th and final year of eligibility for both Clemens and Bonds. Clemens received 65.2 percent of the vote, Bonds 66 percent, shy of the 75 percent needed for election. Clemens' voting numbers had steadily climbed over a decade but never got there.

Clemens' two seasons in Toronto came and went. For as high as those seasons reached into the sky, they never set down roots. Clemens was traded after two seasons to the Yankees, part of a controversial out clause, which further colours his time in Toronto for Blue Jays fans.

Those 1997 and 1998 seasons happened. The numbers are undeniable, but the stories we tell about those seasons and how you contextualize them in your own mind are more sub-jective matters. It's something we're left to wrestle with, and as Clemens' voting numbers over the years show, time can bring change with it. Twenty years from now, we may talk about those seasons in a different tone or acknowledge them more openly, for better or for worse. And 20 years from now, Clemens' num-bers will surely still tower above everything else we've seen on that mound in Toronto.

PART 5

THE GLORY YEARS

24

Almost: The 1980s

The eventual World Series wins took the sting off the heartbreaks of the 1980s, all those great Blue Jays teams that kept falling just short.

There may have been none finer than the 1985 squad. Their 99 wins still stand as the most in Blue Jays history, but they fell just short in the ALCS to the Royals, losing in Game 7. Just that year, the ALCS had expanded from a best-of-five to best-of-seven. Given that the Blue Jays were up 3–1 before the series collapsed, it will forever be one of the great "what ifs" in Blue Jays history.

These teams were stacked with fan favourites, so many of whom were just coming into their own in the big leagues. There was a young Tony Fernández, dazzling everyone as he played a full-time role for the first time. There was that incredible outfield of George Bell, Lloyd Moseby, and Jesse Barfield, all of them just 25 years old at the time. The Blue Jays were set up to be a potential dynasty if it all broke their way.

"Everybody had gotten to a new stage," Buck Martinez remembers. "Bell was better, Moseby was better, Upshaw was good, Barfield had established himself. It was one hell of a team. You had Rance and Garth at third.... Tony was terrific. We just had a great team. Bobby Cox was incredible."

This was Bobby Cox's final of four seasons in Toronto before he returned to Atlanta as general manager. His tenure in Toronto was too brief to stand alongside the likes of a Cito Gaston, but Cox is a Hall of Famer for a reason.

Martinez calls Cox the best manager he's ever played for, no competition, and there's a story he liked to tell to capture why.

"He would tear a strip off of a guy, but the next day it was like it never happened," Martinez explains. "He dressed down some players. We had Dave Collins with us in Boston one year and this is an interesting story, because Davey was intense, intense as hell. He was a really good player, but he was pissed off one day because he wasn't in the lineup. We're in Boston playing the Red Sox and he doesn't have his spikes on. Coxy said, 'Colly, go in there and pinch run.' It was the ninth inning in a close game. I know it, but Coxy doesn't know it yet...he's got his tennis shoes on.

"Collins runs out there, gets the green light, and slips. He gets thrown out. In Boston, where the manager stands right next to the steps, the players have to walk right past him. Coxy is right there and said, 'Hey, good try buddy, way to go.' Then he starts looking at his shoes. He noticed his shoes. We go into the locker room in Fenway, and you know how small that room is. Coxy just goes ballistic. 'What the hell is wrong with you? You don't even care enough to put your spikes on?'"

"Coxy said, 'If you don't want to play, give the money back!' It was right in the middle of the locker room. Collins came to me and said, 'Man, he hates me.' I said, 'No, he doesn't hate you, he hates what you did. He's going to play you tomorrow.'"

The next day, Dave Collins was back in the lineup.

"That was the beauty of Bobby Cox."

Cox actually thought the '83 and '84 teams were better, according to Martinez, but the Blue Jays didn't have much of a bullpen yet. That changed when the Blue Jays, in the free-agent compensation draft of 1985, selected a reliever from the Rangers named Tom Henke.

Henke became known as "The Terminator," which tells you all you need to know about him. He'd been coming off a brutal year with the Rangers, but immediately gave the Blue Jays one of the best closers in baseball. When Henke was eventually paired up with Duane Ward, the duo became nearly unbeatable, a modern super bullpen before we'd even thought of them.

In the rotation, Toronto's pitching was excellent. Dave Stieb was in his prime, posting a 2.48 ERA over 265 innings, but a young Jimmy Key had just burst onto the scene. Key deserves to be remembered among the best pitchers in Blue Jays history, the lefty who pitched nine seasons in Toronto and was sometimes overshadowed by Stieb, but was incredibly talented in his own right.

"Jimmy Key was one of the most intelligent left-handed pitchers I've ever caught," Ernie Whitt said. "He was a true pitcher. He was able to expose the hitters' weaknesses that we found. He was a control pitcher. He changed speeds, had a sneaky fastball, a plus curveball, and a plus changeup. He was very intelligent on the mound.

"His peers knew how good he was. He wasn't explosive like Dave Stieb was, but he was probably a better *pitcher* than

Dave. Dave had the electric stuff and hitters dreaded facing him. Jimmy would get that comfortable 0-for-4 out of a hitter. The hitters would be saying, 'How did I miss that pitch?'"

Even if these great seasons of the '80s didn't lead to a World Series run, they set the stage for what was about to come and announced Toronto as a legitimate baseball presence in the process. So many of the building blocks for 1992 were already forming.

Cito Gaston was in the dugout as the hitting coach, working with the young players on their craft. Key and Stieb were at their best, both barreling toward 1992, which would be their final in Toronto, along with Henke, for the time being. Fernández would eventually be dealt, along with Fred McGriff, for Roberto Alomar and Joe Carter. A 20-year-old Manuel Lee was just breaking in.

The Blue Jays, just nine years into their existence, had arrived. It wasn't their moment yet, but their moment was coming.

25

World Champions in 1992

Cito Gaston remembers the caravan tours the Blue Jays would go on each winter. At fan events, they'd play highlights of the year prior, often with Tom Cheek or Jerry Howarth hosting. Year after year, those moments were another reminder, in the cold of winter, that the Blue Jays were still chasing something.

Those teams of the '80s had evolved into a new Toronto Blue Jays. The trade of Tony Fernández and Fred McGriff for Roberto Alomar and Joe Carter has long taken most of the credit for the Blue Jays getting over the hump, but there was so much more that went into it.

John Olerud, just 23, was coming into his own. Devon White was catching every single ball hit in the air. Dave Winfield, after 18 seasons chasing a ring, had come to Toronto to hunt one down. Jack Morris, who'd just won the 1991 World Series, joined him.

"We had a good team. A good team, a good offensive team and a good bullpen," Cito Gaston said in 2022, celebrating the anniversary of those championships. "When we got to the seventh inning, it was pretty much a lockdown with Wardo and Tom Henke. Guys like Dave Winfield came in and had my back a lot of times when I didn't see what was going on. He got those guys straightened out."

This had been building, of course, for years.

"We can go back to the '91 season, winning the AL East. That got us over the hump," Joe Carter said at that same anniversary celebration. "At that time, not a lot of us had experienced a championship season. That was our first time winning the division. Getting beat by the Twins, man, that was depressing. I'm like, 'Making the playoffs is good, but it is *not* fun when you lose.' From that day forward, in '92, we were there to win the whole thing."

Players who had been with the organization for a few seasons saw the same growth. Duane Ward was just coming into his prime in 1992, pairing with Tom Henke to form an incredible tandem at the back of the Blue Jays' bullpen, a group that was so important to that World Series run.

"We were starting to get a lot of pieces together and we built it slowly through '89, '90, '91," Ward said. "Seeing that team develop, grow, and come close together, I just think about how good a team we had, how good a pitching staff we had. That's what I go back to. God, we were pretty good."

"You didn't really see a weakness. Looking back on it, a lot of guys that I've talked to or run into over the years, they always say, 'If we didn't get to your starters, which was hard enough in the first place, we were definitely not going to beat that bullpen.' They'd put a lot of pressure on themselves to try scoring off the starter. Once we started running out that bullpen, they knew the game was over. Teams knew they were in trouble when they got to our bullpen."

No team wins a World Series, though—especially their first one—without some surprise heroes.

Ed Sprague's pinch-hit home run in Game 2 of the World Series is a landmark moment in this organization's history. Sprague had played in just 22 games in the regular season and wasn't seen as an offensive threat, but in that Game 2, the pitcher's spot was coming up in the batting order in the top of the ninth inning. Derek Bell had just walked, so Sprague stepped to the plate with the Blue Jays down 4–3.

Gaston had given Sprague a heads up that he would be hitting in this spot, but this was 1992. He couldn't pick up an iPad and type in 'Jeff Reardon,' the pitcher he was about to face. Instead, he leaned on the veterans in the dugout, particularly Rance Mulliniks, who huddled up with Sprague.

"He was going to try to get ahead with a high fastball," Sprague remembers. "He liked the top of the zone with his heater and [Rance] said, 'He's going to try to get ahead of you at the top of the zone.' I was a low ball hitter, so it wasn't an ideal matchup for me in that spot."

Next, it was Pat Borders. The 29-year-old catcher had established himself as a solid big-leaguer with the Blue Jays, but when you thought about that 1992 roster, your mind didn't exactly jump to Borders. He had the series of a lifetime in that World Series against Atlanta, going 9-for-20 (.450) with three triples and a home run, winning the World Series MVP Award.

"I remember how tired I was at the end of the series," Borders said at the anniversary celebration. "I was happy that the series was over. I was worn out. I was ready to go home and sleep. People were saying they wanted to go out and party? No, I wanted to go to bed. I was just drained mentally from the concentration. I didn't, personally, notice any crowd noise. Nothing. It was a tunnel vision. It was a fun place to be. You just can't recreate that during the regular season."

"I take pride in it, but maybe because we had so many superstars and good players, they felt like they had to get me out. Maybe that helped me get better pitches than someone like a Winfield, Carter, the stars we had all around us. It might have played to my advantage that way."

When the Blue Jays finally sealed it—complete with a 4–3 win in extra innings and powered by a two-run double off the bat of Dave Winfield that may just be the most underrated moment in this organization's history—an estimated half-million people flooded into the streets of Toronto, closing most of the major downtown roads to traffic. The celebration was on.

"CHAMPIONS," read the front page of *The Sunday Star,* atop a photo of Mike Timlin and Joe Carter celebrating the moment.

All these years later, Carter continues to relive those moments. This was his first. He hadn't yet touched 'em all. That was a year away.

As he gathered with old teammates to celebrate yet another anniversary going by, another round number passing them without another Blue Jays World Series to celebrate, he paused for a moment to think about what it all means.

"...It means I'm old. That's what it means," Carter said, smiling. "It means I'm still around, still healthy, which is great. But it just shows you that you never know when that opportunity will come. If you had told me when I left here in '97 that the Blue Jays would not get to another World Series since '93, I wouldn't have believed that. It just goes to show you that, if you have the opportunity, you have to take advantage of it. In any game, especially baseball, you have a five- to six-year window when you have a chance to really elevate yourself, to become a champion. You take advantage of that. You do whatever it takes."

26

Going Back-to-Back: 1993

WINNING IS HARD. THE ONLY THING HARDER IS DOING IT again.

The Blue Jays didn't just run it back in 1993. What makes it so impressive is that the Blue Jays rebuilt their roster and came back *different*, but perhaps that was the genius of it all from Pat Gillick and the Blue Jays' front office.

"We had two different teams in '92 and '93," Cito Gaston said at an anniversary event in 2018. "The '92 team? We had the whole package from starting pitching to the bullpen, defence, offence, just a really balanced team...then we got rid of 14 guys. We came back the next year with 14 different guys. It was a different team. We overpowered people, which is impossible to do in Major League Baseball. It helps when you have John

Olerud finishing first in the league, Molitor finishing second in the league, and Robbie finishes third."

That 1993 offence was a freight train. It all started with WAMCO.

White, Alomar, Molitor, Carter, and Olerud, a one-through-five that opposing pitchers feared with every ounce of their being. After scoring 780 runs with a league-best .747 OPS in 1992, the Blue Jays came back in '93 and scored 847 runs with a .786 OPS. They were unstoppable, but even after Gillick and the front office rebranded this team over the winter, they didn't stop there.

Gone was Dave Winfield, but in was Paul Molitor. Gone was Dave Stieb, but in was Dave Stewart, filling out a rotation that now featured a young Pat Hentgen. The Blue Jays turned over their depth, too, but two of the biggest moves came in-season.

In June, the Blue Jays brought back their old friend, Tony Fernández, from the Mets. It's only right that Fernández got to be part of one of the World Series runs and he was fantastic down the stretch. The big move came at the trade deadline, when the Blue Jays acquired Rickey Henderson from the A's. They already had WAMCO, but now they had the greatest base stealer to ever live.

"Are you kidding me? We hated Rickey when he played against us," Joe Carter said in 2018. "He was a nuisance. He was like that mosquito, 'bzzzz' all the time. He wouldn't go away. When we got him and realized he's going to lead off that ninth inning? I was hitting fourth, so I knew I was going to hit because we knew he was going to walk. I was surprised he didn't steal any bases there because that's what he's known for, that's what he does. He's Rickey. He was a great addition."

The Blue Jays were already a complete team, but they didn't settle.

"I felt almost sorry for the opposing pitchers," Pat Hentgen said.

"We had a lot of confidence on that team, too. I think there are 15 guys that have two rings. There was a little bit of turnover, but the core guys stayed. Alomar was incredible. Devo was incredible. We had a great defence and people forget how excellent our defence was. It was excellent."

The Blue Jays were a team without a real weakness, and their offence was completely overwhelming.

John Olerud chased a .400 average deep into the season, his average still sitting at .400 on August 2. He fell shy, batting .363, but it was still one of the great all-around offensive seasons in Blue Jays history. What makes it even more incredible is that Blue Jays batters finished 1-2-3 for the American League batting title.

John Olerud (.363)
Paul Molitor (.332)
Roberto Alomar (.326)

It was a cleanup hitter's dream. No wonder Joe Carter drove in 121 runs that season and eight more in the World Series.

"People will look at Robbie and look at myself, but we wouldn't be there without Duane Ward. We wouldn't be there without Dave Stewart, Paul Molitor, Devon White," Carter said, looking back. "This was a collective effort. Every time we went out there, it was an All-Star game. It was just one guy doing their job. Everybody did their job, exactly what they were supposed to do. Rickey was supposed to get the walk and get to first base. Molitor was supposed to get the hit. I was supposed to drive them in. These are the things we did the whole year. We knew our job and we stayed in our lane. We complemented one another and that's what great ball clubs do. We had great pitching. We had a great closer in Duane Ward. That's what 25 guys do. They come together. You need that karma, that charisma inside the locker room and the accountability we had with one another."

This team was built so boldly, Pat Gillick shaking the old "Stand Pat" nickname to deliver move after move that simply worked.

It gave us the greatest moment in Blue Jays history, too, Joe Carter's walk-off home run in Game 6 of the World Series.

"Touch 'em all, Joe. You'll never hit a bigger home run in your life."

Since 1993, there hasn't been a bigger home run hit in any life. Baseball players will be chasing a moment like Carter's forever, just like the Blue Jays will be chasing a season like 1993 until the next World Series win comes around.

These moments are so rare, which is so hard to appreciate in the moment. With each year that passes, each new anniversary celebration for '92 or '93, the glory years of the Toronto Blue Jays drift further away.

"You never know when that chance is going to come again," Carter said. "It may never come again."

27

Return to Glory: 2015–16

WHEN THE DROUGHT FINALLY ENDED, 22 YEARS OF RAIN FELL all at once.

Those 2015 and '16 Blue Jays teams mattered. They'll always matter. Even with each season falling short in the ALCS, those years brought baseball back to life in Canada.

A city and a country had been waiting for those teams, spectacularly talented with an edge, an attitude that made it all so cinematic.

"We weren't boring," John Gibbons said, breaking into a laugh. And that's all you need to know.

Kevin Pillar puts it more bluntly.

"We were going to be bad motherfuckers on the field and the expectation was to win."

This is why those Blue Jays teams mattered so much, beloved for how they won as much as the wins and losses themselves. They set down roots in the hearts and minds of Blue Jays fans, and for the younger generation of fans who were either not born in 1993 or too young to remember, they finally had a team that belonged to them. They finally had a team that, even in the moment, you know you'd be telling stories about for decades.

It's only been one decade now, but that's long enough. Of the younger players on those teams, those still in the game are well into the autumn of their careers. Most, like José Bautista, Edwin Encarnación, and Josh Donaldson, are beyond their playing days. They cannot look down to their hands and see a ring, shimmering with diamonds in the light, but with those postseason runs, they created something of permanence, something that will last for decades more.

"I appreciate those days even more now because now, I see it from the other side," said Edwin Encarnación. "What we did for the city was unbelievable, especially me and Bautista. We came from teams that were in last place to bringing the city back to the playoffs. It was a big change for the city, for the team, for the organization. When we made the playoffs, it was very impressive for us, and we were so happy to make that turn for this team. I appreciate everything, especially the fans, how they show us the love that they have for us. That is one thing I am never going to forget."

The Blue Jays, long trapped in the foggy middle of the league, suddenly mattered again. They were cool. The younger crowd, which had long abandoned Rogers Centre, started to flood back in. It was a social destination again, a place to spend $45 on three beers before walking up to King St. West.

Bautista, Encarnación, and Donaldson were the faces of it all, a dominant trio of hitters who had all been late bloomers.

The most vivid sense of those seasons, though, comes from some of the players who did not stand as squarely in the spotlight as those stars. These rosters were overflowing with talent, from that incredible trio to Troy Tulowitzki, Russell Martin, Marcus Stroman, Aaron Sanchez, David Price, R.A. Dickey, Mark Buehrle, and more. Young stars, breakout stars, and players who had already been stars for a decade came together and fit just perfectly, even if John Gibbons had to wrangle that clubhouse together every other day, its massive personalities banging and clanging against one another.

The fan favourites, as has often been the case in Toronto, existed a step outside of that group.

Kevin Pillar, the outfielder who never met a wall he couldn't climb, became beloved in Toronto. He became "Superman," making a string of catches that changed his life overnight. Pillar carved out a long, impressive career after leaving Toronto, but like so many other players from those years, he looks back on 2015 and '16 with so much love.

They're the good old days.

"I can't put it in a moment," Pillar said. "I can put it in a word, and that would be 'magical.'"

Ryan Goins, another defensive maestro, was also thrust into the middle of it all. In another lifetime, Pillar and Goins could have been grinding it out for a 70–92 team, playing in front of sparse crowds but happy to be there. Instead, they got the baseball experience of a lifetime, almost immediately.

"My mind goes to the most fun two years of my career," Goins said. "The guys, the clubhouse, playing in Toronto and playing for a whole country, that was the most fun baseball I've ever played. To have passionate fans who are showing up every night, you're on national television every night and everyone wants you to win. The city was so connected in that way. It was so special, man. It was so fun to come to the field every day."

We'll remember those seasons for their incredible moments. José Bautista's bat flip is one of the three or four most famous moments in this franchise's history. Josh Donaldson's mad dash home. Edwin Encarnación's walk-off home run in the AL wild card.

Goins was standing on third base when Bautista launched the biggest, loudest home run Toronto has witnessed since 1993. The image of Goins, coming down that third-base line in full celebration, is burned into the history of this team.

"Honestly? I remember nothing. I was blacked out. I just blacked out in time," Goins said. "Watching it back, when you play the whole inning back, you do all of that and then *that* happens? That's the moment I thought our team was invincible. No one can beat us. Everything can go wrong, and we can still do this."

"It was iconic. That was an iconic swing. I'm not taking anything away from Joe Carter's home run in the World Series, but I would say that Bautista's is more of a known thing now just because of where we're at."

"I tell people, when they ask me what the best moment of my career was, that I didn't even do anything. I was just there. It was the best moment of my career."

Just by existing in the same orbit as José Bautista, Goins experienced the moment of a lifetime.

If the day ever comes when statues are built outside the Blue Jays' stadium—either Rogers Centre or the next one—Bautista's bat flip will be among them. The only design challenge will be figuring out how to make Bautista's bat appear as if it's suspended in the air.

Next to it, you should find Encarnación, standing right on top of home plate with his arms stretched straight up, above his head. His walk-off home run against Ubaldo Jiménez in the bottom of the 11th to send the Blue Jays to the 2016 ALDS was a legendary moment, one that can never be taken from him.

"That is something I am never going to forget," Encarnación said. "I am always going to live with that. When you look at that home run José hit, he hit so many homers for the organization, but that one changed everything for everybody. You will never forget that. Then, the same thing happened to me. I hit a lot of homers for that organization, even in the playoffs, but the one I hit in the wild card to advance to the ALDS was something I will never forget. I will always live with that. The people recognize you for moments like that. It was very special for me to have that opportunity and hit that homer in the perfect moment. It's something that…in the city? They'll never forget."

The Blue Jays are chasing that again.

Even as more recent teams went to the postseason—think about the 2021 near-miss, then 2022 and 2023—it hasn't felt the same.

There wasn't nearly as long a wait, which matters in all of this, but it's also about how these teams feel. A fan base wants to feel a connection to teams, to see that teams are fighting for them, even if that means fighting the other guy every once in a while. Those teams demanded to be loved.

They were cool. They were renegades. They belonged to Toronto, and for a moment, Toronto belonged to them.

PART 6

THE STORYTELLERS

28

Tom and Jerry

MORE THAN 40 YEARS AGO, JERRY HOWARTH WAS BEING introduced as Tom Cheek's full-time radio broadcast partner at an event at a hotel in downtown Toronto when he noticed two men coming through the crowd wearing costume masks.

It wasn't a robbery. They were dressed as Tom and Jerry, the cat and mouse from the famous series that began in the 1940s. It was the beginning of the Tom and Jerry era in Toronto.

"I'd grown up watching Tom and Jerry, and sure enough, my partner Tom was the big cat and there I was, the little mouse running around," Howarth said, laughing at the memory. "It all seemed to work out perfectly."

For over two decades, the beauty of this two-man radio booth was its balance. Cheek was the strong, serious voice of the game, his baritone cutting through the noise of the crowd behind him, so easy to trust. Howarth's voice was so much different, more high-pitched, nasal, and enthusiastic. He learned to control this over the years—the "runaround mouse"—and let the crowd come in.

Back and forth they went between their voices, their styles, their innings.

"We were two opposites who, as we sat down in the radio booth, had come from different areas. When we left, we went into different areas, as well," Howarth said. "Our lives were totally different. But when we came together for those three hours, it was wonderful unity."

It's difficult to know when you've struck gold with a broadcast booth, though. Howarth first called games on a part-time basis with Cheek and eventually took over for Early Wynn, but a good booth needs time, something that isn't afforded as freely to most broadcast teams today.

One mention of Howarth's hire appeared in a story by longtime *Toronto Star* baseball writer Neil MacCarl on January 29, 1981. At the end of that notebook, underneath a note about how young outfielder Paul Hodgson of New Brunswick planned to get married and squeeze in his honeymoon before flying south for spring training, was this small note about the radio booth:

"Jerry Howarth of Salt Lake City has been added to Jays' broadcast crew. Howarth, who subbed for Early Wynn in a few games last season, will work 40 games."

Little did we know.

* * *

Howarth had a front-row seat to not only the glory days of the Toronto Blue Jays but to Cheek's career. In Canada, in broader baseball circles and in the broadcasting world, the 2013 Ford C. Frick Award winner, Cheek, is a giant. In 1974, he started as a backup announcer to Dave Van Horne on Expos broadcasts, then in '76, a 37-year-old Cheek was tapped as the voice of the Blue Jays.

Any conversation about Cheek's career, of course, leads quickly to the Streak.

It's a number that's burned into the brains of so many who knew and loved Cheek. The moment Howarth hears the word "streak" mentioned, he cuts in: "4,306 games. Wow."

"Tom's consecutive streak of 4,306 games was remarkable from a number of standpoints. For me, my streak was 35–40 days to start my career. Then, I got laryngitis and missed a week," Howarth remembered. "Everybody bursts out laughing when I tell that story, but that's what streaks are all about. Can you avoid that illness or sickness? I was unable to do that, but Tom, for all those years, he just continued to broadcast well, and he overcame whatever might have come into his day."

It was almost unfathomable, to call every Blue Jays game from the first moments the Blue Jays took the field at Exhibition Stadium on April 7, 1977, right up to June 3, 2004.

On luck and logistics alone, it's remarkable. Like Howarth said, all broadcasters have their horror story of losing their voice. Speak in your fullest voice for three, maybe three and a half hours straight tonight, and listen to yourself in the morning. The voice is a muscle, developed by broadcasters over the years, and each has their own trick. Some have a certain tea they'll drink. Others have a certain beer or food they know they can't touch the night before a broadcast. In most cases, they learned it the hard way.

Travel was another aspect of this. Life on the road is not easy, even when you're taking nicer flights and sleeping in nicer hotels than the average Joe.

Let's not pretend Cheek felt fresh every day. He was, like the players, going through the grind of a 162-game season, over and over again. During the streak, on an old CFTO broadcast, Cheek shared one of the stories from the journey.

"One night in Milwaukee, I had two big pieces of bubble gum in my mouth, sitting in the clubhouse before the game working on my scorebook because it was very cold outside. I chomped down on the gum, and I felt this big explosion in my head. I pulled this gigantic filling out of one of my back teeth."

It was freezing in Milwaukee that night, causing Cheek terrible pain nearly each time he opened his mouth. He demonstrated how he pushed a finger on the outside of his cheek to apply some pressure to the tooth, and somehow, got through the broadcast.

Then, one day, it ended.

The Blue Jays had just landed in California for a series against the A's in Oakland when Howarth got a call from Cheek.

"Jerry, I won't be at the broadcast tonight. My father just passed away in Monterey," Howarth remembers.

Cheek's father, Tom, was a fighter pilot in World War II and fought in the Battle of the Midway. It's fateful the Blue Jays were nearby in California. In the days that followed, an emotional Cheek spoke with *Toronto Star* reporter Geoff Baker about his relationship with his father.

"I think that a lot of what I've done in my life and a lot of how I approach things was done so that he could be proud of me. We never really discussed it, but I truly hope that he was, because he was a good man."

Upon returning to the booth soon after, Cheek didn't feel right physically. Tests discovered a brain tumor, which Cheek underwent surgery for on June 13. Cheek still called some home games in Toronto while undergoing chemotherapy, but the cancer eventually worsened and he died on October 9, 2005, at 66.

Cheek's name still hangs above the field at Rogers Centre, "4,306" forever alongside it as a reminder. The Blue Jays added his name to the Level of Excellence while Cheek was still alive, in late August of 2004.

Cheek had said over the years that the only streak that mattered was Cal Ripken Jr.'s, who played in 2,632 consecutive games from 1982 to 1998 to pass Lou Gehrig, "the Iron Horse" himself.

That day, Paul Godfrey, then president and CEO of the Blue Jays, read Cheek a letter that Ripken had written him. As a montage of Cheek's great calls rolled, Frank Sinatra's "It Was a Very Good Year" played inside SkyDome.

"I could never really get the point until somebody said, 'Since I was a little kid, you have been the sound of summer,' Cheek said. "I say from the bottom of my heart, thank you and God bless you. To everybody…to everybody."

* * *

Those lucky enough to have grown up with Cheek on the mic—before and throughout his partnership with Howarth—spent thousands of hours with those voices.

Newer generations of fans still have their connection, though, through the calls made famous by some of the biggest moments in Blue Jays history, the back-to-back World Series wins. Let's start in 1992, a moment that Howarth still remembers so fondly as his favourite call.

The Blue Jays were one win away from their first World Series title in 1992, with Game 6 against the Braves set for Atlanta-Fulton County Stadium on October 24, 1992. Tied at two, the game rolled into the 11th inning, which was supposed to be Howarth's inning as the play-by-play man after Cheek had called the ninth and 10th.

With two outs in the top of the 11th, Dave Winfield pulled a two-run double down the line, past the third baseman. It's one of the biggest moments in Blue Jays history, kept on a shelf below the others only because it wasn't a home run.

"A ground ball hit over third, a base hit! Down the line! White scores!" Howarth said into the microphone as Devon White ran home, waving behind himself for the next runner. "It's picked up and bobbled by Gant. He dropped the ball in the corner. Alomar scores on a Dave Winfield two-base hit!"

After Candy Maldonado popped out, the Blue Jays carried a 4–2 lead into the bottom of the 11th, the first World Series in the organization's history just three outs away. It was still Howarth's inning to call play-by-play, but in the commercial break, he had a feeling.

"I said to myself, 'Jerry, Tom's been here since Day 1.' When I glanced to my right, he was sitting back in his chair. We came back and this is what I said…"

"It's the bottom of the 11th inning. The Blue Jays lead Atlanta 4–2. I've had the pleasure of calling Dave Winfield's two-run double. Tom Cheek, my partner, has seen every game for the Blue Jays. As we go to the bottom of the 11th, it's my pleasure to give Tom Cheek the opportunity to take the Blue Jays home. Tom, you take it."

There was that baritone voice again, the one that had called those thousands of games that had come before it. So many of those games were forgotten—most of them, really—but now Cheek's voice lives alongside a moment that will never die. As Atlanta scraped back a run, making that left-field bobble on the Winfield double all the more important, Mike Timlin came in for the final out.

"Timlin to Carter, and the Blue Jays win it! The Blue Jays win it! The Blue Jays are World Series champions!" Cheek called. "They come pouring out of the dugout and they are mobbing Carter. And they go down in one big, collective heap."

That inning still means so much to Howarth. He first shared that story with me in May 2020. Without a ball game to turn to each night during the early days of the COVID-19 pandemic, we turned to old games and old stories to pass the time. I'd heard the famous calls so many times, as we all have, but so much existed in between.

With help from the great staff at Sportsnet 590 The FAN, we were able to find some of this old audio in their deep archives. The joyous calls of a new championship feel so familiar, but the back-and-forth between Howarth and Cheek—up to that seamless handoff for the bottom of the 11th—made it feel so alive again, even all these years later.

"I was so happy to do it, to do the right thing and to have Tom enjoy that moment," Howarth said, reflecting on a memory that's still emotional for him. "That's my favourite call, because it includes Tom."

That call came 5,679 days after Cheek called the first moments of Blue Jays baseball on a snowy afternoon in 1977 at Exhibition Stadium. Of course, he only needed to wait 364 days for the next one, the call that lives forever.

"Here's the pitch on the way. A swing and a belt. Left field! Way back! Blue Jays win it! The Blue Jays are World Series champions as Joe Carter hits a three-run home run in the ninth inning and the Blue Jays have repeated as World Series champions. Touch 'em all, Joe, you'll never hit a bigger home run in your life!"

Only two men have hit a walk-off home run to win the World Series: Carter and the Pirates' Bill Mazeroski in 1960. Mazeroski's walk-off brought down a giant in the Yankees, who had won eight of the last 13 World Series, that '60 team led by Mickey Mantle and Roger Maris in their prime.

Those two historic home runs were connected by a thread. Howarth, who was and still is a baseball encyclopedia, later shared with the audience that when Mazeroski reached home plate in 1960 and was mobbed by his teammates, his shortstop, Dick Schofield, was among them. Thirty-three years later, the crowd awaiting Carter at home plate included shortstop Dick Schofield Jr., who had been out since May with a broken arm but was in the dugout with his team, in uniform, for the World Series. What are the odds that a father and son were there for something that's only happened twice in baseball history? Moments like these are why Howarth loves baseball.

Cheek's call wasn't canned and corny. You know what those sound like, when a broadcaster has scripted their call—so often overwritten—for when the big moment arrives. It can take the air out of a moment, putting an artificial glaze over it.

Instead, Cheek was doing what he always did. He called the game in front of him. That day, the game gave Cheek one of its greatest moments.

"Some things, you can't rehearse. You don't know what's going to happen. You can't pre-plan those moments for what you're going to say when it happens," Joe Carter remembered at an event years later, marking the moment's anniversary.

"I asked Tom, 'What were you thinking when you made that call?' Tom said to me, 'You were jumping up and down on the bases and I was telling you to make sure you touched all the bases.' That's ironic, because if he remembers, when I got to first base and started jumping, the first thing on my mind was to touch all of the bases. We had that moment there when we were on the same page. Touch all of the bases. I've got the proof on all of the film. I touched all of the bases."

* * *

Howarth retired prior to the 2018 season after 36 years in the booth. After undergoing surgery for prostate cancer in 2016, he'd returned to the booth with all the energy of that "runaround mouse," but in 2017, he was again forced to miss 21 games after a battle with laryngitis. Eventually, Howarth chose to step away from the microphone on his own terms, taking a long and joyful career with him.

Still, you couldn't keep Howarth away from the ballpark. For half his life, that had been his second home.

In 2018, the Blue Jays' press box was still behind home plate, up on the 300 Level. When you walked in the door, you could veer right toward the dining area and the rows of seats taken up by writers. Make a left turn, you'd find the TV booths and the radio booth, Howarth's home for all those years.

I was new to the Blue Jays' beat at the time, just two years in, still dressing as if each day were a job interview. In my first year covering the team, I'd worn an argyle sweater to the ballpark one day early in the season, and as Howarth passed me in the hallway, he commented, "Hey, I have those socks!" The sweater was retired that day.

Being junior on the beat, I tucked myself away in the farthest end of the press box, the second of three rows along the right wall. This was beyond the dining room, beyond the tables with scattered chairs, and as far from Sportsnet 590 The FAN's radio booth as you could get in the press box.

Early that season, Howarth walked over unexpectedly and asked if he could join the row for a game.

"Oh, I can picture that like it was yesterday," Howarth said, his voice trailing off in thought.

He'd made a point to try to come to the first game of each series at home. Over his decades in the game, his contacts stretched well beyond the Blue Jays' organization. Each team that came through town had a manager he'd interviewed 40 times, a player he knew from 12 years ago or a staff member who'd once spent time in Toronto. He was so well connected.

Howarth wanted to stay involved, but with a catch. He didn't want to intrude.

"When I went upstairs, I said to myself, 'Jerry, you're retired, get as far away from the radio booth as you can because now, it's not your baby. It's Ben Wagner's.'"

Growing up, I spent time on lobster boats in Nova Scotia. I was an imposter there, working on the backs of boats like so many in my family had before me, the backup to the backup when a friend needed an extra set of hands to haul traps out of the water and band the lobsters. Feeling like a tagalong those days, I'd watch as the men around me tilted their bodies to the sea, anticipating each wave before I could see it. They stood steady as I stumbled for footing, their bodies rocking and swaying with the motion of the water, always one step ahead in their dance.

Looking to my left that day in 2018, I saw the same.

There was Howarth, watching the game from an angle a few degrees to the right of what he'd known for so long. There's a physicality to calling a game. Broadcasters use their posture, their arms, their fists, and the tilt of their bodies into that microphone to get the most out of their voices.

I'm still so sure of it now—even these years later—that I saw Howarth leaning into the microphone during a few of that game's biggest moments. As the inning ended, I wondered, did his mind go to the between-inning advertisement read for whichever lawn seed company or car dealership had bought that season's ad package?

He took in the game silently, though, the man whose voice had filled so many rooms, cars, and cottage patios over the years. It felt right.

"I would sit at the far end of the press box to take in the game in my own private way and there you were, right next to me. I said to myself, 'This is what I like,'" Howarth said. "I was always a very quiet person. People say that I'm an extrovert, but I tell them that I'm not. I'm an extroverted introvert. I've always been an introvert. It's just something in my life, all the way back to the University of Santa Clara, where I graduated in 1968. I love my quiet time."

Howarth has earned this retirement that he's embraced so well, still living such a full life with his wife, Mary.

The game has changed so much since Cheek and Howarth first read you the lineup and set the stage for first pitch. The genre of radio, itself, holds such a different place now, but the standard was set by these two.

Yes, sir...there...she...goes.

29

Alison Gordon

THERE'S A TRADITION, EVEN IN THESE FADING DAYS OF sports media. When it's time for an old writer to catch the ferry to the other side—whether that be retirement or a communications job—all of the writers gather for a night of drinks, stories, and drinks.

There have been moments over the years, as our veteran writers have moved on, that I've caught myself in a quiet moment, looking around the room with a sense of awe. Every story in the history of the Toronto Blue Jays, or at least damn close to it, has been told by someone standing in this room. In these moments, you also see a room almost entirely full of men.

You cannot tell the history of this organization, or how it's been covered, without telling the story of Alison Gordon.

She was the first woman to cover an MLB beat full-time, hired by the *Toronto Star* for the 1979 season. Gordon covered the Blue Jays for five years, the early days of an organization

266

that was still trying to stand on its own two feet at Exhibition Stadium. Even today, you can count on one hand the number of women who cover the Toronto Blue Jays regularly. The same still applies in many MLB markets. In Gordon's day, she was one of one.

Gordon became close with the women who had begun working the baseball beats in other cities, too. After Gordon's passing in 2015, Claire Smith, winner of the BBWAA Career Excellence Award, wrote these beautiful lines for ESPN:

"Toronto was a safe harbor because of her. It was a place to decompress because she had done all the heavy lifting."

Gordon began covering the Blue Jays full-time soon after Melissa Ludtke had first entered the New York Yankees' clubhouse in New York, an accredited reporter with *Sports Illustrated*. At that year's World Series, though—1977 in New York—Ludtke's clubhouse access was taken away. SI's parent company, Time Inc., later sued, and by late 1978, District Judge Constance Baker Motley ruled in favour of Ludtke.

This was a crucial moment for women in baseball media, but clearly, not all involved saw it that way.

In a chapter of her 1984 book, *Foul Balls*, titled "Token Broad," Gordon writes about that day.

"The day may have been semi-historic, but it was also a mess. Coincidentally, the Blue Jays were playing at Yankee Stadium when the barrier crashed down, and the reporters who were there remember the scene as a zoo, with the Yankees doing everything they could to embarrass the women. Sparky Lyle brought out a phallus-shaped cake with pink frosting and posted a sign next to it: 'for women sportswriters only.' The Blue Jays, mainly younger players, were simply embarrassed."

In her book and much of her writing following her beat days, Gordon praised the Blue Jays for their response. Prior to her first season, Blue Jays players were given a lecture on how they would be expected to treat Gordon or any other woman who walked through those clubhouse doors. Many did so with respect or, at the very least, weren't outwardly hostile.

Not all players rolled out the welcome mat, of course.

"I also met less savoury types that spring, one in particular who I will never forget," Gordon wrote of her first spring training in *Foul Balls*. "His name is irrelevant, since only his mother remembers him."

Gordon's writing was injected with such a sense of life and humour, the voice of someone who had a life and interests outside of baseball but still knew the game so well. That balance is what makes the best sports writers.

In 2001, Gordon wrote a piece for the *Toronto Star* looking back on her time covering the Blue Jays, her humour once again on display.

"There's a lot you can say about the 1979 Blue Jays. The words that leap immediately to mind are ones like inept, laughable, pathetic, just plain bad—words like that."

"The *Star* was the first newspaper to hire a woman, me, for the baseball beat. My main credentials were a love for and understanding of the game, a facility with the written word and, in hindsight, a naive belief this particular challenge was within my grasp.

"The first few months on the beat would sorely test that belief. Reactions as I set the first female foot into press boxes and clubhouse around the American League ranged from acceptance to hostility."

Some players would never be won over. Younger players, Gordon soon found, were often easier to work with than the older players who had called those clubhouses home for a decade, the boys' clubs. Following Gordon's death, Lloyd

Moseby spoke about his experience playing on those Blue Jays teams for four of the five years Gordon worked the beat.

"She was relentless," Moseby told the *Toronto Star.* "A lot of women that are in the profession right now should be very thankful for what Alison did and what she went through. She took a beating from the guys. She was a pioneer for sure."

"We had four or five guys that really rallied around not letting her in the clubhouse, but I don't think Alison gave a damn, to tell you the truth. She could have very easily taken the words that a lot of guys said and took it to heart and went back to her bosses and said, 'I'm not doing this. I don't get paid to take abuse.' But she never did. She kept showing up. And it was amazing, really. I'm just proud to have known Alison."

Gordon's book, *Foul Balls*, is essential reading for any fan of the Blue Jays and anyone who works in the media. Everything is aired out and laid bare, from players to coaches, staff to other media members.

Later in life, Gordon published a series of murder mysteries with titles like *The Dead Pull Hitter* and *Safe at Home.* They followed a main character, Kate Henry, a sportswriter and amateur detective who solved murders in the baseball world.

So much of how we remember Gordon has to do with the clubhouse. It represents something—a door that opened, both literally and figuratively. As she writes in *Foul Balls,* though, that was only part of it. Gordon was not held to an equal standard to her male colleagues. The bar was so much higher.

"The obsession with the locker room completely ignored the most serious problem of being a woman reporter in those early days. For us, the real challenge of the job was having to do it better than everyone else or risk failure on behalf of the whole female sex. An inexperienced male reporter could ask a dumb question and get away with it. An eyebrow would be raised here or there, perhaps, and some might think him awfully dumb. If a woman asked the same question, it would be further proof that broads didn't know anything about baseball."

Around baseball, press boxes bear the names of famous ball writers or longtime PR reps from the teams. The Orioles recently named theirs after Jim Henneman, the longtime Baltimore writer who later became the Orioles' official scorer. In Boston, the Red Sox call theirs the "Bresh Box" after Dick Bresciani, the club's longtime public relations head.

Gordon's name belongs above the door of the Blue Jays' press box at Rogers Centre. From all the stories—and all of the storytellers—we must never forget Alison Gordon in Toronto.

30

Dan Shulman

THIS WAS NOT DAN SHULMAN'S MASTER PLAN.

He was a kid growing up in Toronto who loved sports—that's it—and the Blue Jays arrived at the perfect time.

This never entered his mind, though. Forget doing play-by-play for the Blue Jays, being the voice of *Sunday Night Baseball*, or calling the Olympics. Forget being named a finalist for the National Baseball Hall of Fame's Ford C. Frick Award. Forget winning the Canadian Baseball Hall of Fame's Jack Graney Award on one side of the border and the National Sports Media Association National Sportscaster of the Year on the other.

No chance. That wasn't even a thought.

Growing up, Shulman was "a math geek."

"Here's how fun the parties I went to were…. My math ability was like a party trick. That's the crowd. We were the cool kids. Everybody knew I was going to do something in math, but I couldn't figure out what. In Grade 12, I was driving around with a buddy of mine, and I said, 'I don't know what to do, I guess I'll be an accountant.' He asked me, why not become an actuary, so I asked him what everybody said: '...What's an actuary?'"

Good question. Even actuaries have trouble telling you what an actuary does. The short version is that actuaries use math and data to determine how likely an event is to occur. It's intentionally broad, but applies to insurance issues, pensions, investments, and more.

"One of the lines was that actuaries were accountants with personality, which I think insults both of us?" Shulman said.

While Shulman was studying math to become an actuary at Western University, he made a point to get involved in something, anything, extra-curricular. It's a lesson he'd taken from his parents. Get out there. Do something outside of classes to stay involved. Strolling by the office of the campus radio station, CHRW, a young Dan Shulman, who'd never called a second of sports, knocked on the door and asked if they were looking for volunteers.

Soon enough, he was calling Western Mustangs football and basketball games, later hosting his own sports talk show called *From the Cheap Seats* on the station. Year four of Shulman's studies came, though, and becoming an actuary—like going through law school—required him to write outside exams to qualify. He'd have too much on his plate, so he stepped back from the radio station. Even then, he didn't have this grand idea of fame and success in broadcasting. He was there to become an actuary. Period.

Then, the real world came. Shulman started to work as an actuary. It was...fine.

But Shulman had this one memory of his father burned into his mind growing up. His father, Arnie, was a dentist. Each

Sunday, he would watch and notice his father's stress creeping up, knowing that a new work week and all its challenges waited for him the next morning. Shulman knew then that he had to do something he enjoyed, fully and completely, not just something that could get him through the day. Still just 22 years old, he met with his parents and grandparents and told them what every family member dreams of hearing, that he'd like to leave his stable, sensible job to go into broadcasting.

"I had that moment of truth, and it came quick. I was two months into my job. The people were wonderful, and the job was exactly what it was supposed to be. I just decided to have my mid-life crisis at 22, which I strongly recommend for everybody. Have it before you have any dependents."

He went to work sending tapes across Ontario. We're still talking about the early 1990s here, so he was stuffing cassettes into envelopes, walking them down to the post office, and waiting. There was no immediate gratification in any of this, but eventually, Shulman caught on at CKBB in Barrie, Ontario, and soon moved to Fan 1430 in Toronto, which would later develop into Sportsnet 590 The FAN.

This is where Shulman got his first lucky bounce. Even the greats get a few bounces along the way.

One night in 1993, Shulman was hosting a show from 8 PM to midnight on Fan 1430 when the phone in the studio rang.

"My name is Al Jaffe," the voice said. "I'm calling from ESPN. I'd like to talk to you about coming down to audition for ESPN Radio."

At Western, Shulman had a roommate named Rob. He thought this was a prank call.

"That's pretty good, Rob. You gave yourself a not-very-good New York accent and everything."

There was silence on the other end of the line, then the voice cut through again, speaking slowly.

"I'm going to say this one more time. My name...is Al Jaffe..."

Here's the thing, though. Jaffe wasn't looking for Shulman that night. He was looking for a 1420 station somewhere in Albany or Rochester, maybe Syracuse. Shulman was just up the dial at 1430, so ESPN had stumbled upon Shulman hosting this show by total accident. This was like a music executive finding the next great country music star by walking into the wrong bar on a Monday night for open mic. It was the perfect collision of luck and talent.

This was when everything started to accelerate for Shulman, who worked shows on Fan 1430 through the week and did ESPN Radio on weekends until, after the 1994 season, a job opened up with the Blue Jays on TSN. Jim Hughson was leaving the booth, where he'd called games with Buck Martinez, and TSN needed a new play-by-play guy. Shulman doesn't quite remember who contacted who, but either way, he got an audition.

He and Buck Martinez still remember every detail of the game they called together in that sound booth at TSN's studios for Shulman's audition.

They remember every detail...because there weren't many.

* * *

When Shulman auditioned for the play-by-play job with the Blue Jays in November 1994, he had called one inning of baseball. One.

As the pre- and post-game host on Fan 1430, he'd be the "other guy" in the booth at times with Tom Cheek and Jerry Howarth calling the games. When he was down in Dunedin for a few weeks of spring training games in 1994, the legendary Cheek turned to Shulman in the middle of the game and said to him:

"Danny, come on up front. You ever done an inning? Come on up front."

As Shulman tells this story, his voice breaks into a Cheek impersonation, Shulman's already-classic voice weaving in with Cheek's trademark baritone, one great artist covering another. What a sound.

"Buck and I were in this little studio looking at a television, and I'm so green that I don't even realize that in the corner office on the fifth floor, all the bosses are listening. I was so young. I was 27. I was sick as a dog."

That's Martinez's first memory, too. This kid auditioning to be his partner in the booth was sick as hell.

Oh, and one more thing.

"A radio guy?" Martinez remembers thinking. "Radio?!..."

This was Shulman's big chance to show that he could hang on TV, not just the radio, but nothing happened in this game. Not a damn thing. They'd given Shulman a game from the prior season to call with Martinez, a May 3, 1994, matchup between the Blue Jays and Royals that ended 1–0. The teams combined for five hits. Sure, Pat Hentgen struck out 14 batters and threw a complete game shutout on 116 pitches—just a brilliant performance—but this was Shulman's one chance to make an impression and they'd only given him white paint to work with.

"Nothing happened. Nothing," Shulman remembers. "It was like a *Seinfeld* episode. What if we auditioned him with a game and nothing happened?"

Martinez still lights up at the memory, almost like it was Shulman's unintentional initiation in retrospect. Frankly, Martinez knew before anyone else did that he was standing next to the next play-by-play voice of the Toronto Blue Jays.

"It was the stupidest game they could have pulled to audition someone, a 1–0 game, Kevin Appier against Pat Hentgen," Martinez said, grinning. "Back and forth, back and forth, nothing to nothing with nothing to talk about. Bob Hamelin hit a double down the left-field line that scored the only run of the game and Dan picked up on it perfectly. I walked out of the booth and said, 'There's your guy.'"

But TSN didn't listen to him.

Two days later, Shulman got a call. Thanks, but no thanks. They'd decided to pursue someone else for the job, and depending on who you ask, TSN may have pursued a couple. A few months later, though, in February, Shulman's phone rang. They offered him the job.

"I don't know who Plan A, B, and C were," Shulman said, "but I'm happy to be D."

* * *

So it began, the first era of Buck and Dan on your television. Back then, networks shared the broadcast rights to the Blue Jays. It's not like today, where all 162 games belong to Sportsnet. There were times that, on a 10-game road trip, the TSN crew would travel along with the club for the whole ride but only call four of the games.

First, the two needed to get to know one another. Shulman had been around Martinez, but the two hadn't even had a beer together before. Martinez was nearly 20 years older than him, already a respected broadcaster after his long playing career.

The MLB strike was still rolling at the time, leaving teams—and broadcasters—unsure what this season would look like. Would there be replacement players? Would it start on time?

That spring, Shulman and Martinez rode around Florida with their producer, Rick Briggs-Jude. They'd call a game into a tape recorder in Lakeland or Sarasota, then listen to the tape on the way back to the hotel. The two had immediate chemistry, which isn't nearly as common as you'd expect in a broadcast booth. Styles can clash, personalities can clash, even voices, but something about these two fit.

That doesn't mean Shulman hit the ground running, though. There are always going to be growing pains and you never forget your first.

"My first game, they were playing Baltimore. It was a spring training game in Dunedin. Brady Anderson was the first batter. To this day, I cannot see the damn ball in the sky in Dunedin. Brady Anderson hits a high fly ball to deep right-centre field. Devon White is the centre fielder, the most graceful man who has ever played centre field. I say, 'He's setting up underneath it…' and it was 20 feet over the wall. The first batter hit a home run and I screwed it up. It was instantly just sweat pouring out every part of my body. I can't do this! I won't be able to! Buck helped calm me down 100 times that first year until I got comfortable."

It was in these days that Shulman and Martinez became so close. Neither could have imagined where their careers would take them from there, both working with ESPN at different points through the '90s and 2000s before coming back together on Sportsnet all those years later.

"He meant the world to me. One of the things he said to me that I'll always remember, and this was probably early, early in that 1995 season. Maybe I was trying too hard or something like that. He said to me, 'Listen, if you and I can make this sound like two guys sitting at the bar watching the baseball game up on a little TV, we're doing fine.' It was 29 years ago he said that to me and I think of that every time I do a game."

"The world was different in the '90s, but we used to have this little game where we would just decide to stop talking. We would call it a lull. We'd go into a lull. I'd mouth it to him, or he'd mouth it to me. We'd have bets on how long it could be until whoever the producer was that night would say, 'What the hell is going on up there?' You could do that stuff back then and nobody would shred you on Twitter. You could be silly and do things that you could never do now, harmless little things like that with inside jokes. Sometimes, one of the directors I've worked with over the years would give me a word. He'd say, 'Your word is *oscillate*,' or something like that, but it had to be used in context. I couldn't just force it in. I could feel the money changing hands in the production truck, even though I couldn't hear it or see it. We had fun."

When you think of Shulman, you can hear his voice immediately. Like so many of the great broadcasters, it's confident without being brash, assuring and steady in every way, so easy to trust. It's so difficult to picture that young, green Shulman all those years ago, heart racing before a broadcast.

In an April 1995 story by the *Toronto Star*'s Ken McKee, introducing readers to the new guy in the booth, Shulman said, "I am nervous. I hope people will be patient."

"It was television, not radio. It was national, not local. I skipped a couple of steps. I was very nervous. I think I got comfortable pretty quickly and a lot of that was because of the crew I worked with. Buck was enormous in that. I didn't even know what I didn't know. Buck would say to me, 'Actually, when the umpire does *this*...stuff like that.' I was learning TV, too. I had done a little bit of play-by-play on TV, too, but not a ton. I knew baseball, but I was learning the finer aspects of baseball and I was trying to get comfortable talking to players. That team in '95 still had a lot of older, established, intimidating players. What was a huge help to me was that in the next couple of years, Dan Plesac, Paul Quantrill, Ed Sprague, Pat Hentgen, Shawn Green, Carlos Delgado, all of those guys came up. They were phenomenal. They saved me. They would put up with my questions and sit with me. We did about 80 games back then because there were three networks. I learned then that you go into the clubhouse every day. Don't stand around for a half-hour, but show your face every day."

Before Shulman even got through his first season on the mic calling Blue Jays games, though, it was time for another late-night phone call out of the blue.

* * *

The Blue Jays were playing a series in New York that September 1995, and Shulman was staying with the broadcast crew at the Hyatt Grand Central hotel. TSN had the Tuesday and Thursday night broadcasts for that series, with Wednesday's game airing on another network.

After the Tuesday game, Shulman got back to his hotel and walked into his room to see the red light on his phone flashing. This was back when hotel phones were more than just something that got in your way on the nightstand. He picked up the phone and pressed the button to hear the message. Here's how he remembers it:

"'Dan, my name is Jed Drake. I'm the coordinating producer for baseball at ESPN. Call me immediately, no matter how late it is.' And I'm thinking…I'm just an actuary, right? So I called Jed and I didn't know Jed, but he said that someone was sick, and they needed a play-by-play guy in Kansas City tomorrow.

'I understand you're not doing the Blue Jays game tomorrow. Can you go to Kansas City?'"

That moment is such a great snapshot of how Shulman's job has changed. How all jobs in sports media have, really, especially in baseball, which comes with the most relentless travel schedule and the demands of covering 162 games.

It was 1995. The internet wasn't anything close to the internet of today. He couldn't just fire up Baseball Reference or pull up everything written about the Royals over the last week. He just had to get from New York to Kansas City, show up to the field early, and figure it all out on the fly, notebook in hand. That's after showing up to the airport in New York and walking up to the counter, hoping everything had been arranged by ESPN and that a ticket was waiting for him.

In the chaos of it all, Shulman called home to his parents. That night his father, Arnie, walked into a sports bar downtown, and for the first time in Toronto's history, a man spoke the words: "I need the Royals game on."

"He sat at the bar by himself and watched that baseball game, which is the guy he was. That's who he was," Shulman said, smiling at the memory.

Two weeks later, Shulman got another call from ESPN. Could he call basketball? Sure!

As Shulman continued to call Blue Jays games and do work for ESPN, he eventually took on a much larger role on the basketball side. ESPN acquired the NBA rights going into 2002, which moved their top college basketball broadcasters up to the big leagues, if you will, which bumped Shulman to the top of the NCAA list. He'd also just gotten the *Sunday Night Baseball* radio gig, a massive opportunity for him, and all of this required him to make the full-time move to ESPN. He stayed there for 15 years before coming back to Blue Jays broadcasts on a limited basis in 2016–17, then returning to Sportsnet full-time following the '17 season.

It's come full circle now. Shulman's son, Ben, was named the new radio voice of the Blue Jays in 2024. He even worked his first spring training television game and first regular season television games alongside Martinez, who continues to span generations.

In spring training, 2024, Ben Shulman took over for a couple of games on television while Dan was bouncing around the United States, calling NCAA basketball games for ESPN. When Dan returned from that trip, he took play-by-play duties back over in Dunedin. After a few days of standing next to Ben, Buck Martinez was standing next to Dan again. He turned to his partner in the booth and said, "Wow. You've aged terribly."

* * *

Shulman has already made so many memorable calls over the years, both in the slow build of a baseball game and the frantic pace of basketball. Many American fans in particular remember the night of May 2, 2011, when Shulman was calling *Sunday Night Baseball* between the Phillies and the Mets, a nationally broadcast game. Midway through the broadcast, his partner in the booth, Bobby Valentine, gave him a nudge and showed him a message on his cell phone. Stunned by what he'd just read, Shulman and the booth confirmed the news with their ESPN colleagues and Shulman went to the air with the following, a Canadian speaking to the biggest audience in the United States that night.

"ABC News is reporting that Osama Bin Laden has been killed and a presidential news conference is upcoming momentarily. We ask all of you to go to your ABC stations for further details on that situation. For those of you staying with us, we'll be back with the ninth inning momentarily here in Philadelphia with the game tied at one..."

That's going to be hard to top.

Shulman's voice is going to continue to live alongside the biggest moments in sports, though, and it would just sound so right calling the Blue Jays' return to glory one day.

One call many don't remember was José Bautista's bat flip. Shulman was there, calling the game for ESPN Radio.

He'd been working the series between the Cubs and Cardinals, which ended the night before Game 5 of the ALDS between the Blue Jays and Rangers, one of the wildest, most memorable games in the history of this franchise. Shulman's phone rang, which, if you're keeping score at home, has tended to bring good news.

Someone was sick, and while we should really investigate whether Shulman was behind any of these well-timed illnesses, ESPN Radio needed a broadcaster in a pinch once again.

Shulman was supposed to be at the game that night. He had four tickets, but as he rushed home to Toronto to suddenly prepare for a major game on the mic, he arranged for his mother and father to go to the game with two of his sons.

All hell broke loose in the seventh inning of a game that was already teetering on the edge of chaos when Russell Martin's throw back to the mound bounced off the bat of Shin-Soo Choo, allowing the go-ahead run to score. Debris rained onto the field, and as Shulman called the incredible scene playing out in front of him, he was waiting for a break in the action to reach for his cell phone.

Shulman texted them mid-game while on the air: "Whatever you do, do not leave the ballpark after the game. There could be a riot outside. Let me come get you and we'll go out together."

Then, Bautista hit that home run and he texted back, "We're good. See you at home."

"*The 1–1...Bautista! Drives it! Deep left field! Gone! Suddenly, it is 6–3 for Toronto. The Blue Jays dugout has erupted as they greet Bautista at the edge of the track.*"

What a gift it is to have Shulman and Martinez together in the same booth now. So much has changed since 1995. Martinez used to have the best hair in the booth, for example, and now he has the only hair. But their chemistry is what makes this work. They've spent thousands and thousands of hours together, some with the mics on, so many more with the mics off. They can say more with a silent look than most colleagues can say with a full sentence. With the twitch of an eyebrow or the shake of a head, they communicate with one another on the broadcast, bouncing back and forth, never getting too far ahead or falling too far behind one another.

We're living in another golden era of the Blue Jays broadcast. Martinez, the longtime player, manager, and broadcaster, belongs on the Blue Jays Level of Excellence. Shulman, who still has so many years of broadcasting ahead, should find a Ford C. Frick Award in those years, enshrining him as one of this generation's truly great broadcasters. Another former player turned broadcaster, Joe Siddall, has added a fantastic element to the broadcasts with his analysis and ability to communicate that expertise to every level of fan, often filling in for Martinez alongside Shulman. Sideline reporter Hazel Mae, so beloved by Canadian baseball fans, brings outstanding access and stories from field level, where her relationships with the players and coaches—and their trust in her—shine through on the broadcast. Regardless of what the product on the field looks like, Blue Jays fans are being brought these stories by a crew that most other major markets would dream of.

If you're lucky, Shulman will be on the mic to call the next generation of Blue Jays games, the next big wins, the next bat flip, the next "Touch 'em all, Joe."

Not bad for the math geek. Not bad for an actuary.

"For not one millisecond did I think this would be a career," Shulman said, still shaking his head.

31

Buck Martinez

THERE ARE THESE MOMENTS IN BUCK MARTINEZ'S LIFE THAT seemed so small at the time.

Coming into the 1981 season with the Brewers, Martinez was 32 years old. He'd spent his career in Kansas City and Milwaukee, sometimes a backup, sometimes splitting the catching duties. He had a .594 OPS in 595 career games. He was buried on Milwaukee's depth chart, and as other clubs took a look at their own catching, one called the Brewers.

"They had a deal to trade me to the Yankees in spring training," Martinez remembers.

The deal never happened, though. The Brewers were in the same division with the Yankees at the time, which eventually held up the trade. That could have sent Martinez's life spinning off in another direction entirely, but at the time, it was just another day, another story that wasn't a story. Martinez had already been in the big leagues for over a decade. He knew how these things worked.

Instead, he started the season with the Brewers as their fourth catcher. He didn't play in a game in April. Then May started, and he just kept tagging along.

"I literally just rode around the American League with the Brewers."

Eventually, Martinez got called into the office of manager Buck Rodgers while they were in Anaheim playing the Angels. Milwaukee needed to get a pitcher onto the roster and Martinez was the odd man out, designated for assignment. He called his wife, Arlene, at the team hotel and told her not to come to the ballpark that day. He'd be there soon, he told her.

The two had just sold their house and were still in the middle of deciding where they'd move next—either Arizona or Florida—so they went to Martinez's parents' house in Sacramento, where they stayed for the next 10 days. He exercised to pass the time, his body still set to the schedule of a big-league season, and on May 10, he returned to the house from a run to find Arlene waiting for him at the door.

Inside, on the table, was a bottle of champagne.

Buck Martinez had just been traded. That moment, on May 10, 1981, changed his life forever. He just didn't know it yet.

"Arlene said, 'You got traded to Toronto,' and I went, 'Oh, fuck. Really? That's the best they could do?'"

Arlene was ecstatic, though. Pat Gillick had called her directly and her first question was where the Blue Jays held their spring training each year. She hated Arizona, so the word "Florida" was all Martinez's wife needed to hear. She was sold.

Martinez's memory of these moments is amazing all these years later. He pulls back the smallest details, but more than anything, he pulls back how it all felt. The Blue Jays were the new kids, only five years into their existence, and they hadn't won more than 67 games in a season yet. Sure, the franchise was in the early stages of building those great teams of the 1980s, but they had no reputation yet, no identity. They were just that team up north.

"I went to Toronto, and I landed on a cold May night. Rick Amos picked me up at the airport and it was raining, just miserable. You know how Toronto is when it's raining in May. I thought, 'What the fuck have I gotten myself into?' I thought I'd be there for a year. I thought that was the end of the line for me. I thought it doesn't get any worse than coming to Toronto."

The early days didn't come easy, either. The Blue Jays already had a backup catcher, Dan Whitmer, who was beloved by the other players and their families. Gillick called Martinez into his office on one of those early days, though, and made it clear that he was in Toronto for a reason. Well, two reasons. He was there to help the pitching staff get better and help Ernie Whitt become a better catcher.

This should have been what Martinez expected it to be, a one-year trip to retirement's waiting room.

It's an unspectacular story we've seen over and over again in baseball, it doesn't matter the year. Martinez was the grizzled veteran catcher, brought in to manage a pitching staff and help out the new kid for a few months until someone else came along. If he slapped a few hits while he was there, great.

That's not what happened.

Sitting in a diner in Dunedin, Florida, in the spring of 2024, near where he and Arlene have made their home for years, Martinez smiles and shakes his head, all these memories flowing back through his mind. If only he could have known when he landed in Toronto on that rainy May night what was about to happen.

"Sitting here now…it's probably the best thing that ever happened to me."

* * *

As a player, Martinez was beloved for all the same reasons a backup catcher falls into favour with a fan base. He was tough.

Over those first three years, he put up some numbers, too. From 1981 to '83, Martinez had three of his best seasons at the plate, batting .243 with a .740 OPS. The Blue Jays had gotten far more than they could have expected out of Martinez, even as he approached his mid-thirties.

The Blue Jays were blossoming into baseball's newest powerhouse in those years. By 1985, when they won a franchise-record 99 games under Bobby Cox, that rotation was led by the great Dave Stieb in his prime, and a young Jimmy Key behind him with Doyle Alexander and Jim Clancy. The bullpen, led by closer Tom Henke, was magnificent. Tony Fernández, George Bell, Lloyd Moseby, and Jesse Barfield were no older than 25. A golden age of baseball was dawning as Martinez, at 36, was the second-oldest player on the roster behind Cliff Johnson.

Midway through that season, Martinez was involved in the iconic play. It's the moment he's asked about most from his career, and how could it not be? It was the Broken Leg Double Play, which tells you everything you need to know about what happened.

Martinez was behind the plate with a runner on second when the Mariners singled, and on the throw home from Jesse Barfield, Martinez was involved in a massive collision, badly injuring his leg. He'd held onto the ball for the out, though, and as he sat up, still in a daze, he noticed that Gorman Thomas was still running, so he fired the ball to third. When that throw went past Garth Iorg and into the outfield, George Bell scooped it up and threw home to Martinez for a second time on the play. Martinez, still flat on his backside after the first major collision, reached up and tagged the runner for the second out.

A 9-2-7-2 double play. A career-defining play.

"Before I broke my leg I had a similar play in the same game," Martinez remembers. "Jesse threw me a ball on the first-base side of the plate. I grabbed it, dove across the plate, and tagged out Jim Presley. Jesse came in after that double play to end the inning and it was a scoreless game. We hadn't scored a run in a month. We were dying on the west coast. I said, 'Jesse, next time, throw it on the other side of home plate.' The very next inning, that's when they hit the ground ball to right and Jesse comes up throwing. Phil Bradley hits me and dislocates my ankle and breaks my leg. I threw the ball past Garth down the left-field line. That's when George Bell picked it up and threw it back to me to tag that runner."

Martinez had to miss the rest of that season, watching on as his teammates lost to the Kansas City Royals, his first team, in Game 7 of the ALCS. Until the Blue Jays won their first World Series in 1992, this '85 team was the greatest they'd ever fielded.

Even though Martinez didn't want to look this in the eye at the time, he knew that he was coming to the end.

The 1986 season came and went. Martinez, now 37, played in 81 games that season, but hit just .181. On the final Sunday of the season, manager Jimy Williams called him into his office. He turned to Arlene and said, "Well, this is probably the end of the line."

When Martinez walked into the office that day, Williams was seated with Pat Gillick and Paul Beeston. He still remembers his eyes meeting Gillick's, the man who had brought him to Toronto six years ago, the GM who'd called his wife and assured her that, no, she wouldn't need to move to Arizona.

"Pat was very, very emotional. He was always tied to his players. It was unbelievable. He literally had tears in his eyes while he said, 'I don't know how to tell you this. You've been a wonderful guy for us–'"

That's when Martinez cut him off.

"Pat, I came here six years ago expecting to play one year. It has been a fabulous six years. I couldn't ask for more. You guys have been great with me, treated me wonderfully. I had a wonderful time."

The four talked, and toward the end, Paul Beeston's unmistakable voice cracked through.

Martinez's full name is John Albert Martinez, and Beeston, always the eccentric, calls him Albert. When even Beeston remembers this meeting today, nearly 40 years later, that's the first word out of his mouth: "Albert!"

Beeston had an idea.

"Albert..." he said, "do you want to do TV?"

Martinez said thanks, but no thanks. He'd known the life of big-league baseball for 17 seasons now. He'd built such a life in this game and thought he still had another year or two left before he'd have to hand up his catcher's gear.

Martinez, like he's done in so many of these moments through his life, made his first call home to Arlene.

"Call him back. You can't play anymore," Arlene told him.

He listened to her. Thinking back on that phone call, he can only shrug and smile.

"Once again, she made the right decision."

* * *

This was always one of his wife's greatest gifts, Martinez said, her incredible feel for people.

They'd met on a beach in Puerto Rico. Martinez was playing winter ball, which was more common in that era for big-leaguers.

"She was on the beach with her girlfriend, and I had a dog, a stray dog that I had befriended, so I'd take him down to the beach and throw tennis balls on the beach. He'd run and chase them."

Here, I had to cut him off. *You knew exactly what you were doing, Buck.*

"I'd always throw them over toward the pretty girls. 'Excuse me! I'm sorry, my dog! I can't control my dog!'"

Martinez invited Arlene and her friend to the game that night. Just last year, the two went back to that same beach in Puerto Rico and took the same pictures they'd taken 50 years ago. There's something he didn't know that first day they met, though.

"About 10 years later I found out they were stone broke," Martinez remembers, breaking into a laugh. "They'd gone to St. Thomas that day and they had no money, so they had to go with us!"

In Martinez's early days of transitioning out of the game and into the broadcast booth, it took some time for him to wrap his head around things.

"I didn't want anything to do with it," he remembers, almost echoing his early thoughts on his trade to Toronto in 1981. "When you're a player for so long, there's only one thing you want to do: play. Anything short of that isn't meaningful. 'Shit, anyone can do this. This isn't a job.'"

Paul Beeston knew he'd found the right guy, though. The two had a great relationship over the years. At one point, when

Martinez was re-upping with the Blue Jays, Beeston playfully slid him a blank cheque and told him to sign his name on the bottom. He'd fill out the number later, he said. When Martinez picked up the pen and went to sign, Beeston jumped up and said, "Don't get any fucking closer to that thing!"

"Buck was the guy that studied the game, he was the catcher. He had a supreme amount of confidence and he got along with everybody. He'd played the game at a high level in the major leagues, and he knew everybody in the major leagues. If there's a guy that can do it, Buck can do it."

Arlene was an actress. She'd done three years at the Lee Strasburg Theatre and Film Institute in New York City. When she saw Martinez on television, she saw a different version of him than she'd known for all those years.

"I came home after one of the first broadcasts and she goes, 'You sound just like Ted Knight.' He was on the *Mary Tyler Moore Show* with the big TV voice like, 'Hellooo, everybody!'"

She had a suggestion. Acting classes. Martinez needed an acting coach, Arlene said, to teach him how to be himself on the air. He met with a speech pathologist, too. It's a tricky game, trying to sound like "yourself" on television. The sweet spot is finding a version of your own voice that is slightly more polished. Not a big, fake television voice—and not Ted Knight—but something that still feels true.

Well, it all worked.

Martinez's voice is unmistakable. It lends itself to impressions so well, but no one can quite pull off a proper Buck Martinez. It's become an iconic sound over the years as Martinez grew as a broadcaster, eventually left the booth to manage the Blue Jays for the 2001 season and part of 2002, then returned to the mic following that. He's called games for ESPN, TSN, and Sportsnet over the years, teaming up with Dan Shulman in his early days of the booth beginning in 1995 and the two have reunited again, all these years later.

These job titles don't capture him, though. They can't.

Martinez has become one of this organization's most beloved personalities. He's an icon in Canadian sports and media.

"He's been a leader in spreading the gospel of baseball across the country," said Paul Beeston.

"You're not going to find a finer human being," said John Gibbons, who got his first job with the Blue Jays as Martinez's bullpen catcher in 2001.

"I don't think I get where I've gotten without him," said Shulman. "He helped me in so many different ways. It could even be as simple as introducing me. 'Hey, Danny. This is Bobby Cox.' He helped me in more ways than I could ever articulate to him."

It's too rare for someone to hear how loved they are when they're still around to hear it—to truly sense it and feel it—even someone of Martinez's stature. The day will come, hopefully many years from now, when Martinez will step away from the broadcast booth, when his voice is no longer keeping you company each night, summer after summer. There will come a day when we honour his career, every remarkable turn of it, a day when the thousands of people he's crossed paths with in baseball, in media, and in life will tell their stories of what he's meant to them.

He doesn't feel like he needs that moment, though. He's already had it.

* * *

It feels too formal to continue calling Buck by his last name. He's Buck.

It doesn't matter if you played with him for a season, shared a broadcast booth with him for a decade, or just tune into the odd ball game. He's Buck.

That's the beauty of what he means to baseball fans. Even if you've never met him, you feel like you're on a first-name basis with him. It's that intimacy only allowed by the game of baseball.

"Buck always brings a smile to my face. He's always positive," John Gibbons said. "He's just one of those guys who, when he comes around, you feel good. When you see Buck, you feel better. He's a legend. He's done it on the field and in the broadcast booth. He's really a special man."

In April 2022, the news came. Buck had been diagnosed with cancer. He announced on April 17 that he would be leaving the booth "for a little while" to undergo treatment.

This is Buck Martinez, though, the guy who pulled off a double play with a broken leg and a busted ankle.

"My doctor told me that I was going to miss the whole season and I said, 'No, I'm not. You do your job and I'll do my job.'"

There he is.

Just over two months later, on July 26, Martinez was back in the booth for the first time. It was one of the most memorable days I'll ever cover at Rogers Centre. I can still see it in my mind, Buck walking through those sliding clubhouse doors so casually, as if he'd just missed a few games to handle some appointments.

Buck wanted everything to be normal. He was there to check back in with the players, get the lay of the land in the manager's pregame media session, and sneak back up to the broadcast booth. He missed his perch, high above home plate.

Then, it happened.

"When I got back in the booth, it was the second inning and it felt like a regular game, it felt great. Then, I noticed that we weren't going to commercial. I started to look around, then I looked up at the scoreboard. I get emotional thinking about it...but it was special because my son and his family was there. Then, when I saw the players come out of the dugout, that's when it really hit me. I thought to myself, 'Wow, you must be doing something right.'"

The entire stadium stood and turned toward the broadcast booth, cheering. The Blue Jays walked out onto the field, young stars like Vladimir Guerrero Jr. and Bo Bichette raising their arms to the sky to wave at Buck, others holding their caps in the air.

It's a scene anyone there that day will always remember. Most days at the ballpark are, frankly, forgettable. By the time the next day's game is over, not much sticks from the day prior. This existed so far outside of that.

"It was probably the most emotional day of my career. When you have cancer, you don't know if you're going to work again. You don't know if you're going to live.... You don't know. To come back and see that reception...wow."

After the game, Buck walked out of the Gate 13 exit with his son, Casey, his three granddaughters, and Casey's wife. This is the moment that Buck, pausing to remember every detail, will never forget.

"We walked out of the gate, down the ramp, and started to walk through the crowd. Nobody said anything. They just started clapping.... It was unbelievable. They just started clapping."

Buck's work outside of what you see each night is remarkable. He doesn't advertise it, but he's been deeply involved with charity work throughout his career, both in Canada and at home in the United States. He's probably been to half of the small towns in Canada at this point, spreading the game of baseball or speaking at events. Buck stays formally involved with MLB's BAT program, as well—Baseball Assistance Team—a group that confidentially helps players, coaches, staff, and their families. Their work ranges from addiction recovery and treatment to food and housing, medical expenses, and career training.

Since Buck's cancer diagnosis, he's found a new community. He's already begun to travel to participate in ribbon-cutting ceremonies at cancer treatment facilities or speak at events. It's something that Buck hadn't thought about until cancer touched him, but he's been overwhelmed by how many new people this has connected with.

He remembers a recent trip to Saskatoon for an event. A grandfather in attendance told Buck that his granddaughter, who was around 25 years old, wanted to speak to him but was nervous to ask. Buck asked to meet her.

"My dad loved you and he died of cancer," she told him. "He and I used to watch the games together and he would always say, 'He's the best. He knows exactly what he's talking about.' I just had to tell you that."

Everywhere he goes now, he makes these connections.

You can't miss Buck, either. If that shock of brilliant white hair doesn't give him away, his voice will. It's been remarkable over the years to see how much Buck means to people who love this team.

Each spring, I spend hundreds of hours on the field or around the clubhouse covering the Blue Jays. Fans can get so close to players in Dunedin, both at their player development complex and across town at TD Ballpark. I've watched as some of this organization's most beloved players, from José Bautista and Josh Donaldson to Vladimir Guerrero and Bo Bichette, walk past these crowds. Even the briefest glimpse of them, poking their head out of the clubhouse, elicits screams.

The reaction to fans seeing Buck might rival all of them.

Even on the road, throughout the regular season, when you step outside of the stadium alongside Buck, you can't walk five feet. Dan Shulman has lived this life for years. Even as one of the most recognizable voices in sports, when Shulman goes out to dinner or walks the halls alongside his booth mate, he's just...the guy with Buck.

"It's unbelievable. I'm often the guy people ask to take a picture of them and Buck, and that's totally fine. I am happy to be back here. It's just unbelievable. There's something about Buck. Without even consciously trying to, he makes connections. I don't even know what the right word is, but he has this way about him. He touches people. There have been times walking with Buck, and I've had a lot of these over my career.... I worked with Dick Vitale for 20 years and if I walked in wearing a clown suit, nobody would even notice. I've seen it with a few people, but Dick and Buck are something completely different. He deserves it. They only do it for people who deserve it. He got to Toronto in 1981, and outside of those four years in Baltimore, he's been here ever since. It's amazing. It really is amazing."

What a career. What a life.

Buck deserves all of this and more. Here he is, 45 years after Arlene broke the bad news to him that he'd been traded to Toronto.

As we sat in a diner in Dunedin that day, just a short walk up the street from TD Ballpark, the seats started to fill around us. You could see the eyes looking over, the unmistakable presence of Buck, leaning back in his chair.

Over and over, as we talk about the old days, he keeps coming back to how fortunate he is, how grateful he is that the Toronto Blue Jays traded for a fourth-string catcher who everyone thought was at the end of the line.

So I asked him, one last time.... *Imagine if you'd been traded to the Yankees?*

Buck just smiles.

Sources

Books

Gordon, Alison. *Foul Balls*. General Paperbacks, 1984.

Newspapers and Periodicals

Associated Press
Globe & Mail
Inside Sports
Toronto Star
Toronto Sun
New York Times
Sports Illustrated
Washington Post

Websites

Baseball Hall of Fame
Baseball Reference
City of Toronto Archives
ESPN
FanGraphs
MLB.com

SABR
Sportsnet 590 The FAN
Toronto Blue Jays
Toronto Public Library
X (formerly Twitter)
YouTube

Acknowledgments

THIS BOOK WOULD NOT HAVE BEEN POSSIBLE WITHOUT SO many people giving me two of the greatest gifts: their time and their stories.

Thank you to the many players, coaches, executives, and broadcasters who made this project successful. Working on this book throughout the 2024 Blue Jays season was difficult—and was made far more challenging than I expected—but that's a chapter for the next book. For now, I am filled with only gratitude.

I joined the Blue Jays beat in 2017. It's important for me to thank the people I have shared this beat with over the years. It's a difficult dynamic to describe to someone outside of our strange little media bubble. We are, by definition, in competition with one another, covering the same team but for different outlets. There is a camaraderie to it all, though, the bond of people slowly losing their minds for all the same reasons. When I started on this beat, I learned so much from standing quietly in the corner of John Gibbons' office and watching the veterans like Richard Griffin of the *Toronto Star* and John Lott of The Athletic do their work. As challenges arose throughout the process of writing this book, writers and broadcasters from other outlets were not only willing to help, but eager to do so. Over the years, some of us have spent more time with one another between February and October than our own families. Thank you for your friendship, your help, and putting up with me.

This work would also not be possible without the beat writers and editorial team of MLB.com. I am someone who takes time to feel the ground grow solid beneath my feet, but I truly feel at home now. Thank you to my editor, Jim Banks, for his encouragement and belief in me. Our editorial group, also led by Alyson Footer and Jenifer Langosch, along with our team of beat writers and producers, have allowed me to find joy in my work, which has not always come easily to me. Thank you to Mark Feinsand, Bryan Hoch, and Todd Zolecki for their guidance and advice in the early days of this project. Thank you to Julia Kreuz, the more talented member of MLB.com's Canadian Bureau, for being the finest friend and colleague I could ask for.

Thank you to Josh Williams of Triumph Books for bringing me in on this project and to Michelle Bruton, who set me on the right path. I am grateful for her guidance along with that of Stacey Glick, who has helped to demystify this new world of publishing to me.

Lastly, to my friends, with love. Without them, my sanity would have left me long ago, lost somewhere in Buffalo during those COVID years, perhaps. Thank you to Josh Rankin, Jeremy Parkin, Drew Domokos, Sacha Parkin, and Brandon Walsh for all of the moments you had my back (and bought me back) through those years. Thank you to Kelti, my little sister who will always be my little sister. Lastly, thank you to Amanda and Daisy, who make it all worthwhile.